TRANS
FORMERS
DARK OF THE MOON

TRANSFORMERS
DARK OF THE MOON

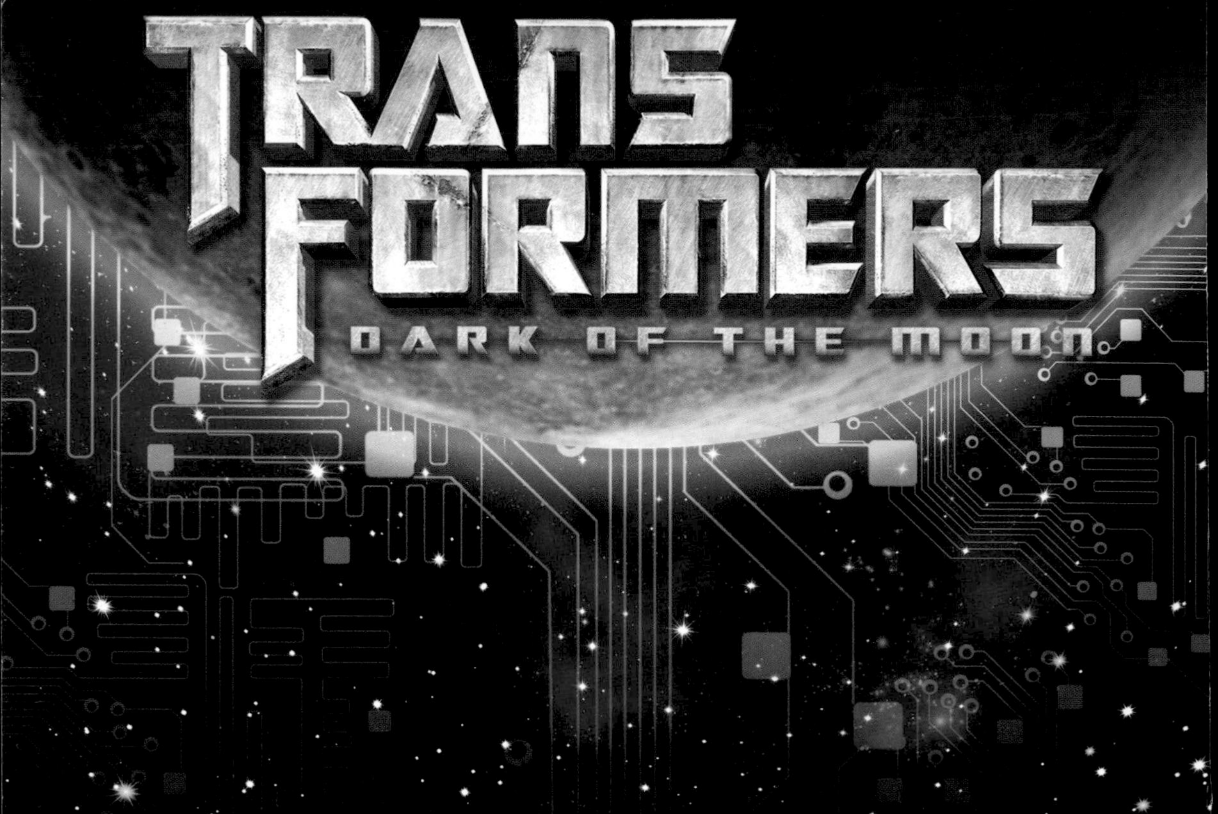

STORY BY **JOHN BARBER**

ART BY **JORGE JIMENEZ MORENO**

COLORS BY **ROMULO FAJARDO** AND **ZAC ATKINSON**

LETTERS BY **CHRIS MOWRY** AND **SHAWN LEE**

SERIES ASSISTANT EDITOR **CARLOS GUZMAN** • SERIES EDITOR **ANDY SCHMIDT**

ADAPTED FROM THE SCREENPLAY BY **EHREN KRUGER**

COLLECTION EDITOR **JUSTIN EISINGER** • COLLECTION DESIGNER **SHAWN LEE**

ISBN: 978-1-60010-917-1 14 13 12 11 1 2 3 4

Special thanks to Hasbro's Aaron Archer, Michael Kelly, Amie Lozanski, Val Roca, Ed Lane, Michael Provost, Samantha Lomow, and Michael Verrecchia for their invaluable assistance.

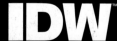

IDW™ Licensed By: Hasbro, Paramount, GM

Become our fan on Facebook facebook.com/idwpublishing
Follow us on Twitter @idwpublishing
Check us out on YouTube youtube.com/idwpublishing

Ted Adams, CEO & Publisher • Greg Goldstein, Chief Operating Officer • Robbie Robbins, EVP/Sr. Graphic Artist • Chris Ryall, Chief Creative Officer/Editor-in-Chief • Matthew Ruzicka, CPA, Chief Financial Officer • Alan Payne, VP of Sales

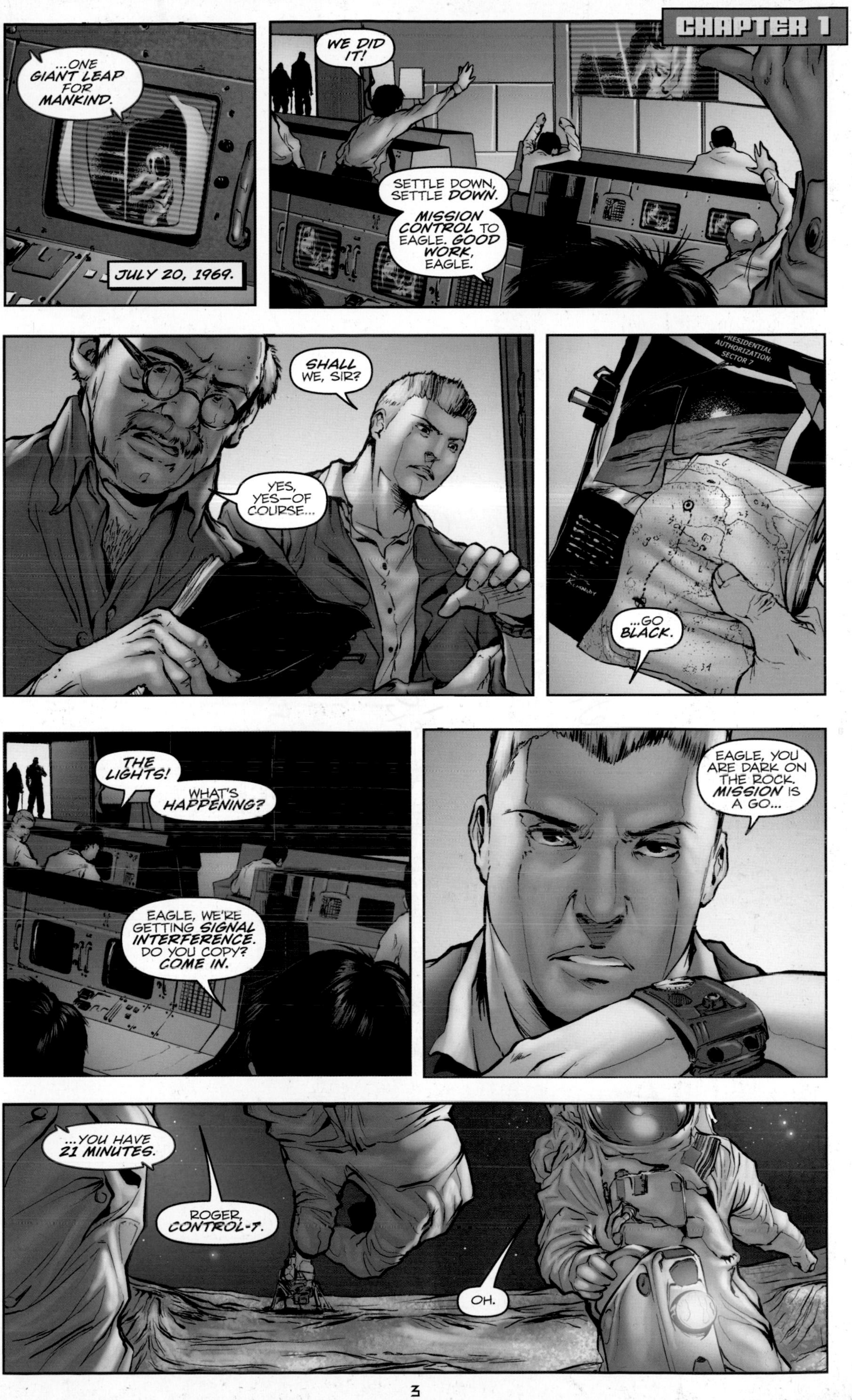
CHAPTER 1
...ONE GIANT LEAP FOR MANKIND.
JULY 20, 1969.
WE DID IT!
SETTLE DOWN, SETTLE DOWN.
MISSION CONTROL TO EAGLE. GOOD WORK, EAGLE.
SHALL WE, SIR?
YES, YES—OF COURSE...
PRESIDENTIAL AUTHORIZATION: SECTOR 7
...GO BLACK.
THE LIGHTS!
WHAT'S HAPPENING?
EAGLE, WE'RE GETTING SIGNAL INTERFERENCE. DO YOU COPY? COME IN.
EAGLE, YOU ARE DARK ON THE ROCK. MISSION IS A GO...
...YOU HAVE 21 MINUTES.
ROGER, CONTROL-7.
OH.

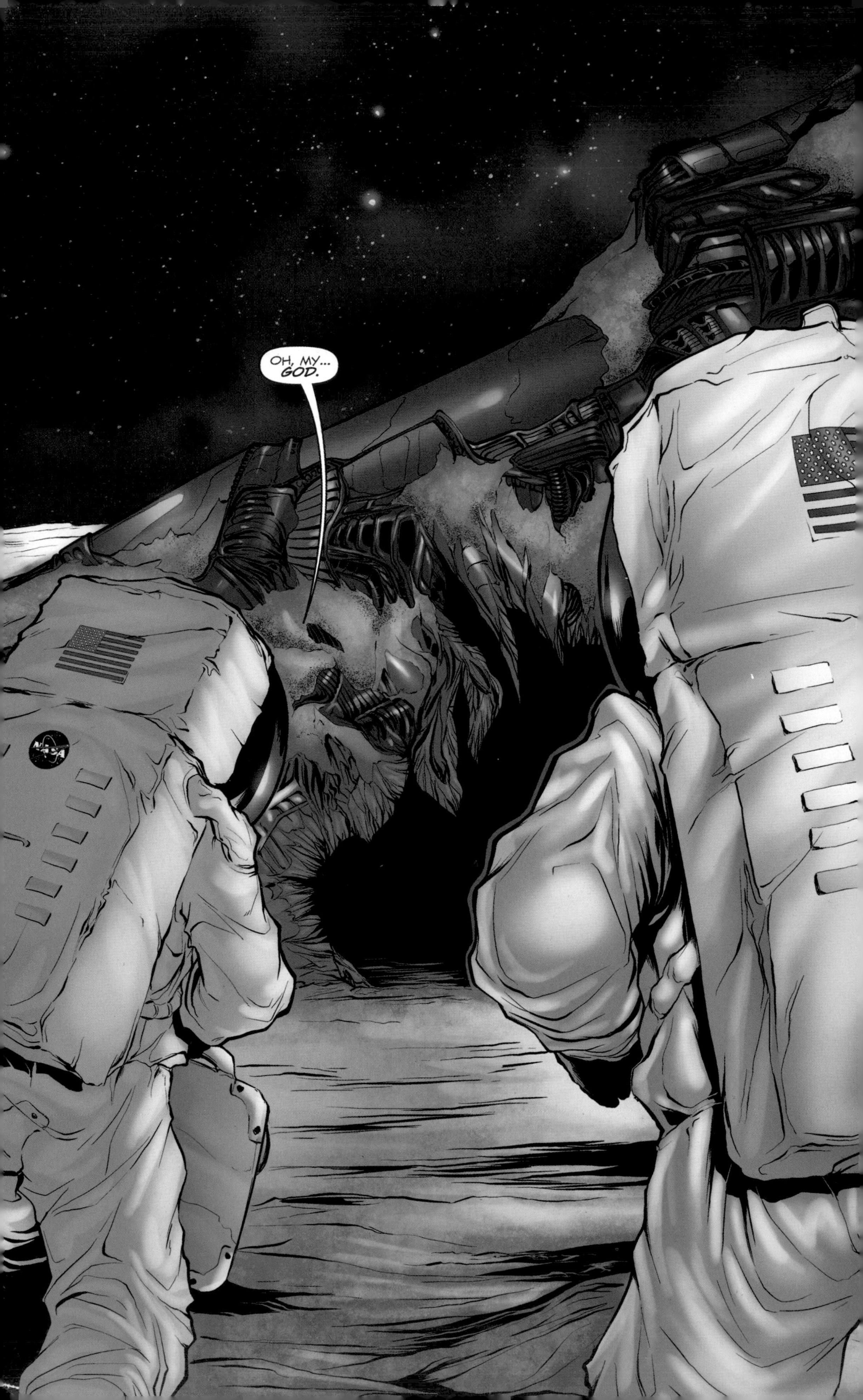
OH, MY... GOD.

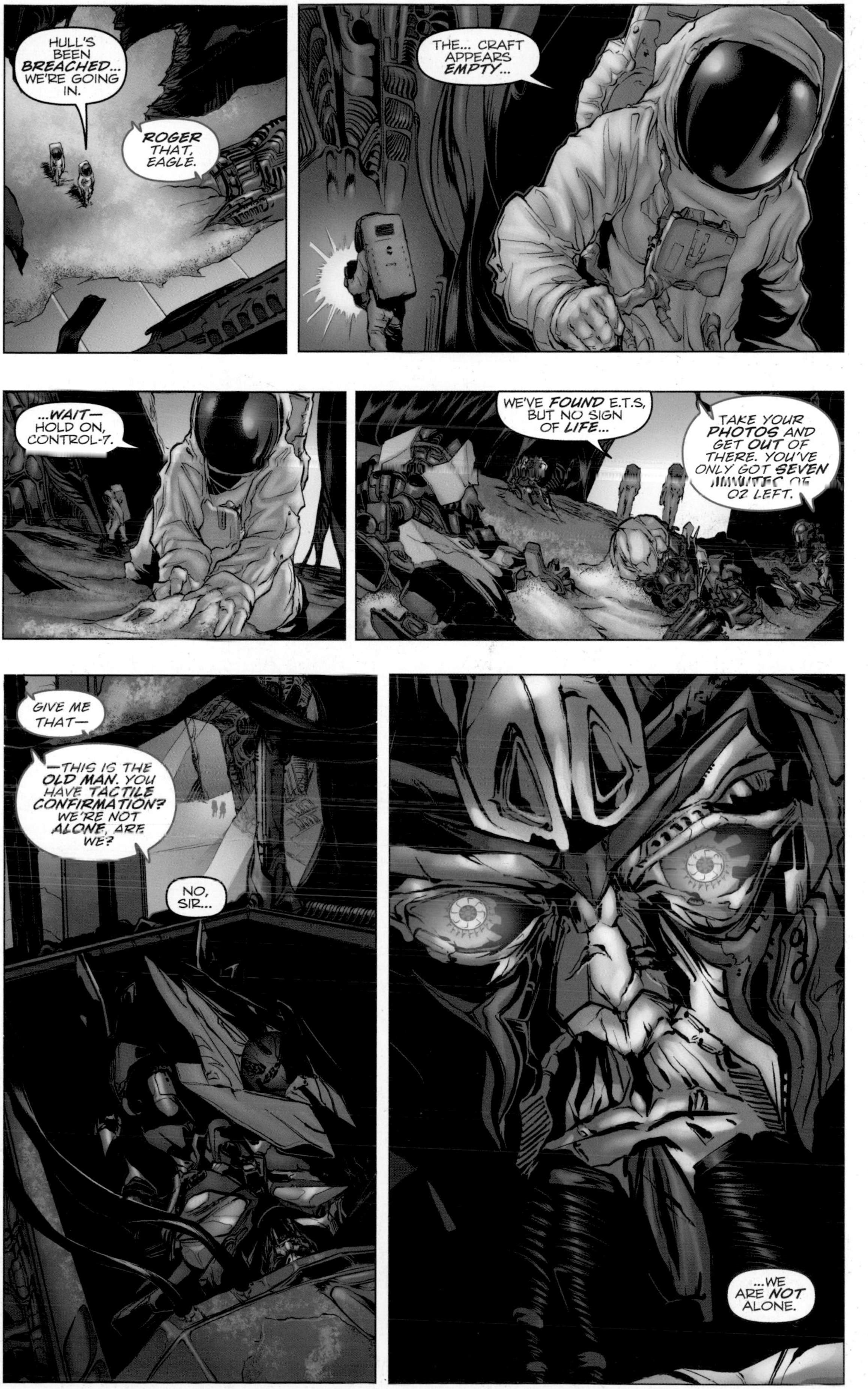
HULL'S BEEN BREACHED... WE'RE GOING IN.
ROGER THAT, EAGLE.
THE... CRAFT APPEARS EMPTY...
...WAIT— HOLD ON, CONTROL-7.
WE'VE FOUND E.T.S, BUT NO SIGN OF LIFE...
TAKE YOUR PHOTOS AND GET OUT OF THERE. YOU'VE ONLY GOT SEVEN MINUTES OF O2 LEFT.
GIVE ME THAT—
—THIS IS THE OLD MAN. YOU HAVE TACTILE CONFIRMATION? WE'RE NOT ALONE, ARE WE?
NO, SIR...
...WE ARE NOT ALONE.

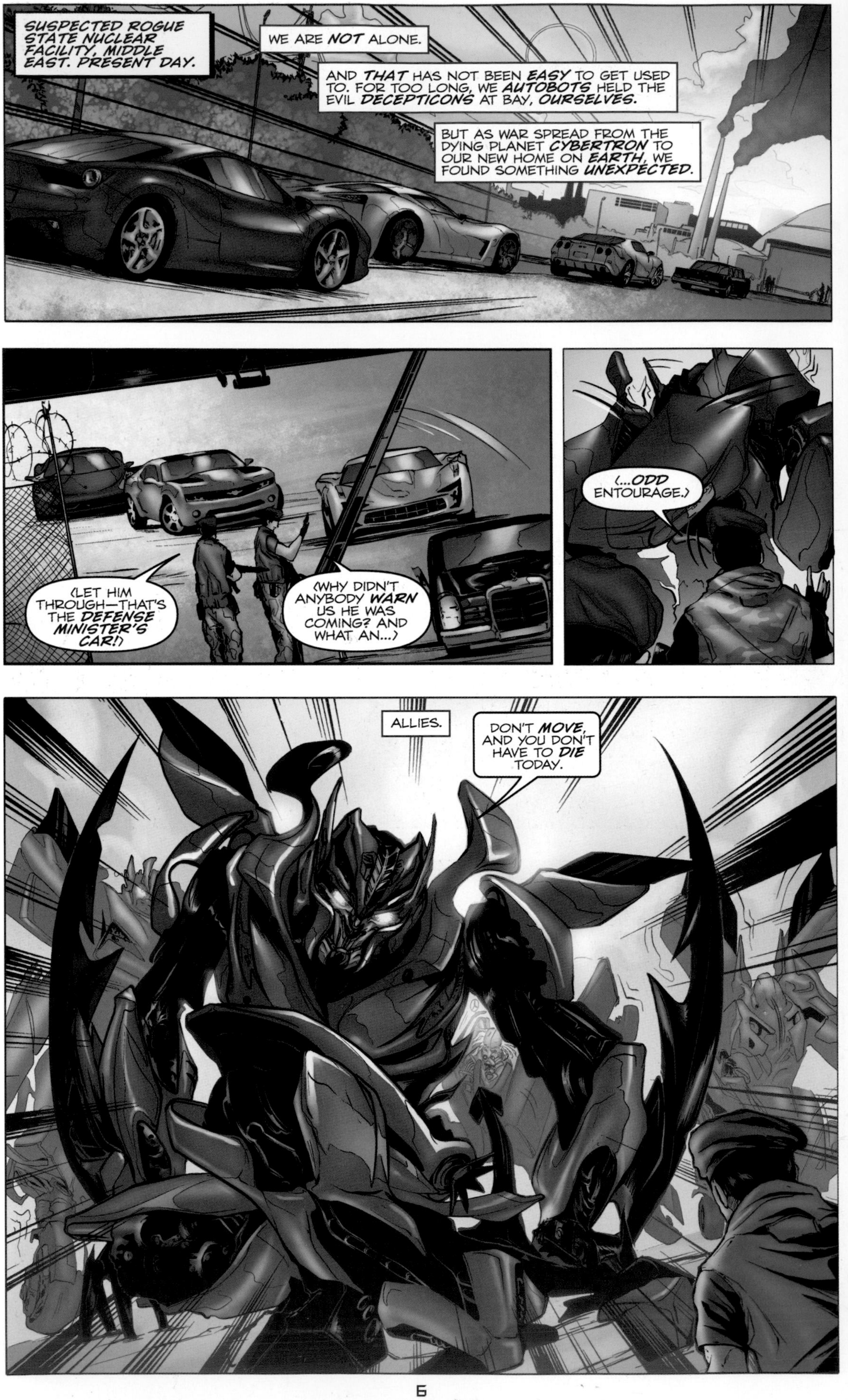
SUSPECTED ROGUE STATE NUCLEAR FACILITY, MIDDLE EAST. PRESENT DAY.
WE ARE NOT ALONE.
AND THAT HAS NOT BEEN EASY TO GET USED TO. FOR TOO LONG, WE AUTOBOTS HELD THE EVIL DECEPTICONS AT BAY, OURSELVES.
BUT AS WAR SPREAD FROM THE DYING PLANET CYBERTRON TO OUR NEW HOME ON EARTH, WE FOUND SOMETHING UNEXPECTED.
(LET HIM THROUGH—THAT'S THE DEFENSE MINISTER'S CAR!)
(WHY DIDN'T ANYBODY WARN US HE WAS COMING? AND WHAT AN...)
(...ODD ENTOURAGE.)
ALLIES.
DON'T MOVE, AND YOU DON'T HAVE TO DIE TODAY.

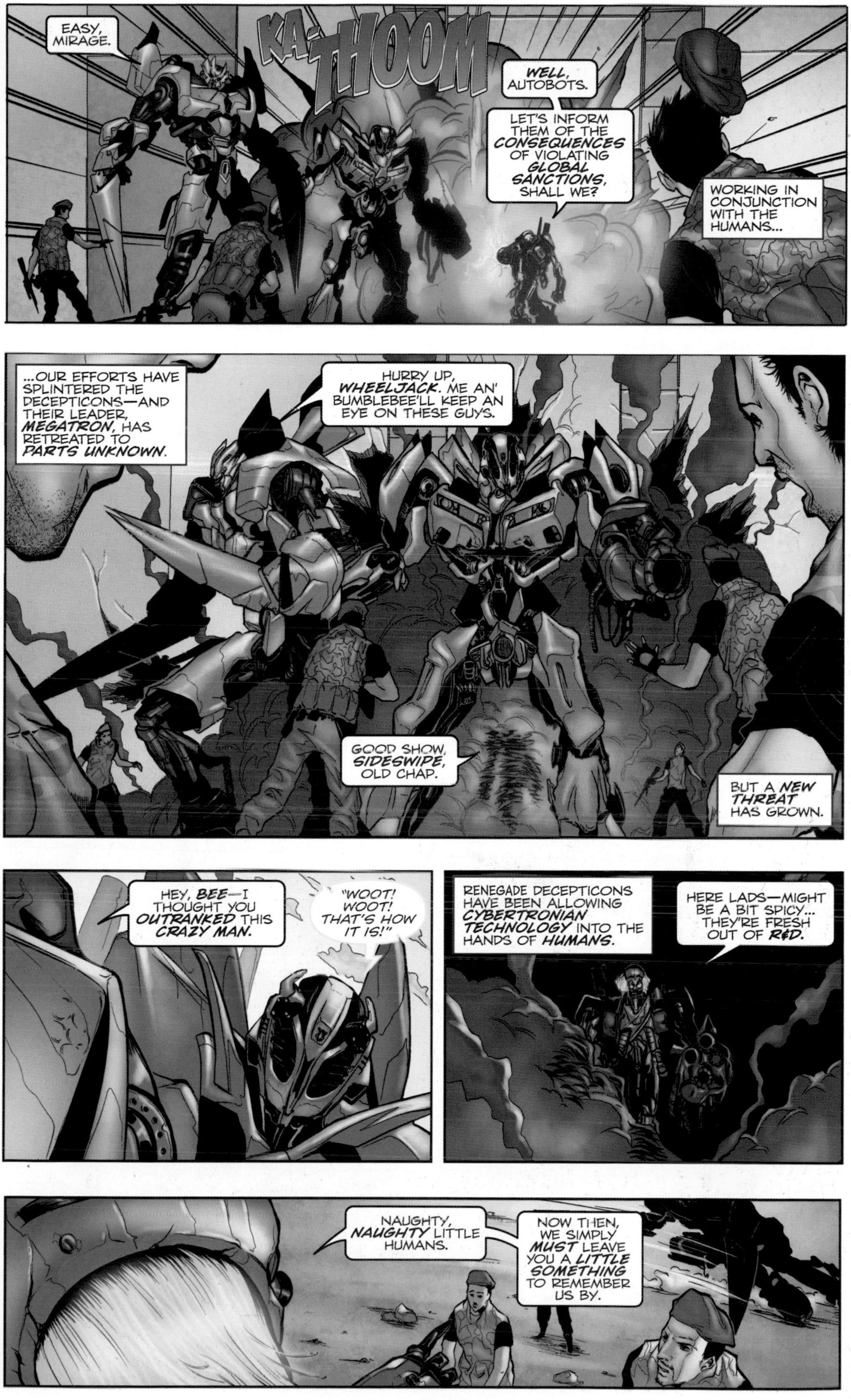

EASY, MIRAGE.
KA-THOOM
WELL, AUTOBOTS.
LET'S INFORM THEM OF THE CONSEQUENCES OF VIOLATING GLOBAL SANCTIONS, SHALL WE?
WORKING IN CONJUNCTION WITH THE HUMANS...
...OUR EFFORTS HAVE SPLINTERED THE DECEPTICONS—AND THEIR LEADER, MEGATRON, HAS RETREATED TO PARTS UNKNOWN.
HURRY UP, WHEELJACK. ME AN' BUMBLEBEE'LL KEEP AN EYE ON THESE GUYS.
GOOD SHOW, SIDESWIPE, OLD CHAP.
BUT A NEW THREAT HAS GROWN.
HEY, BEE—I THOUGHT YOU OUTRANKED THIS CRAZY MAN.
"WOOT! WOOT! THAT'S HOW IT IS!"
RENEGADE DECEPTICONS HAVE BEEN ALLOWING CYBERTRONIAN TECHNOLOGY INTO THE HANDS OF HUMANS.
HERE LADS—MIGHT BE A BIT SPICY... THEY'RE FRESH OUT OF R&D.
NAUGHTY, NAUGHTY LITTLE HUMANS.
NOW THEN, WE SIMPLY MUST LEAVE YOU A LITTLE SOMETHING TO REMEMBER US BY.

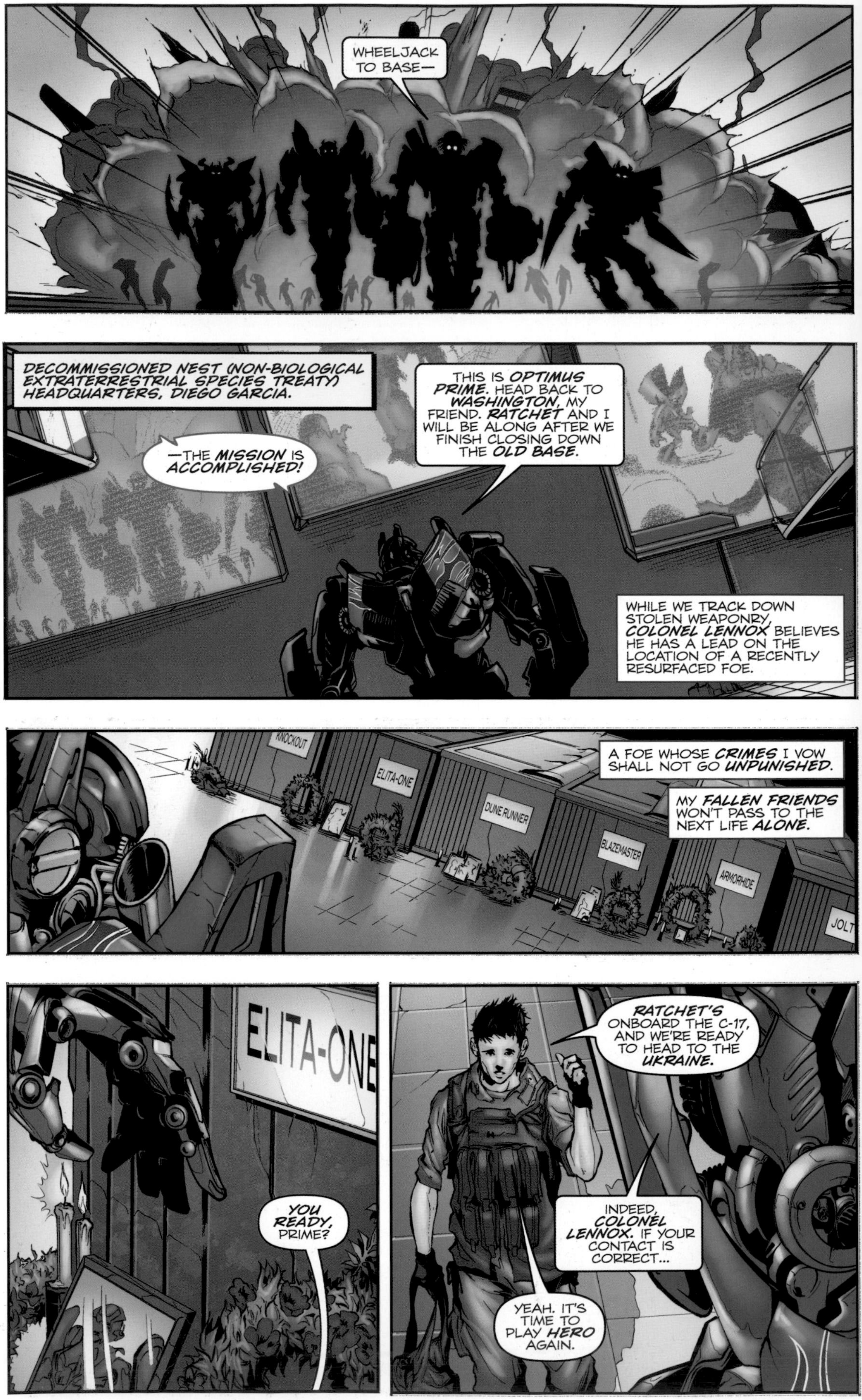

WHEELJACK TO BASE—
DECOMMISSIONED NEST (NON-BIOLOGICAL EXTRATERRESTRIAL SPECIES TREATY) HEADQUARTERS, DIEGO GARCIA.
—THE MISSION IS ACCOMPLISHED!
THIS IS OPTIMUS PRIME. HEAD BACK TO WASHINGTON, MY FRIEND. RATCHET AND I WILL BE ALONG AFTER WE FINISH CLOSING DOWN THE OLD BASE.
WHILE WE TRACK DOWN STOLEN WEAPONRY, COLONEL LENNOX BELIEVES HE HAS A LEAD ON THE LOCATION OF A RECENTLY RESURFACED FOE.
KNOCKOUT
ELITA-ONE
DUNE RUNNER
BLAZEMASTER
ARMORHIDE
JOLT
A FOE WHOSE CRIMES I VOW SHALL NOT GO UNPUNISHED.
MY FALLEN FRIENDS WON'T PASS TO THE NEXT LIFE ALONE.
ELITA-ONE
YOU READY, PRIME?
RATCHET'S ONBOARD THE C-17, AND WE'RE READY TO HEAD TO THE UKRAINE.
INDEED, COLONEL LENNOX. IF YOUR CONTACT IS CORRECT...
YEAH. IT'S TIME TO PLAY HERO AGAIN.

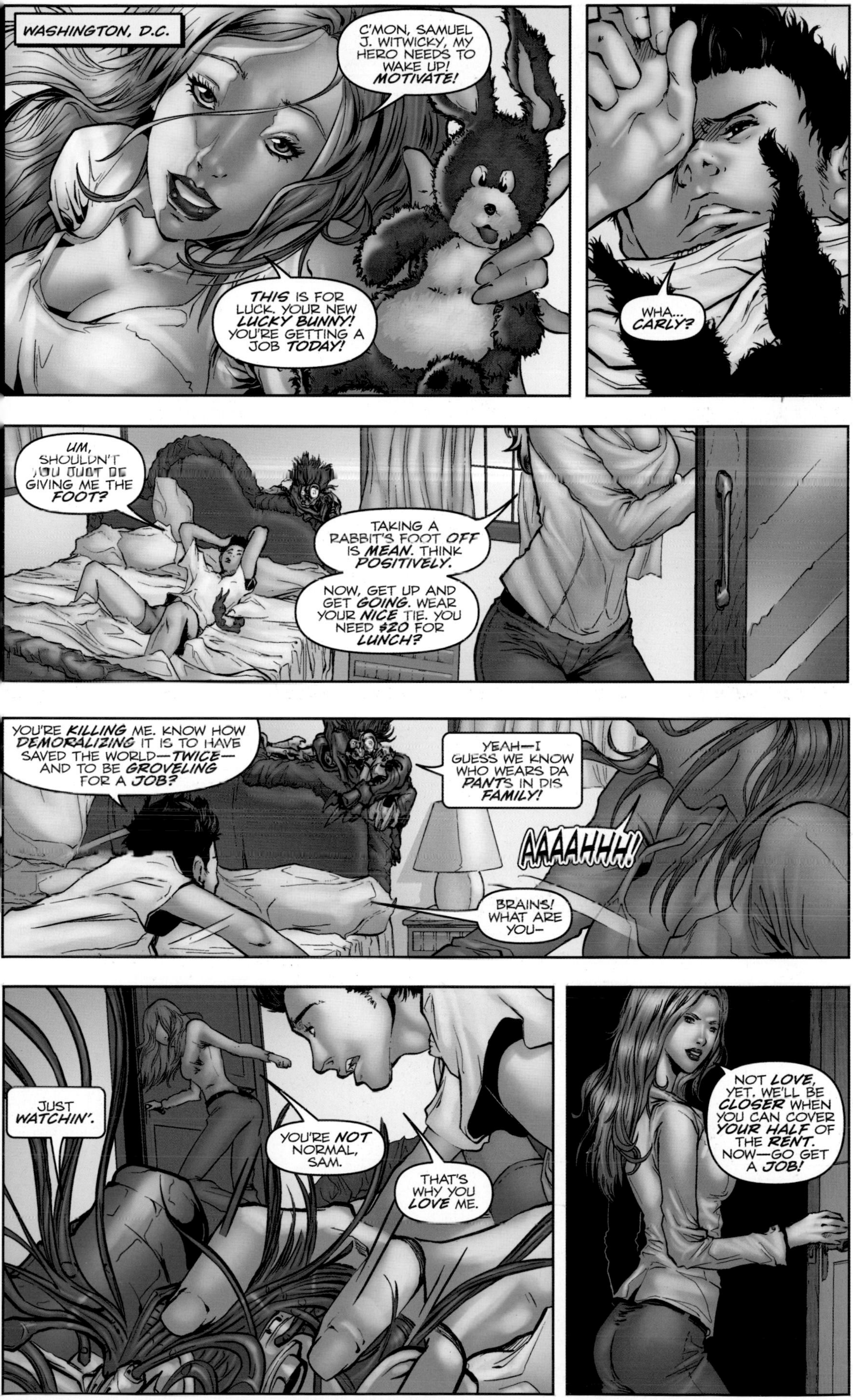
WASHINGTON, D.C.
C'MON, SAMUEL J. WITWICKY, MY HERO NEEDS TO WAKE UP! MOTIVATE!
THIS IS FOR LUCK. YOUR NEW LUCKY BUNNY! YOU'RE GETTING A JOB TODAY!
WHA... CARLY?
UM, SHOULDN'T YOU JUST BE GIVING ME THE FOOT?
TAKING A RABBIT'S FOOT OFF IS MEAN. THINK POSITIVELY.
NOW, GET UP AND GET GOING. WEAR YOUR NICE TIE. YOU NEED $20 FOR LUNCH?
YOU'RE KILLING ME. KNOW HOW DEMORALIZING IT IS TO HAVE SAVED THE WORLD—TWICE—AND TO BE GROVELING FOR A JOB?
YEAH—I GUESS WE KNOW WHO WEARS DA PANTS IN DIS FAMILY!
AAAAHHH!
BRAINS! WHAT ARE YOU-
JUST WATCHIN'.
YOU'RE NOT NORMAL, SAM.
THAT'S WHY YOU LOVE ME.
NOT LOVE, YET. WE'LL BE CLOSER WHEN YOU CAN COVER YOUR HALF OF THE RENT. NOW—GO GET A JOB!

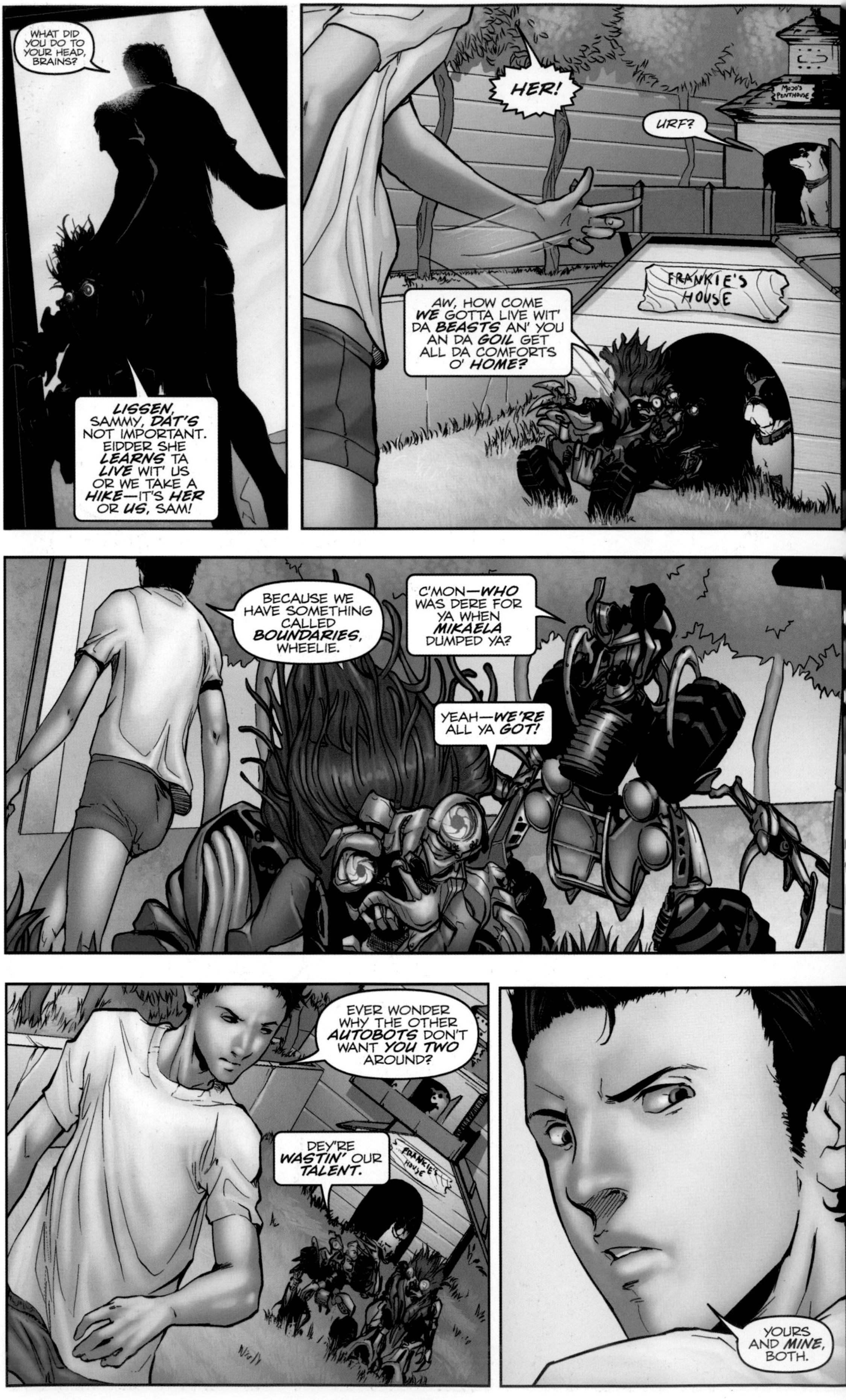
WHAT DID YOU DO TO YOUR HEAD, BRAINS?
LISSEN, SAMMY, DAT'S NOT IMPORTANT. EIDDER SHE LEARNS TA LIVE WIT' US OR WE TAKE A HIKE—IT'S HER OR US, SAM!
HER!
MOJO'S PENTHOUSE
URF?
FRANKIE'S HOUSE
AW, HOW COME WE GOTTA LIVE WIT' DA BEASTS AN' YOU AN DA GOIL GET ALL DA COMFORTS O' HOME?
BECAUSE WE HAVE SOMETHING CALLED BOUNDARIES, WHEELIE.
C'MON—WHO WAS DERE FOR YA WHEN MIKAELA DUMPED YA?
YEAH—WE'RE ALL YA GOT!
EVER WONDER WHY THE OTHER AUTOBOTS DON'T WANT YOU TWO AROUND?
DEY'RE WASTIN' OUR TALENT.
FRANKIE'S HOUSE
YOURS AND MINE, BOTH.

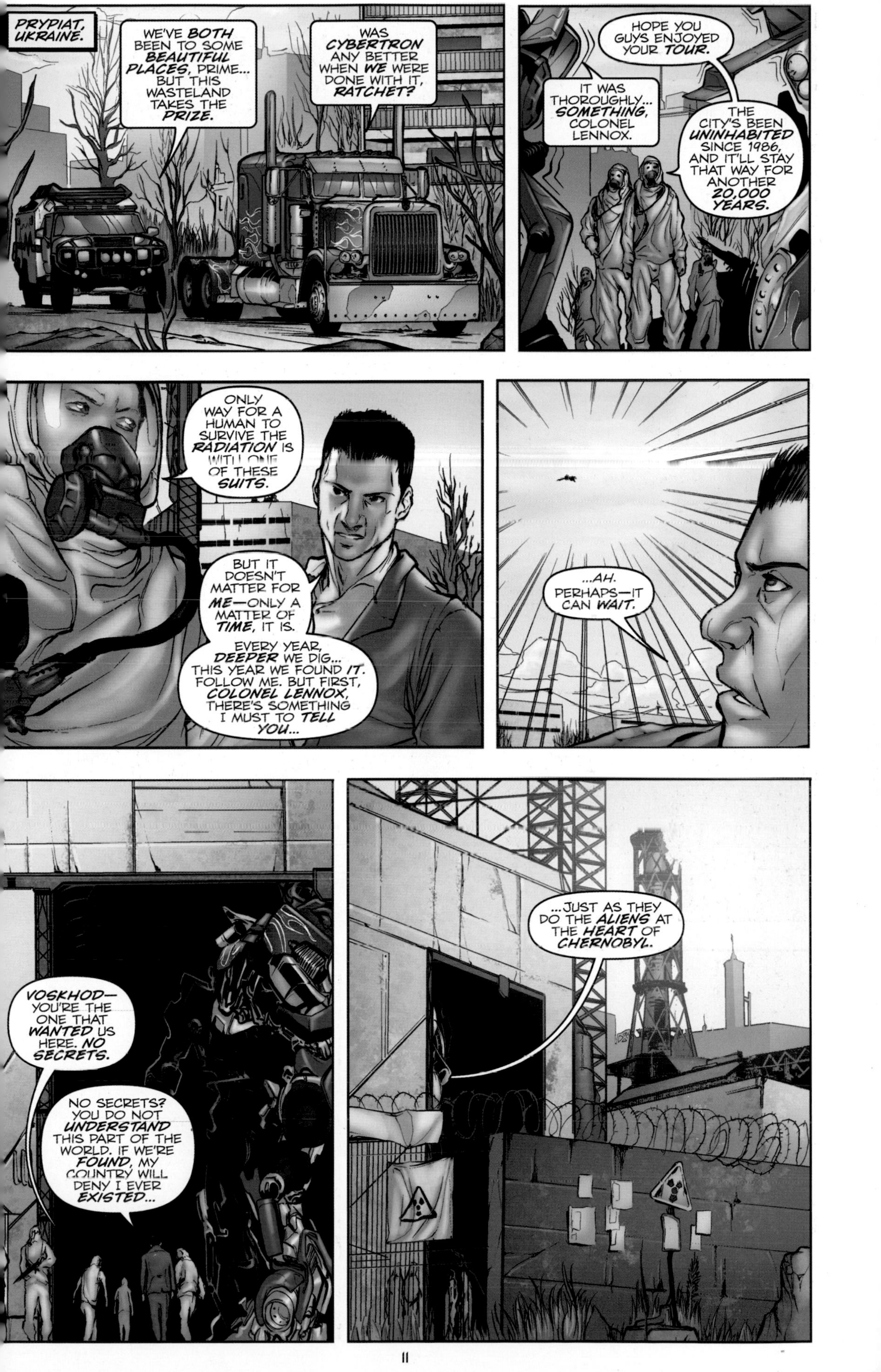
PRYPIAT, UKRAINE.
WE'VE BOTH BEEN TO SOME BEAUTIFUL PLACES, PRIME... BUT THIS WASTELAND TAKES THE PRIZE.
WAS CYBERTRON ANY BETTER WHEN WE WERE DONE WITH IT, RATCHET?
HOPE YOU GUYS ENJOYED YOUR TOUR.
IT WAS THOROUGHLY... SOMETHING, COLONEL LENNOX.
THE CITY'S BEEN UNINHABITED SINCE 1986, AND IT'LL STAY THAT WAY FOR ANOTHER 20,000 YEARS.
ONLY WAY FOR A HUMAN TO SURVIVE THE RADIATION IS WITH ONE OF THESE SUITS.
BUT IT DOESN'T MATTER FOR ME—ONLY A MATTER OF TIME, IT IS.
EVERY YEAR, DEEPER WE DIG... THIS YEAR WE FOUND IT. FOLLOW ME. BUT FIRST, COLONEL LENNOX, THERE'S SOMETHING I MUST TO TELL YOU...
...AH. PERHAPS—IT CAN WAIT.
VOSKHOD—YOU'RE THE ONE THAT WANTED US HERE. NO SECRETS.
NO SECRETS? YOU DO NOT UNDERSTAND THIS PART OF THE WORLD. IF WE'RE FOUND, MY COUNTRY WILL DENY I EVER EXISTED...
...JUST AS THEY DO THE ALIENS AT THE HEART OF CHERNOBYL.

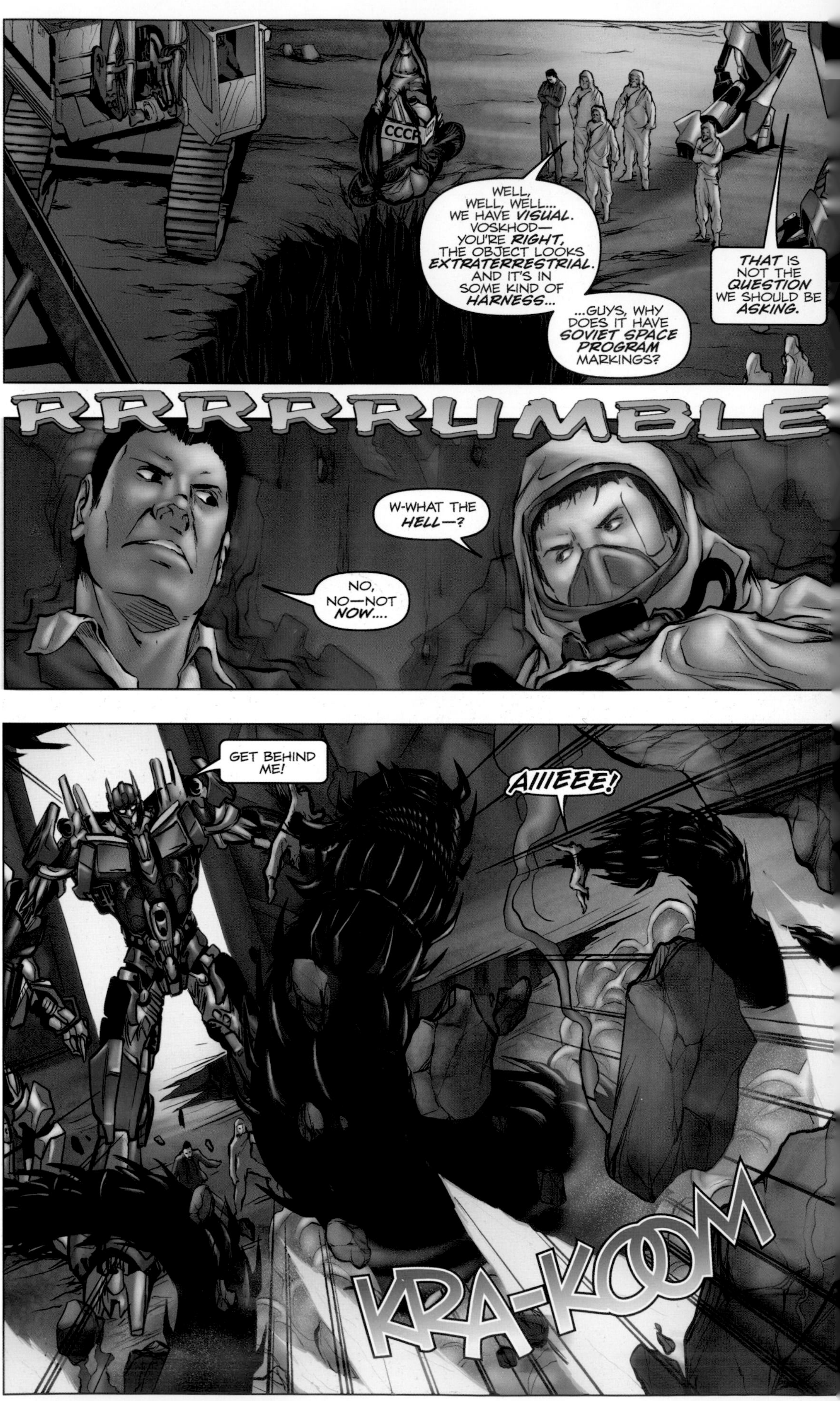
WELL, WELL, WELL... WE HAVE VISUAL. VOSKHOD— YOU'RE RIGHT, THE OBJECT LOOKS EXTRATERRESTRIAL. AND IT'S IN SOME KIND OF HARNESS...
...GUYS, WHY DOES IT HAVE SOVIET SPACE PROGRAM MARKINGS?
THAT IS NOT THE QUESTION WE SHOULD BE ASKING.
CCCP
RRRRRRUMBLE
W-WHAT THE HELL—?
NO, NO—NOT NOW....
GET BEHIND ME!
AIIIEEE!
KRA-KOOM

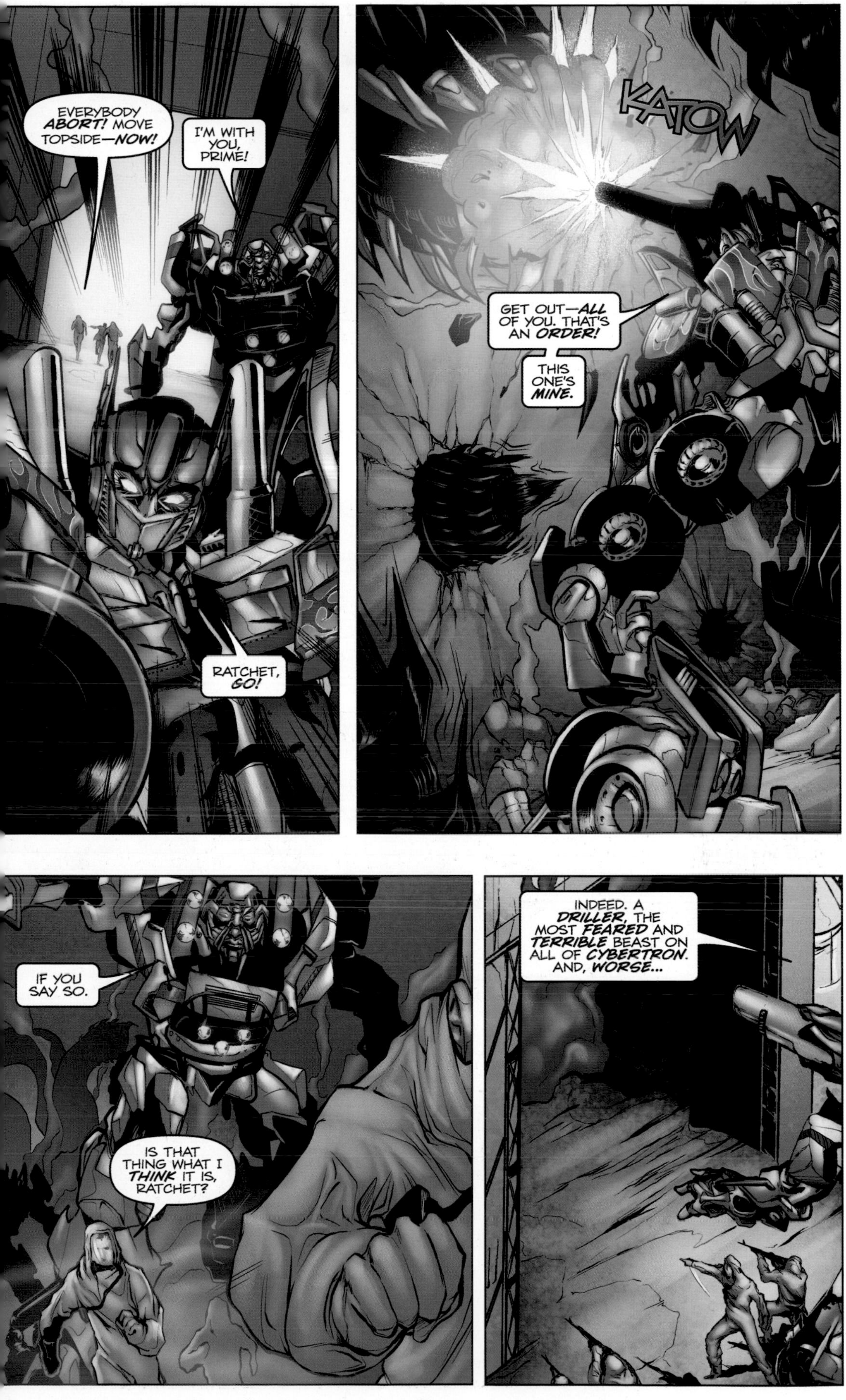
EVERYBODY ABORT! MOVE TOPSIDE—NOW!
I'M WITH YOU, PRIME!
RATCHET, GO!
KATOW
GET OUT—ALL OF YOU. THAT'S AN ORDER!
THIS ONE'S MINE.
IF YOU SAY SO.
IS THAT THING WHAT I THINK IT IS, RATCHET?
INDEED. A DRILLER, THE MOST FEARED AND TERRIBLE BEAST ON ALL OF CYBERTRON. AND, WORSE...

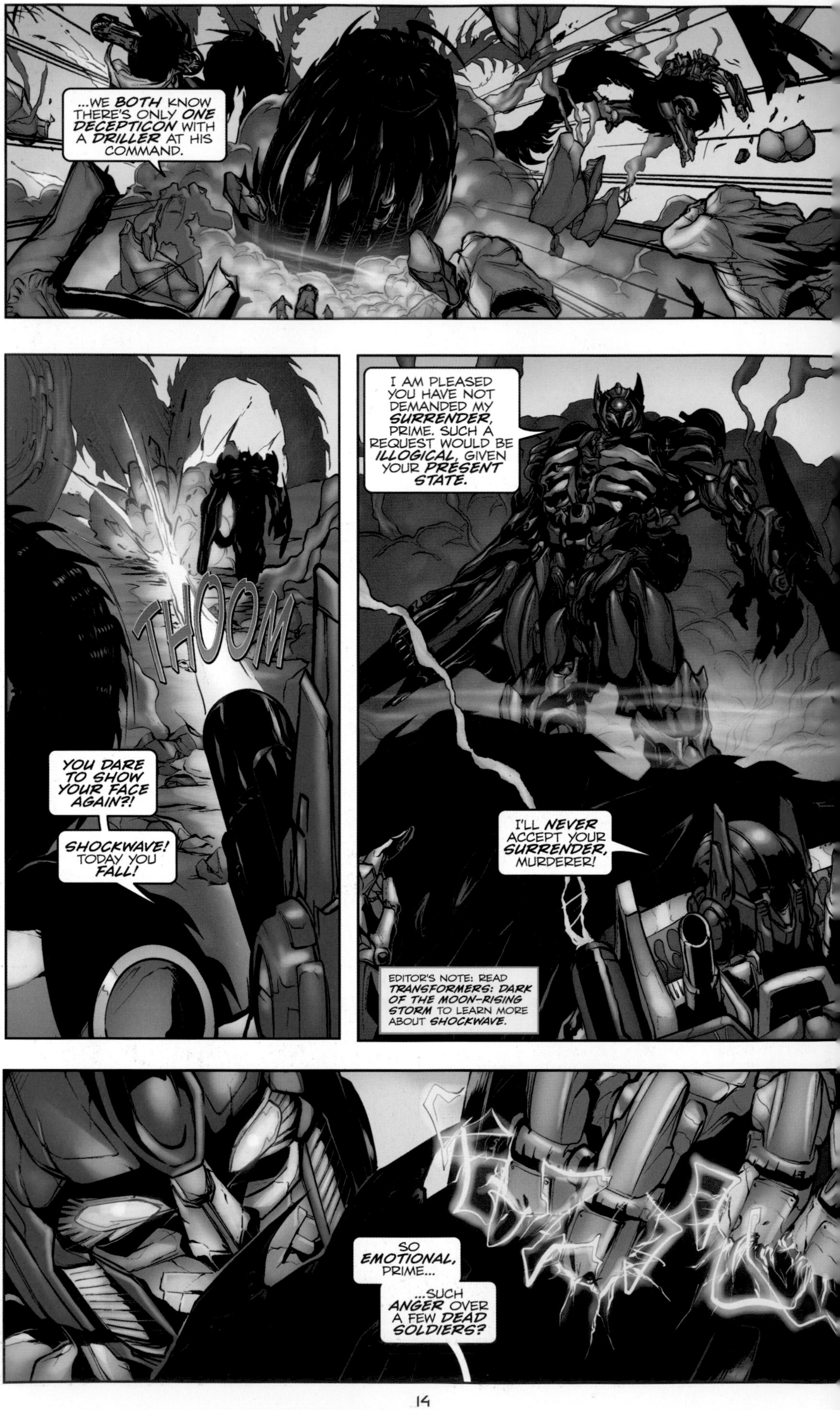
...WE BOTH KNOW THERE'S ONLY ONE DECEPTICON WITH A DRILLER AT HIS COMMAND.
THOOM
YOU DARE TO SHOW YOUR FACE AGAIN?!
SHOCKWAVE! TODAY YOU FALL!
I AM PLEASED YOU HAVE NOT DEMANDED MY SURRENDER, PRIME. SUCH A REQUEST WOULD BE ILLOGICAL, GIVEN YOUR PRESENT STATE.
I'LL NEVER ACCEPT YOUR SURRENDER, MURDERER!
EDITOR'S NOTE: READ TRANSFORMERS: DARK OF THE MOON-RISING STORM TO LEARN MORE ABOUT SHOCKWAVE.
SO EMOTIONAL, PRIME...
...SUCH ANGER OVER A FEW DEAD SOLDIERS?

NO!

THIS IS *WAR*.

WE *FIGHT*. WE *KILL*. WE *DIE*.

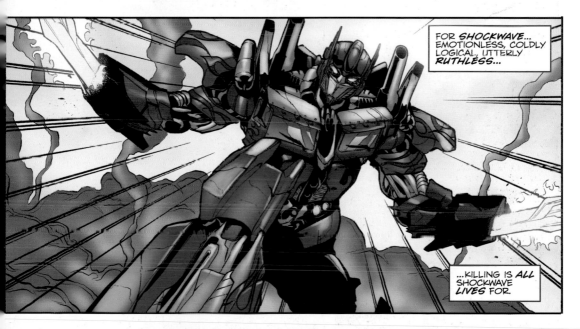

FOR *SHOCKWAVE*... EMOTIONLESS, COLDLY LOGICAL, UTTERLY *RUTHLESS*...

...KILLING IS *ALL* SHOCKWAVE *LIVES* FOR.

BUT NOW... *HERE*, SHOCKWAVE IS *AFTER* SOMETHING.

AND I *CAN'T* LET HIM *HAVE* IT.

CHOOM

HE'S GETTING *AWAY!* FOLLOW HIM *DOWN!*

NO—IT'S *SUICIDE!* WE'LL HAVE ANOTHER CHANCE. PRIME *GOT* WHAT HE WAS *AFTER.*

NNNNH...

YOU *OKAY?*

I'D BE *BETTER* IF I KNEW HOW *THIS* GOT INSIDE A RUSSIAN NUCLEAR POWER PLANT.

WHAT *IS* IT?

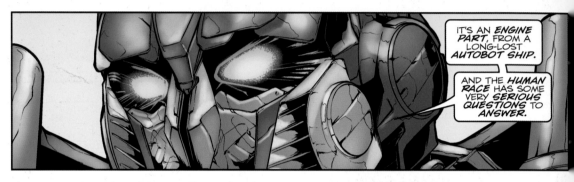
IT'S AN *ENGINE PART,* FROM A LONG-LOST *AUTOBOT* SHIP.

AND THE *HUMAN RACE* HAS SOME VERY *SERIOUS QUESTIONS* TO *ANSWER.*

OF ALL THE *CYBERTRONIAN ARTIFACTS* THAT HAVE MADE THEIR WAY TO *EARTH...*

MAY GOD HAVE MERCY ON ME.

...*THIS* HAS THE MOST *PERSONAL MEANING.*

BRAKKA BRAKKA

BRAKKA BRAKKA

AND FOR *ONCE,* IT REPRESENTS MORE THAN A *THREAT* FROM OUR *HOMEWORLD—*

16

—IT'S A **BETRAYAL** BY THE PEOPLE OF **EARTH**.

OKAY, I GOT MYSELF A *"SAM WITWICKY,"* RECENT COLLEGE GRADUATE—*CLAP, CLAP, CLAP*—PREVIOUS EXPERIENCE NEXT TO ZERO, BUT HMM...

...HE'S GOT A **RECOMMENDATION** LETTER FROM ONE OF OUR **BOARD MEMBERS**.

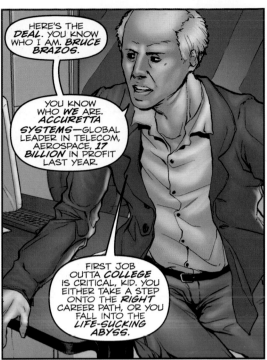

HERE'S THE **DEAL**. YOU KNOW WHO I AM. **BRUCE BRAZOS**.

YOU KNOW WHO **WE** ARE. **ACCURETTA SYSTEMS**—GLOBAL LEADER IN TELECOM, AEROSPACE, **17 BILLION** IN PROFIT LAST YEAR.

FIRST JOB OUTTA **COLLEGE** IS CRITICAL, KID. YOU EITHER TAKE A STEP ONTO THE **RIGHT** CAREER PATH, OR YOU FALL INTO THE **LIFE-SUCKING ABYSS**.

ALL DEPENDS ON HOW YOU RESPOND TO TWO LITTLE WORDS:

IMPRESS ME.

UM. *NOW?*

BUT I DON'T EVEN KNOW WHY I'M **HERE**. I GOT A TEXT—

YOU A **GO-GETTER?** A **RAMROD?** A **TAKE-CHARGE** KINDA GUY?

WE'RE **NOT** LOOKING FOR THAT HERE. I WANT A **MACHINE**. FOLLOWS MY ORDERS, QUESTIONS **NOTHING**.

BUT NO **BROWN NOSING**, NO **SUCK-UPS**. I HATE THAT.

MISTER, I SAVED YOUR LIFE... *TWICE*. I CAN'T TELL YOU **WHEN**, WHERE, OR HOW, BUT REST ASSURED, I HAVE DONE **THINGS** THAT **MATTER**.

AND I'D KINDA LIKE A JOB WHERE I MATTER **AGAIN**. THANK YOU, BUT **GOODBYE**.

YOU REALLY **DON'T** WANT THIS JOB, DO YOU? YOU WANT THE JOB **AFTER** IT.

I LOOK AT **YOU**, AND I DON'T JUST SEE SOME **WEIRD KID** WITH A **STUFFED RABBIT** ON HIS LAP.

I SEE A **YOUNGER** ME.

THE GOULD ESTATE.

CARLY!

THERE YOU ARE. MAN, YOU SAID YOU'RE THIS GUY'S NEW ASSISTANT EVENTS MANAGER, BUT YOU DIDN'T MENTION HE OWNS SPACE MOUNTAIN.

THE RECEPTIONIST POINTED ME DOWN A HALLWAY AND I'VE BEEN WALKING AROUND FOR...

...UM, HANG ON, THAT'S NOT THE MAIN STORY—I GOT A JOB!

SEE? WHAT'D I TELL YOU? IT'S THE BUNNY! YOU. ARE. WELCOME.

WELL WELL WELL...

...JUST WHO DO WE HAVE HERE? IS THIS THE BOYFRIEND I'VE BEEN JEALOUS OF?

UM.

DYLAN GOULD. PLEASURE. CARLY TOLD ME ALL ABOUT YOU.

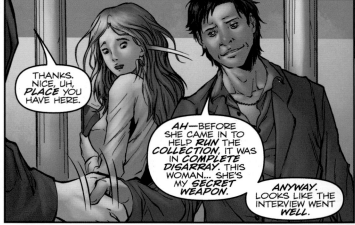

THANKS. NICE, UH, PLACE YOU HAVE HERE.

AH—BEFORE SHE CAME IN TO HELP RUN THE COLLECTION, IT WAS IN COMPLETE DISARRAY. THIS WOMAN... SHE'S MY SECRET WEAPON.

ANYWAY. LOOKS LIKE THE INTERVIEW WENT WELL.

HOW'D YOU...

CARLY MADE IT SOUND LIKE YOU NEEDED A PUSH IN THE RIGHT DIRECTION. YOU DIDN'T THINK ACCURETTA SYSTEMS WOULD JUST CALL YOU OUT OF THE BLUE?

...WELL...

CARLY, TAKE THE REST OF THE DAY OFF. CELEBRATE. BRAZOS WOULDN'T HIRE YOU IF YOU DIDN'T IMPRESS...

...UM, THAT'S NOT YOUR CAR, IS IT?

HEY, DON'T JUDGE A MAN BY HIS CAR. AND, UH, MY OTHER CAR'S...

"...BUSY."

NEST OPERATIONS, WASHINGTON, D.C.

OH GOOD, YOU'RE HERE, COLONEL. I *DO* HOPE YOU HAVE *ANSWERS* FOR HIM. I'VE NEVER *SEEN* HIM SO UPSET.

HE WON'T TALK TO *ME*, TO *IRONHIDE*, TO *ANYONE*...

WHAT'S *THIS*, THE ALIEN SILENT TREATMENT?

SEEN THAT... *THIS* IS NOT *THAT*. THIS IS *WORSE*.

COLONEL LENNOX, ARE YOU IN COMMAND HERE OR *NOT*?

THE AUTOBOTS WORK *WITH* ME, NOT *FOR* ME, *DIRECTOR MEARING*. SOMETIMES THEY DO WHAT THEY THINK IS *BEST*.

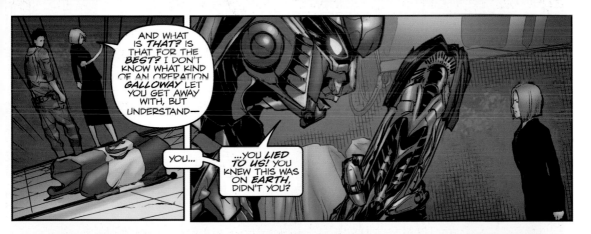

AND WHAT IS *THAT*? IS THAT FOR THE *BEST*? I DON'T KNOW WHAT KIND OF AN OPERATION *GALLOWAY* LET YOU GET AWAY WITH, BUT UNDERSTAND—

YOU...

...YOU *LIED* TO *US*! YOU KNEW THIS WAS ON *EARTH*, DIDN'T YOU?

PLEASE. DO I *LOOK* EASILY IMPRESSED? THIS WAS *CLASSIFIED* ABOVE MY PAY-GRADE UNTIL *SECTOR 7* GOT *SHUT DOWN.*

NOW, YOU WANT TO WAVE *STICKS* AROUND OR DO YOU WANT THE *TRUTH*? BECAUSE I'M FINE WITH *EITHER*. NOW COME ON...

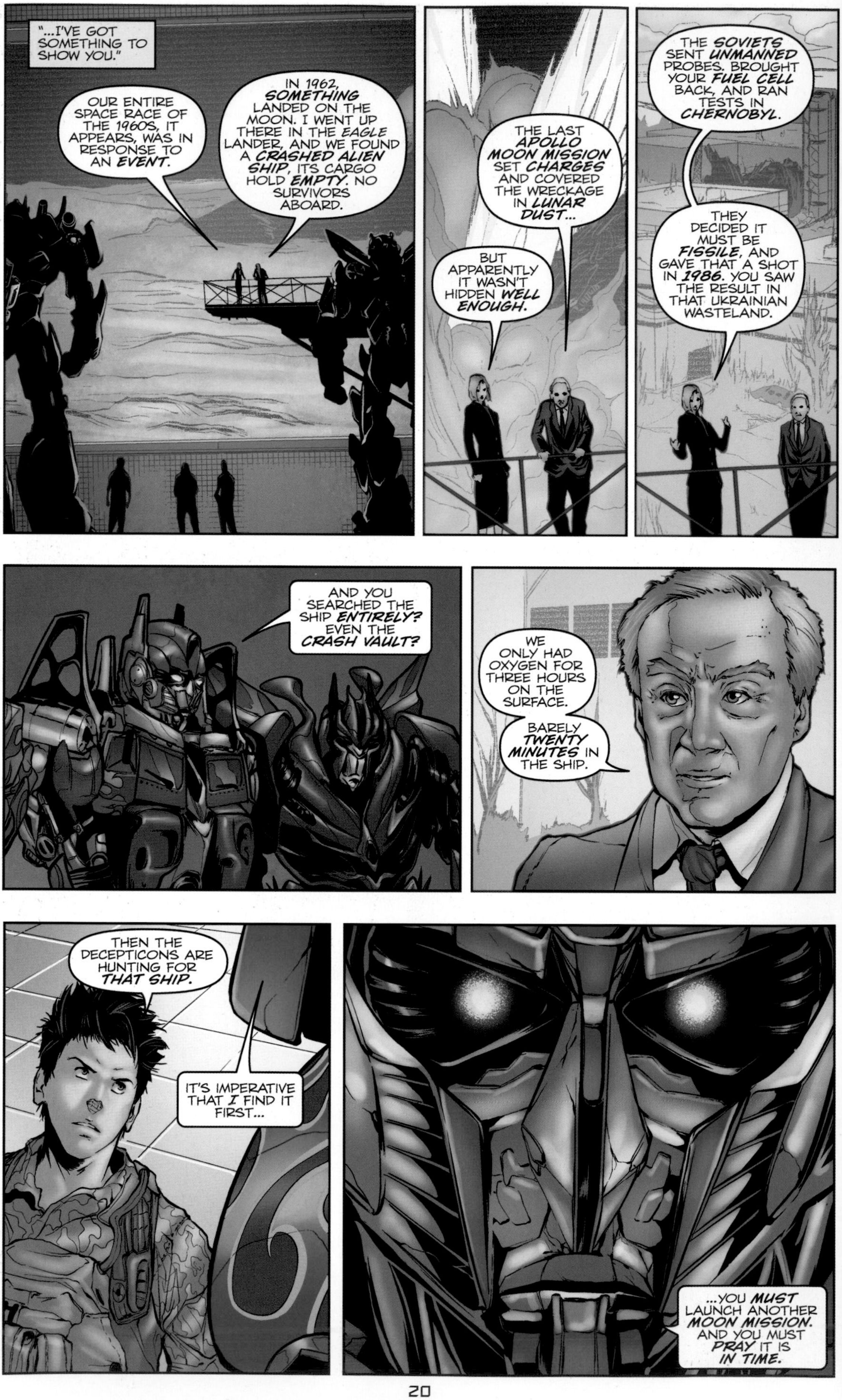
"...I'VE GOT SOMETHING TO SHOW YOU."
OUR ENTIRE SPACE RACE OF THE 1960S, IT APPEARS, WAS IN RESPONSE TO AN EVENT.
IN 1962, SOMETHING LANDED ON THE MOON. I WENT UP THERE IN THE EAGLE LANDER, AND WE FOUND A CRASHED ALIEN SHIP, ITS CARGO HOLD EMPTY. NO SURVIVORS ABOARD.
THE LAST APOLLO MOON MISSION SET CHARGES AND COVERED THE WRECKAGE IN LUNAR DUST...
BUT APPARENTLY IT WASN'T HIDDEN WELL ENOUGH.
THE SOVIETS SENT UNMANNED PROBES. BROUGHT YOUR FUEL CELL BACK, AND RAN TESTS IN CHERNOBYL.
THEY DECIDED IT MUST BE FISSILE, AND GAVE THAT A SHOT IN 1986. YOU SAW THE RESULT IN THAT UKRAINIAN WASTELAND.
AND YOU SEARCHED THE SHIP ENTIRELY? EVEN THE CRASH VAULT?
WE ONLY HAD OXYGEN FOR THREE HOURS ON THE SURFACE.
BARELY TWENTY MINUTES IN THE SHIP.
THEN THE DECEPTICONS ARE HUNTING FOR THAT SHIP.
IT'S IMPERATIVE THAT I FIND IT FIRST...
...YOU MUST LAUNCH ANOTHER MOON MISSION. AND YOU MUST PRAY IT IS IN TIME.

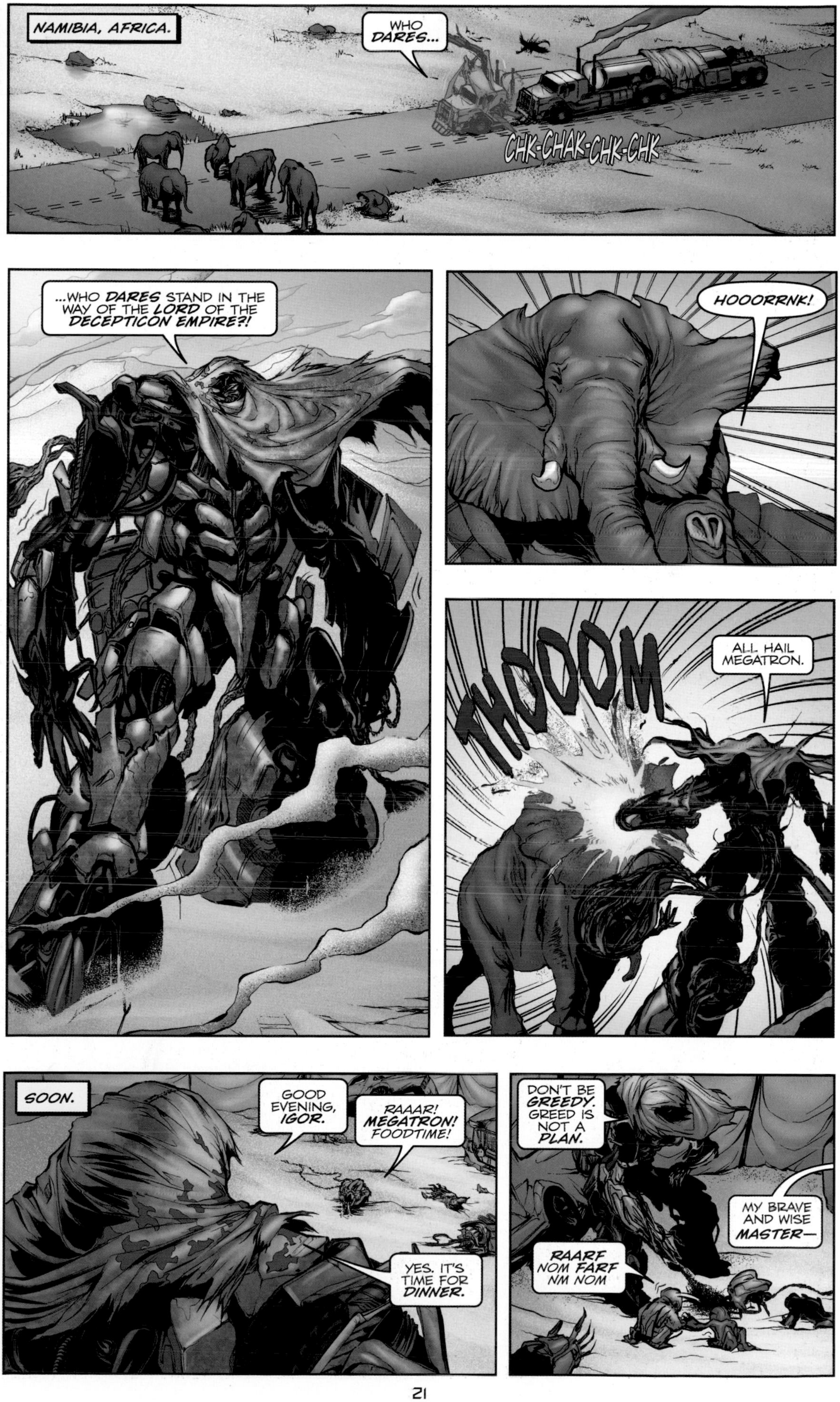

NAMIBIA, AFRICA.
WHO DARES...
CHK-CHAK-CHK-CHK
...WHO DARES STAND IN THE WAY OF THE LORD OF THE DECEPTICON EMPIRE?!
HOOORRNK!
THOOOM
ALL HAIL MEGATRON.
SOON.
GOOD EVENING, IGOR.
RAAAR! MEGATRON! FOODTIME!
YES. IT'S TIME FOR DINNER.
DON'T BE GREEDY. GREED IS NOT A PLAN.
MY BRAVE AND WISE MASTER—
RAARF NOM FARF NM NOM

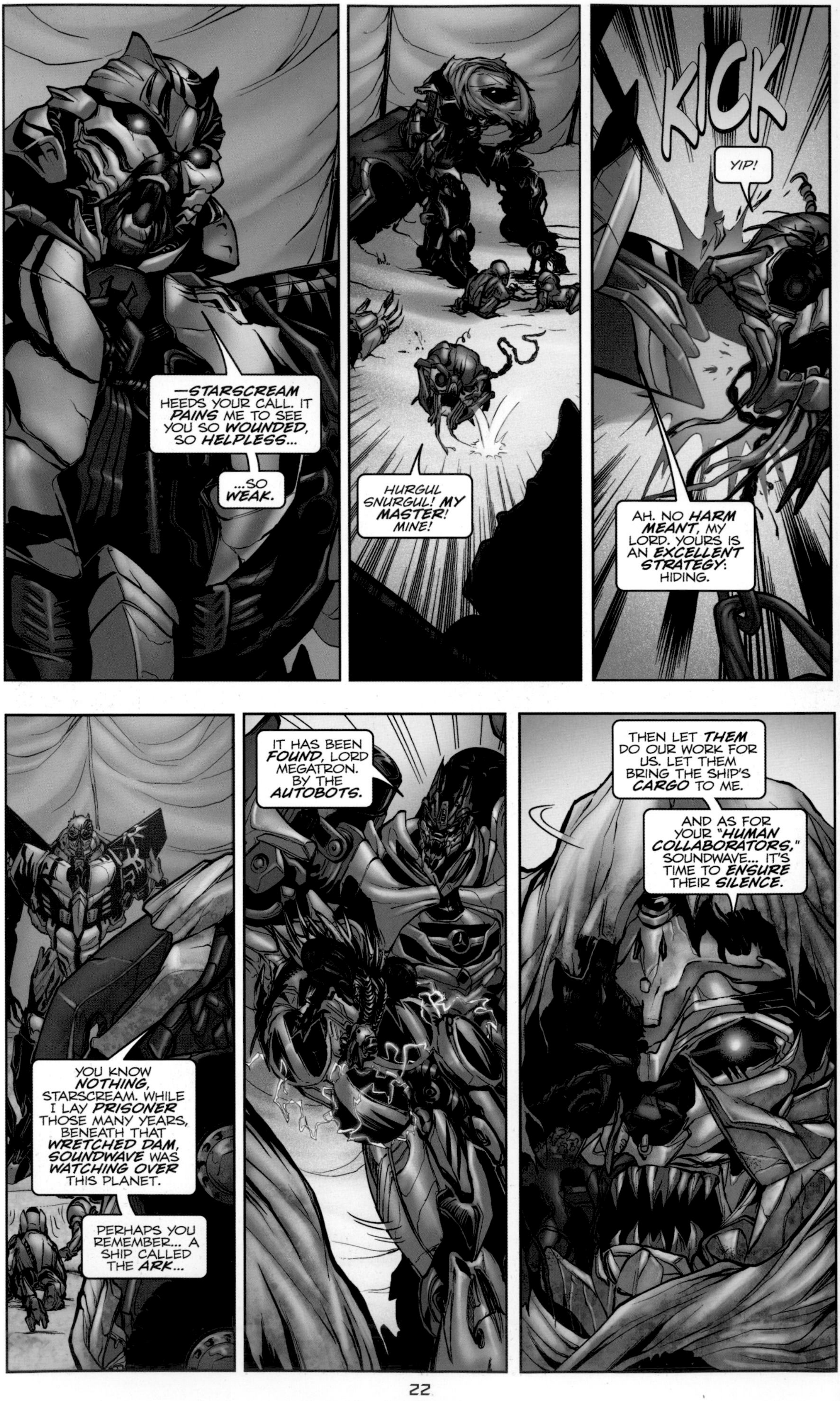
—STARSCREAM HEEDS YOUR CALL. IT PAINS ME TO SEE YOU SO WOUNDED, SO HELPLESS...
...SO WEAK.
HURGUL SNURGUL! MY MASTER! MINE!
KICK
YIP!
AH. NO HARM MEANT, MY LORD. YOURS IS AN EXCELLENT STRATEGY: HIDING.
YOU KNOW NOTHING, STARSCREAM. WHILE I LAY PRISONER THOSE MANY YEARS, BENEATH THAT WRETCHED DAM, SOUNDWAVE WAS WATCHING OVER THIS PLANET.
PERHAPS YOU REMEMBER... A SHIP CALLED THE ARK...
IT HAS BEEN FOUND, LORD MEGATRON. BY THE AUTOBOTS.
THEN LET THEM DO OUR WORK FOR US. LET THEM BRING THE SHIP'S CARGO TO ME.
AND AS FOR YOUR "HUMAN COLLABORATORS," SOUNDWAVE... IT'S TIME TO ENSURE THEIR SILENCE.

KENNEDY SPACE CENTER.

...TWO... ONE...

MISSION CONTROL TO ARES V: YOU ARE GO FOR LAUNCH.

GOOD HUNTING, GUYS.

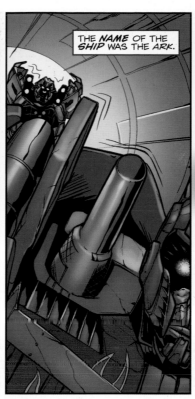

THE *NAME* OF THE *SHIP* WAS THE ARK.

THE *ORIGINAL* ARK... LONG AGO, WE TRAVELED THE *VASTNESS* OF *SPACE* IN A CRAFT NAMED IN *MEMORIAM* OF IT.

BUT HERE IS THE SHIP I ONCE WATCHED CARRY A *TECHNOLOGY* THAT WOULD HAVE *ENDED* THE WAR BETWEEN *AUTOBOTS* AND *DECEPTICONS.*

I WATCHED, *HELPLESSLY,* AS THE CRAFT *EXPLODED* ABOVE ME... IT WAS *GONE.*

ALONG WITH ITS *PILOT.* THE GREAT *SENTINEL PRIME.*

EDITOR'S NOTE: READ *TRANSFORMERS: DARK OF THE MOON—FOUNDATION* FOR THE FULL STORY OF *SENTINEL PRIME* AND HIS ILL-FATED JOURNEY!

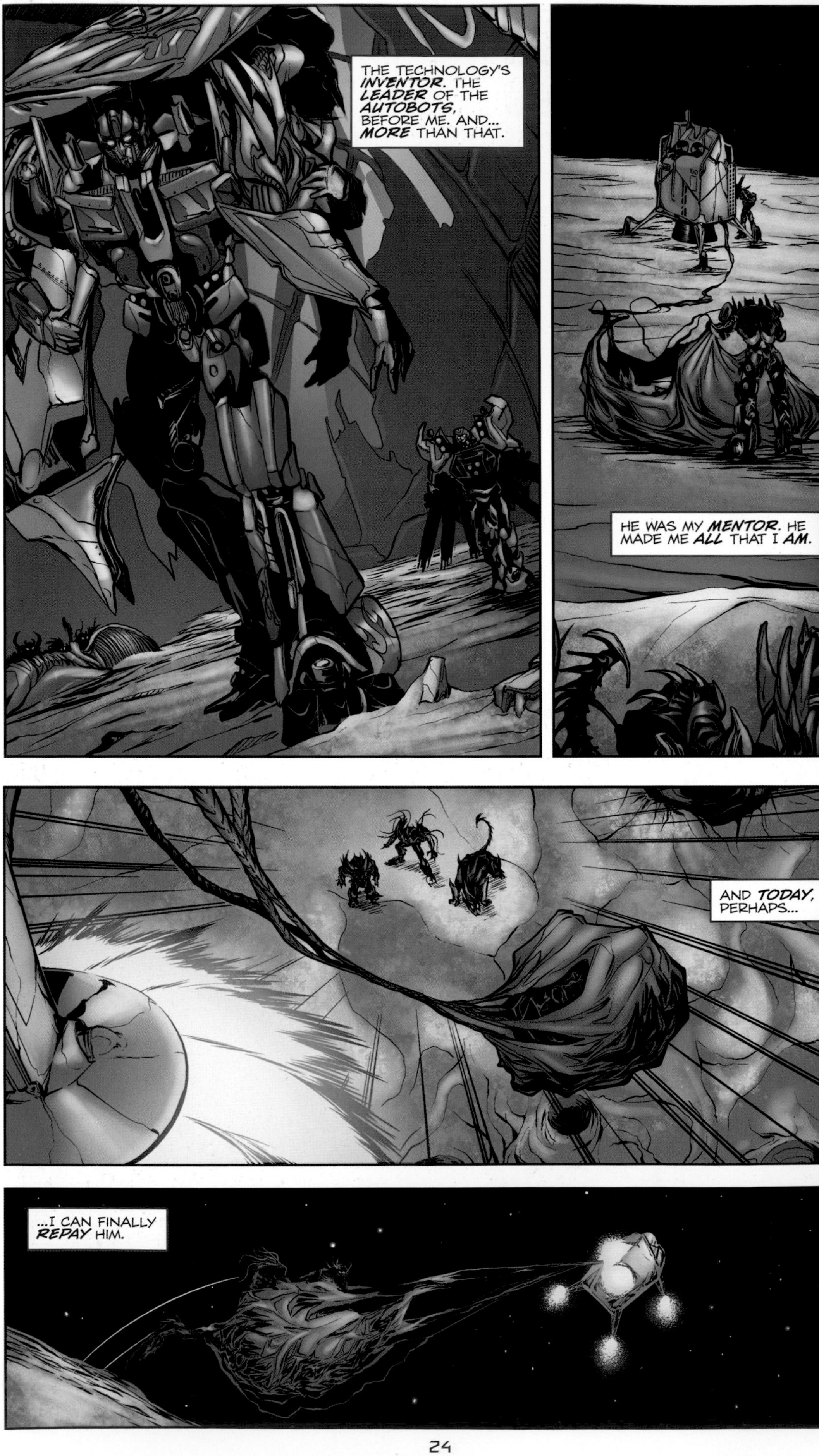
THE TECHNOLOGY'S INVENTOR. THE LEADER OF THE AUTOBOTS, BEFORE ME. AND... MORE THAN THAT.
HE WAS MY MENTOR. HE MADE ME ALL THAT I AM.
AND TODAY, PERHAPS...
...I CAN FINALLY REPAY HIM.

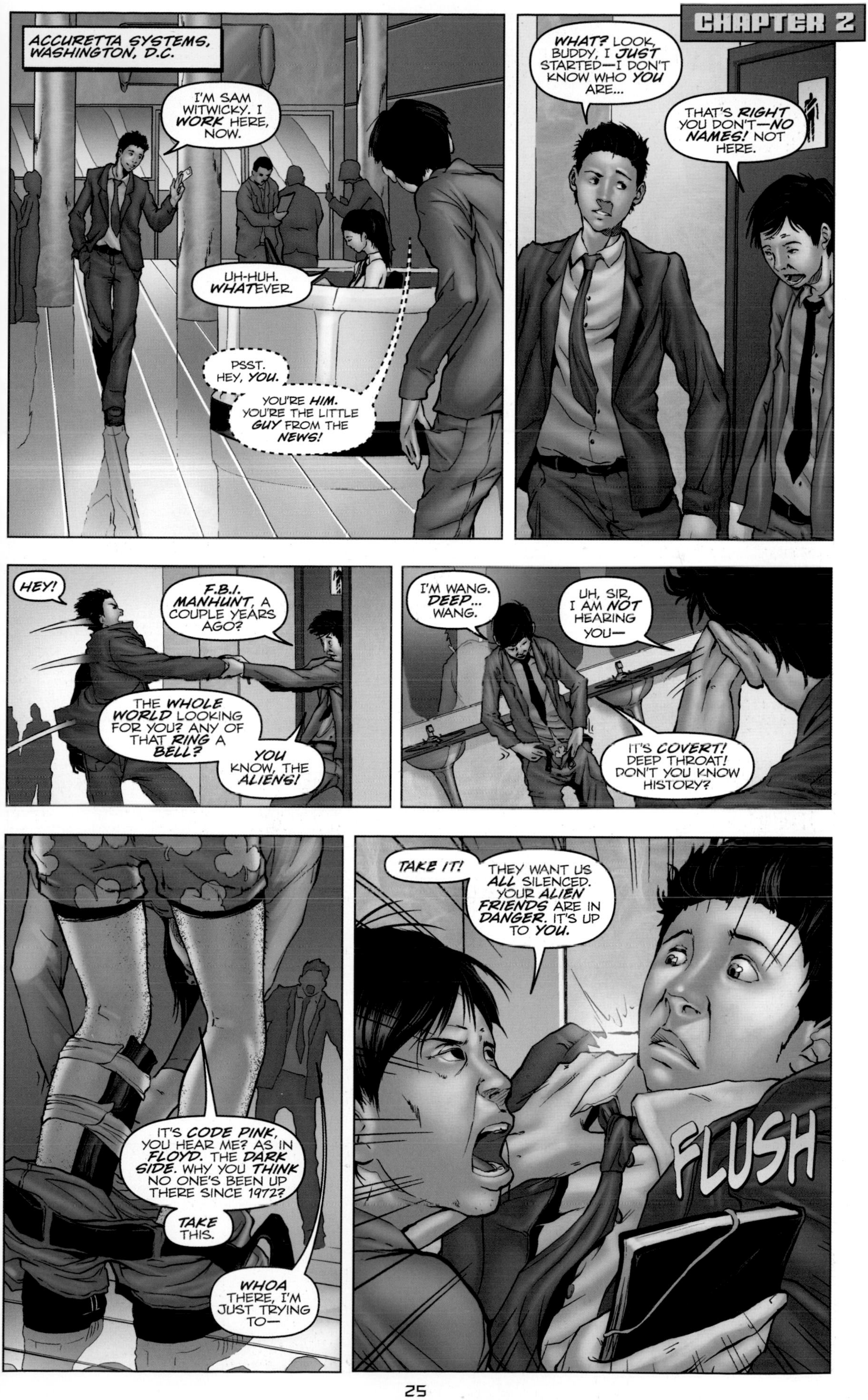
CHAPTER 2
ACCURETTA SYSTEMS, WASHINGTON, D.C.
I'M SAM WITWICKY. I WORK HERE, NOW.
UH-HUH. WHATEVER.
PSST. HEY, YOU.
YOU'RE HIM. YOU'RE THE LITTLE GUY FROM THE NEWS!
WHAT? LOOK, BUDDY, I JUST STARTED—I DON'T KNOW WHO YOU ARE...
THAT'S RIGHT YOU DON'T—NO NAMES! NOT HERE.
HEY!
F.B.I. MANHUNT, A COUPLE YEARS AGO?
THE WHOLE WORLD LOOKING FOR YOU? ANY OF THAT RING A BELL?
YOU KNOW, THE ALIENS!
I'M WANG. DEEP... WANG.
UH, SIR, I AM NOT HEARING YOU—
IT'S COVERT! DEEP THROAT! DON'T YOU KNOW HISTORY?
IT'S CODE PINK, YOU HEAR ME? AS IN FLOYD. THE DARK SIDE. WHY YOU THINK NO ONE'S BEEN UP THERE SINCE 1972?
TAKE THIS.
WHOA THERE, I'M JUST TRYING TO—
TAKE IT!
THEY WANT US ALL SILENCED. YOUR ALIEN FRIENDS ARE IN DANGER. IT'S UP TO YOU.
FLUSH

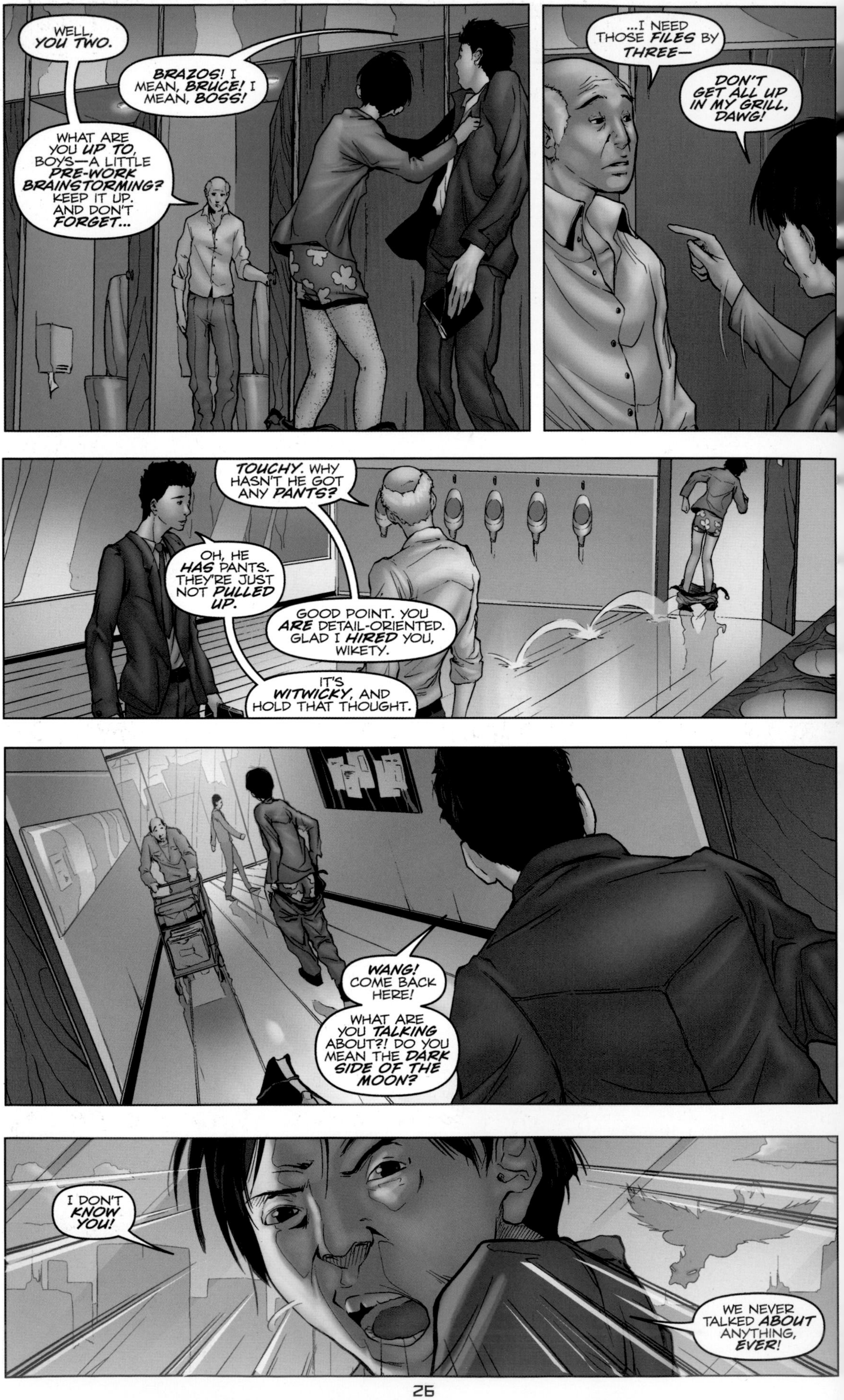
WELL, YOU TWO.
BRAZOS! I MEAN, BRUCE! I MEAN, BOSS!
WHAT ARE YOU UP TO, BOYS—A LITTLE PRE-WORK BRAINSTORMING? KEEP IT UP. AND DON'T FORGET...
...I NEED THOSE FILES BY THREE—
DON'T GET ALL UP IN MY GRILL, DAWG!
TOUCHY. WHY HASN'T HE GOT ANY PANTS?
OH, HE HAS PANTS. THEY'RE JUST NOT PULLED UP.
GOOD POINT. YOU ARE DETAIL-ORIENTED. GLAD I HIRED YOU, WIKETY.
IT'S WITWICKY, AND HOLD THAT THOUGHT.
WANG! COME BACK HERE!
WHAT ARE YOU TALKING ABOUT?! DO YOU MEAN THE DARK SIDE OF THE MOON?
I DON'T KNOW YOU!
WE NEVER TALKED ABOUT ANYTHING, EVER!

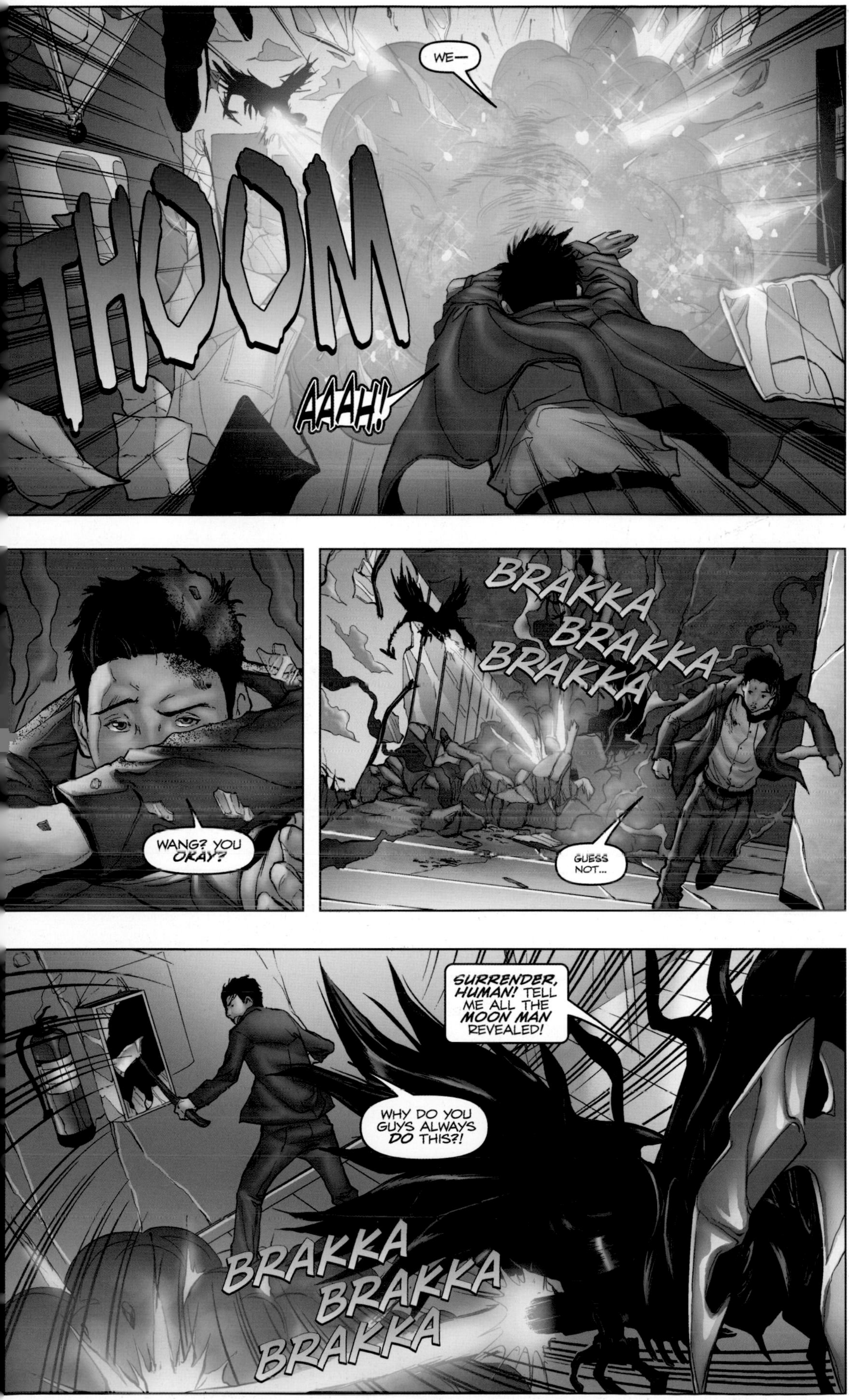
WE—
THOOM
AAAH!
WANG? YOU OKAY?
BRAKKA BRAKKA BRAKKA
GUESS NOT...
SURRENDER, HUMAN! TELL ME ALL THE MOON MAN REVEALED!
WHY DO YOU GUYS ALWAYS DO THIS?!
BRAKKA BRAKKA BRAKKA

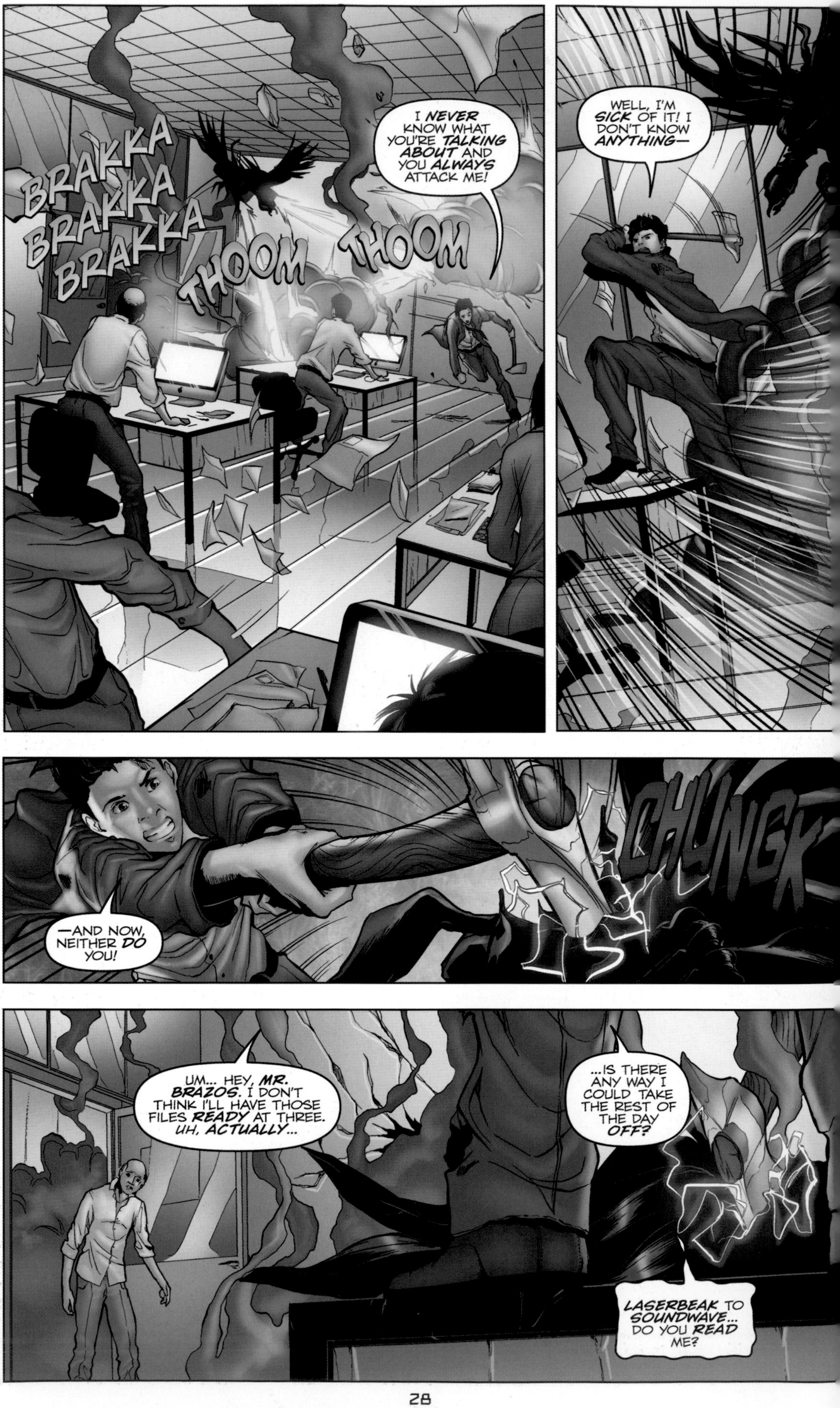
BRAKKA BRAKKA BRAKKA
THOOM THOOM
I NEVER KNOW WHAT YOU'RE TALKING ABOUT AND YOU ALWAYS ATTACK ME!
WELL, I'M SICK OF IT! I DON'T KNOW ANYTHING—
—AND NOW, NEITHER DO YOU!
CHUNGK
UM... HEY, MR. BRAZOS. I DON'T THINK I'LL HAVE THOSE FILES READY AT THREE. UH, ACTUALLY...
...IS THERE ANY WAY I COULD TAKE THE REST OF THE DAY OFF?
LASERBEAK TO SOUNDWAVE... DO YOU READ ME?

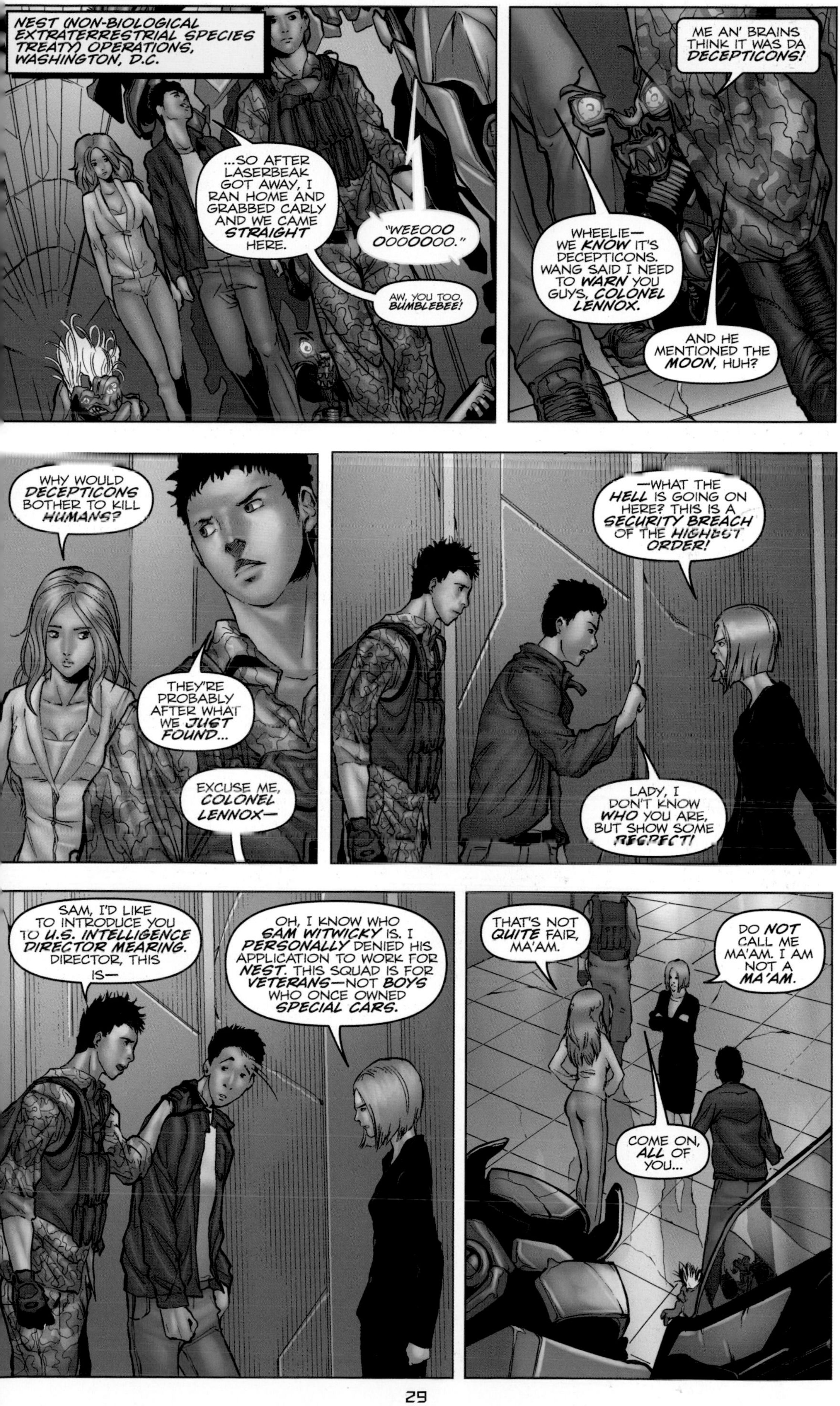
NEST (NON-BIOLOGICAL EXTRATERRESTRIAL SPECIES TREATY) OPERATIONS, WASHINGTON, D.C.
...SO AFTER LASERBEAK GOT AWAY, I RAN HOME AND GRABBED CARLY AND WE CAME STRAIGHT HERE.
"WEEOOO OOOOOOO."
AW, YOU TOO, BUMBLEBEE!
ME AN' BRAINS THINK IT WAS DA DECEPTICONS!
WHEELIE— WE KNOW IT'S DECEPTICONS. WANG SAID I NEED TO WARN YOU GUYS, COLONEL LENNOX.
AND HE MENTIONED THE MOON, HUH?
WHY WOULD DECEPTICONS BOTHER TO KILL HUMANS?
THEY'RE PROBABLY AFTER WHAT WE JUST FOUND...
EXCUSE ME, COLONEL LENNOX—
—WHAT THE HELL IS GOING ON HERE? THIS IS A SECURITY BREACH OF THE HIGHEST ORDER!
LADY, I DON'T KNOW WHO YOU ARE, BUT SHOW SOME RESPECT!
SAM, I'D LIKE TO INTRODUCE YOU TO U.S. INTELLIGENCE DIRECTOR MEARING. DIRECTOR, THIS IS—
OH, I KNOW WHO SAM WITWICKY IS. I PERSONALLY DENIED HIS APPLICATION TO WORK FOR NEST. THIS SQUAD IS FOR VETERANS—NOT BOYS WHO ONCE OWNED SPECIAL CARS.
THAT'S NOT QUITE FAIR, MA'AM.
DO NOT CALL ME MA'AM. I AM NOT A MA'AM.
COME ON, ALL OF YOU...

...YOU NEED TO SEE THIS.

HELLO, SAMUEL.

IRONHIDE, RATCHET! WHAT'S... OH... WHO...?

I SUPPOSE I COULD BE JEALOUS OF THEM.

AFTER ALL, THE AUTOBOTS HAVE FRIENDS.

THAT'S SENTINEL PRIME.

HE WAS OPTIMUS' MENTOR, AND... HE ONCE WAS OUR LEADER.

THE MATRIX OF LEADERSHIP—THE ONLY THING IN THE UNIVERSE THAT COULD POSSIBLY RE-POWER AN AUTOBOT THAT'S BEEN STUCK ON THE MOON FOR SO LONG.

THE MOON, COLONEL LENNOX?

SHH, SAM. THIS IS A SOLEMN MOMENT.

I TAKE SOLACE THAT ONLY FRIENDS...

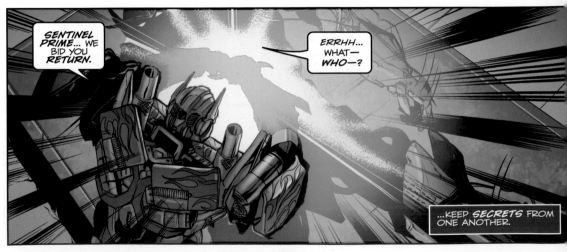

SENTINEL PRIME... WE BID YOU RETURN.

ERRHH... WHAT— WHO—?

...KEEP SECRETS FROM ONE ANOTHER.

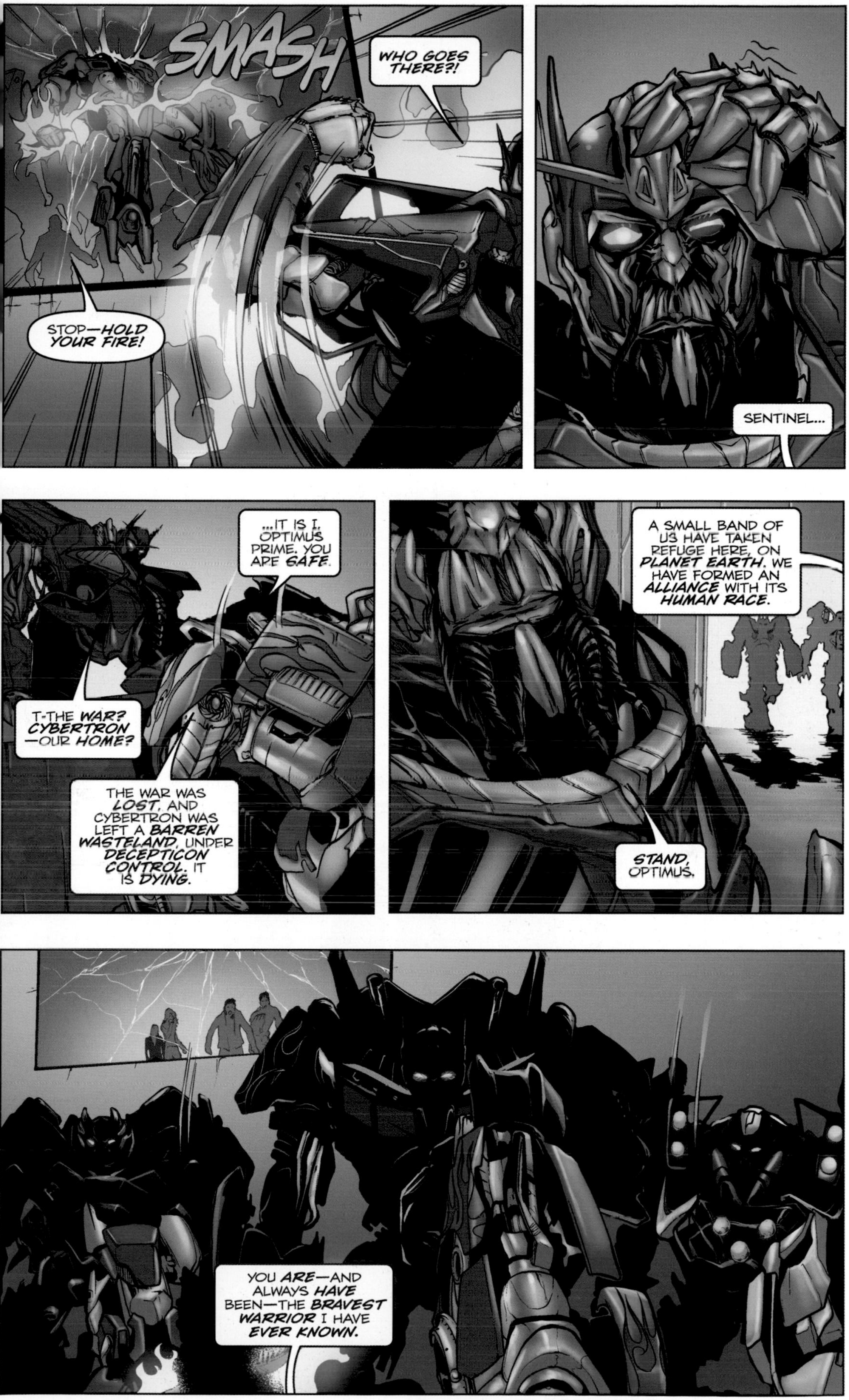
SMASH
WHO GOES THERE?!
STOP—HOLD YOUR FIRE!
SENTINEL...
...IT IS I, OPTIMUS PRIME. YOU ARE SAFE.
T-THE WAR? CYBERTRON—OUR HOME?
THE WAR WAS LOST, AND CYBERTRON WAS LEFT A BARREN WASTELAND, UNDER DECEPTICON CONTROL. IT IS DYING.
A SMALL BAND OF US HAVE TAKEN REFUGE HERE, ON PLANET EARTH. WE HAVE FORMED AN ALLIANCE WITH ITS HUMAN RACE.
STAND, OPTIMUS.
YOU ARE—AND ALWAYS HAVE BEEN—THE BRAVEST WARRIOR I HAVE EVER KNOWN.

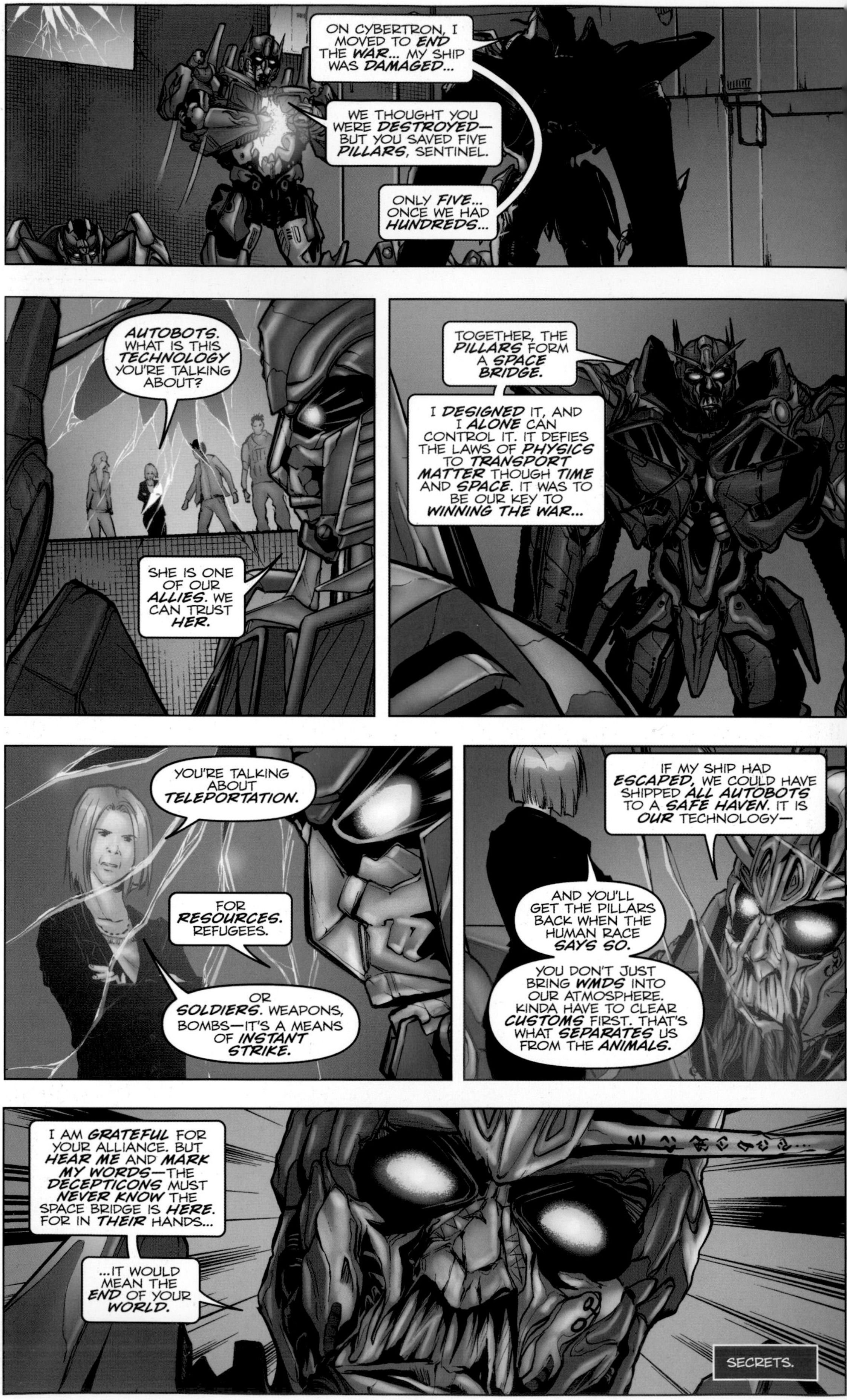
ON CYBERTRON, I MOVED TO END THE WAR... MY SHIP WAS DAMAGED...
WE THOUGHT YOU WERE DESTROYED— BUT YOU SAVED FIVE PILLARS, SENTINEL.
ONLY FIVE... ONCE WE HAD HUNDREDS...
AUTOBOTS. WHAT IS THIS TECHNOLOGY YOU'RE TALKING ABOUT?
SHE IS ONE OF OUR ALLIES. WE CAN TRUST HER.
TOGETHER, THE PILLARS FORM A SPACE BRIDGE.
I DESIGNED IT, AND I ALONE CAN CONTROL IT. IT DEFIES THE LAWS OF PHYSICS TO TRANSPORT MATTER THOUGH TIME AND SPACE. IT WAS TO BE OUR KEY TO WINNING THE WAR...
YOU'RE TALKING ABOUT TELEPORTATION.
FOR RESOURCES. REFUGEES.
OR SOLDIERS. WEAPONS, BOMBS—IT'S A MEANS OF INSTANT STRIKE.
IF MY SHIP HAD ESCAPED, WE COULD HAVE SHIPPED ALL AUTOBOTS TO A SAFE HAVEN. IT IS OUR TECHNOLOGY—
AND YOU'LL GET THE PILLARS BACK WHEN THE HUMAN RACE SAYS SO.
YOU DON'T JUST BRING WMDS INTO OUR ATMOSPHERE. KINDA HAVE TO CLEAR CUSTOMS FIRST. THAT'S WHAT SEPARATES US FROM THE ANIMALS.
I AM GRATEFUL FOR YOUR ALLIANCE. BUT HEAR ME AND MARK MY WORDS—THE DECEPTICONS MUST NEVER KNOW THE SPACE BRIDGE IS HERE. FOR IN THEIR HANDS...
...IT WOULD MEAN THE END OF YOUR WORLD.
SECRETS.

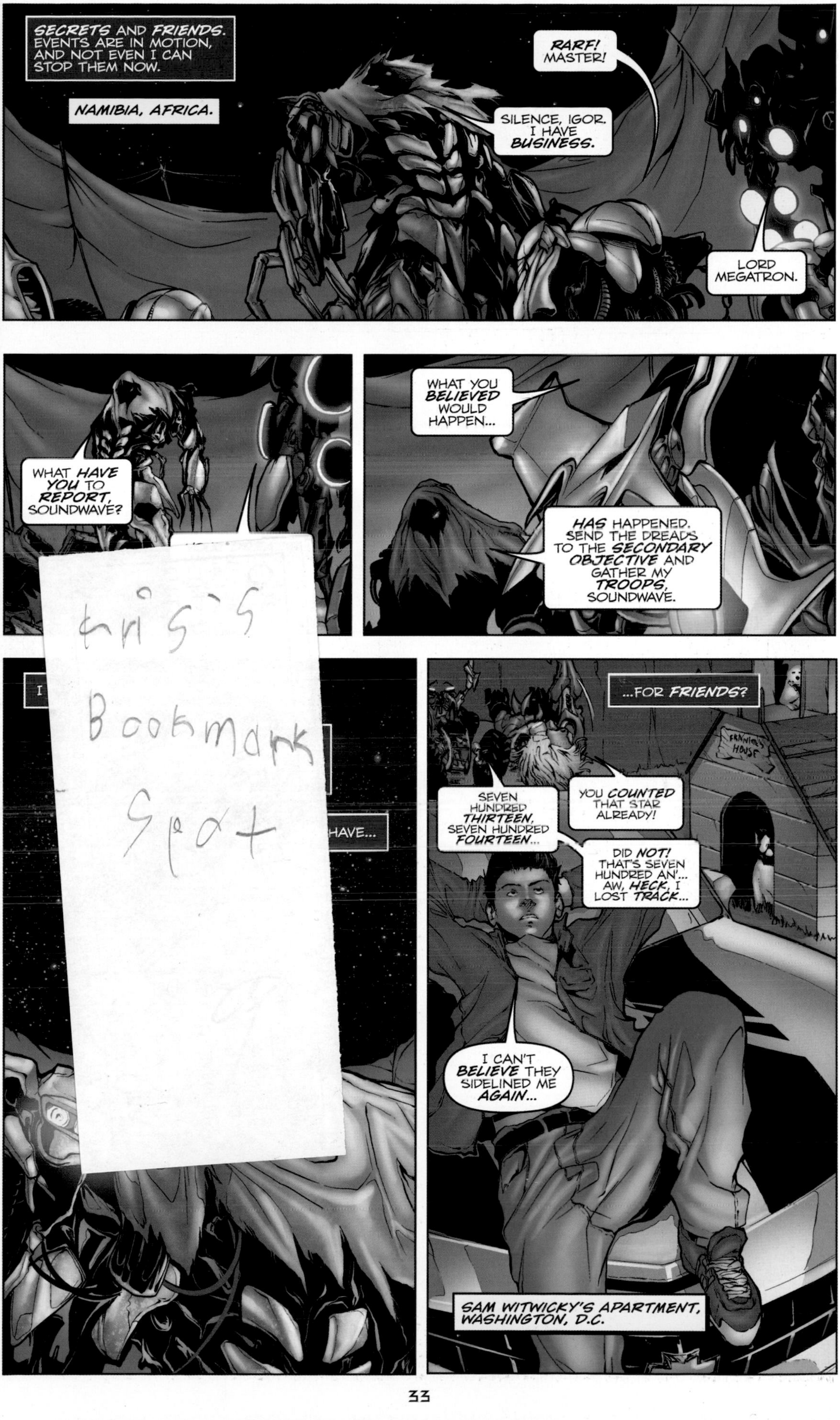
SECRETS AND FRIENDS. EVENTS ARE IN MOTION, AND NOT EVEN I CAN STOP THEM NOW.
NAMIBIA, AFRICA.
RARF! MASTER!
SILENCE, IGOR. I HAVE BUSINESS.
LORD MEGATRON.
WHAT HAVE YOU TO REPORT, SOUNDWAVE?
WHAT YOU BELIEVED WOULD HAPPEN...
HAS HAPPENED. SEND THE DREADS TO THE SECONDARY OBJECTIVE AND GATHER MY TROOPS, SOUNDWAVE.
this is Bookmark Spot
...FOR FRIENDS?
FRANNIE'S HOUSE
SEVEN HUNDRED THIRTEEN, SEVEN HUNDRED FOURTEEN...
YOU COUNTED THAT STAR ALREADY!
DID NOT! THAT'S SEVEN HUNDRED AN'... AW, HECK, I LOST TRACK...
I CAN'T BELIEVE THEY SIDELINED ME AGAIN...
SAM WITWICKY'S APARTMENT, WASHINGTON, D.C.

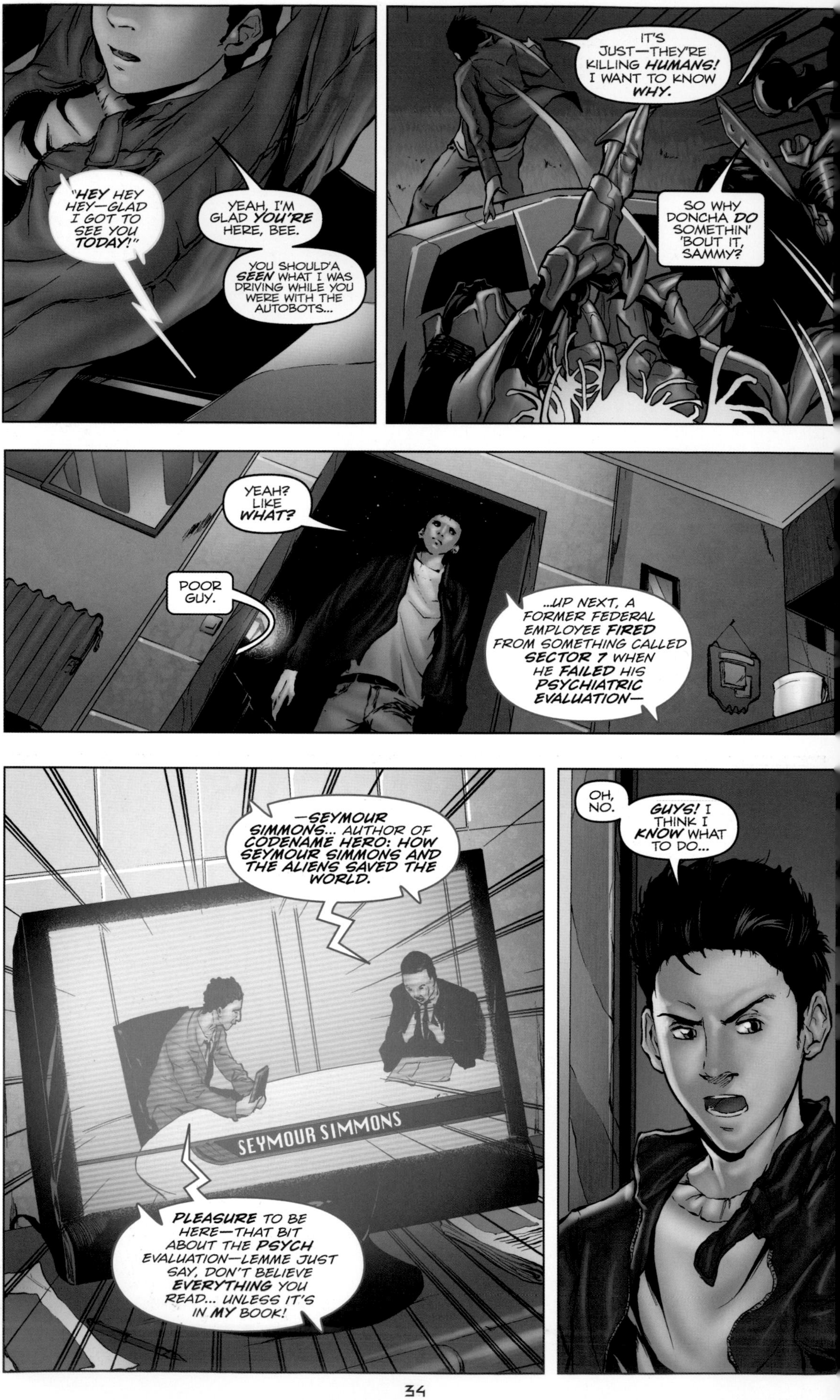
"HEY HEY HEY—GLAD I GOT TO SEE YOU TODAY!"
YEAH, I'M GLAD YOU'RE HERE, BEE.
YOU SHOULD'A SEEN WHAT I WAS DRIVING WHILE YOU WERE WITH THE AUTOBOTS...
IT'S JUST—THEY'RE KILLING HUMANS! I WANT TO KNOW WHY.
SO WHY DONCHA DO SOMETHIN' 'BOUT IT, SAMMY?
YEAH? LIKE WHAT?
POOR GUY.
...UP NEXT, A FORMER FEDERAL EMPLOYEE FIRED FROM SOMETHING CALLED SECTOR 7 WHEN HE FAILED HIS PSYCHIATRIC EVALUATION—
—SEYMOUR SIMMONS... AUTHOR OF CODENAME HERO: HOW SEYMOUR SIMMONS AND THE ALIENS SAVED THE WORLD.
SEYMOUR SIMMONS
PLEASURE TO BE HERE—THAT BIT ABOUT THE PSYCH EVALUATION—LEMME JUST SAY, DON'T BELIEVE EVERYTHING YOU READ... UNLESS IT'S IN MY BOOK!
OH, NO.
GUYS! I THINK I KNOW WHAT TO DO...

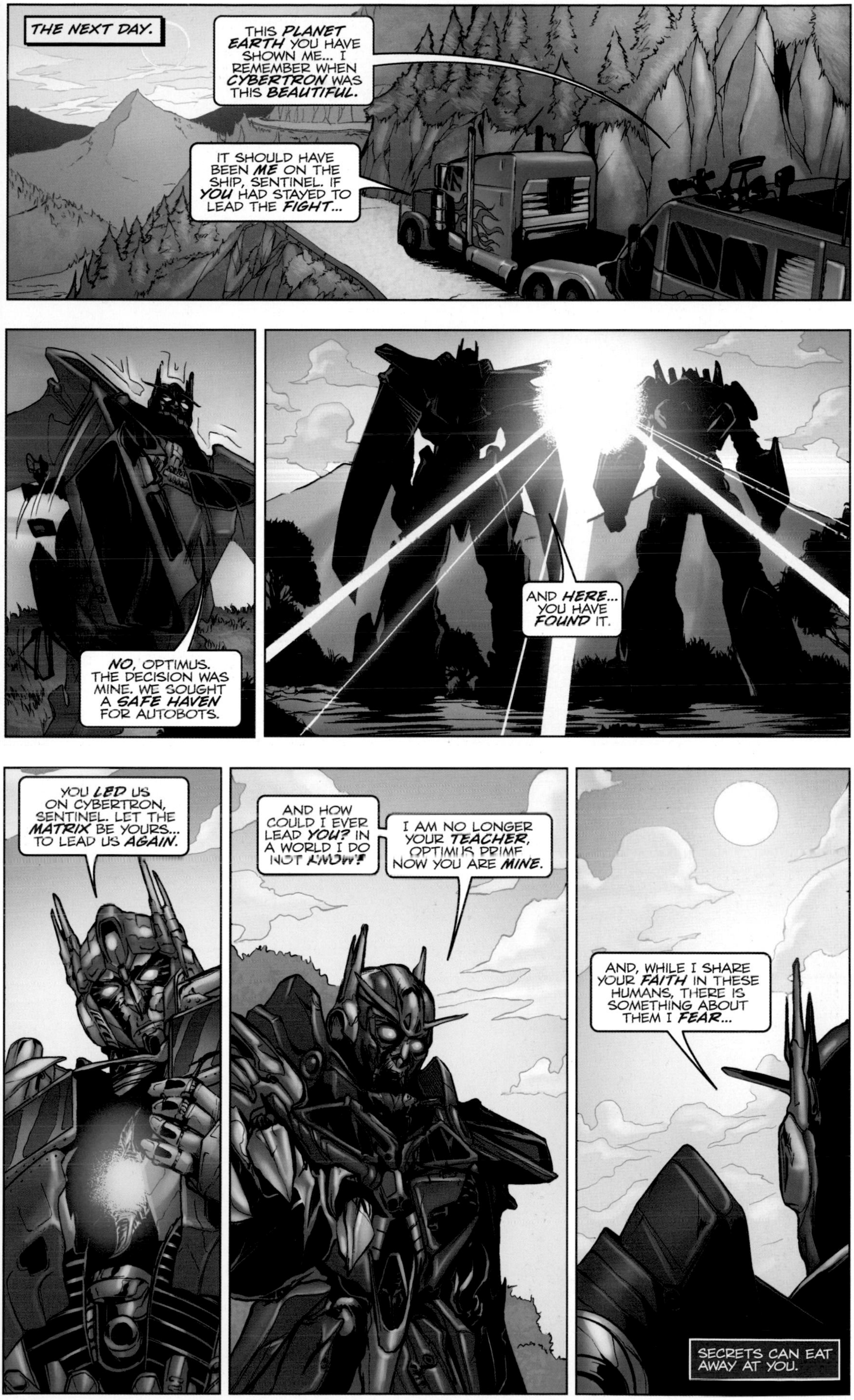
THE NEXT DAY.
THIS PLANET EARTH YOU HAVE SHOWN ME... I REMEMBER WHEN CYBERTRON WAS THIS BEAUTIFUL.
IT SHOULD HAVE BEEN ME ON THE SHIP, SENTINEL. IF YOU HAD STAYED TO LEAD THE FIGHT...
NO, OPTIMUS. THE DECISION WAS MINE. WE SOUGHT A SAFE HAVEN FOR AUTOBOTS.
AND HERE... YOU HAVE FOUND IT.
YOU LED US ON CYBERTRON, SENTINEL. LET THE MATRIX BE YOURS... TO LEAD US AGAIN.
AND HOW COULD I EVER LEAD YOU? IN A WORLD I DO NOT KNOW?
I AM NO LONGER YOUR TEACHER, OPTIMUS PRIME. NOW YOU ARE MINE.
AND, WHILE I SHARE YOUR FAITH IN THESE HUMANS, THERE IS SOMETHING ABOUT THEM I FEAR...
SECRETS CAN EAT AWAY AT YOU.

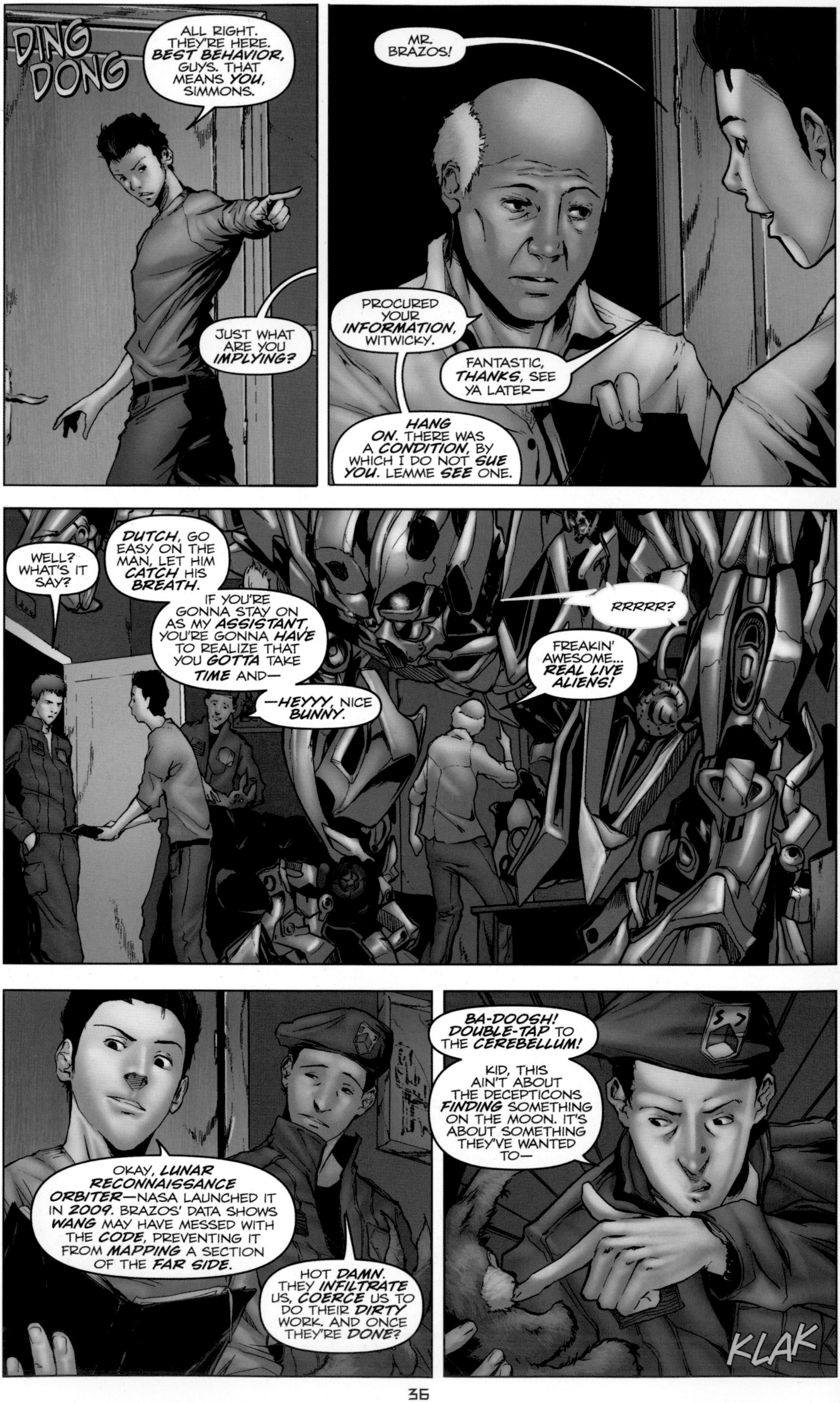
DING DONG
ALL RIGHT. THEY'RE HERE. BEST BEHAVIOR, GUYS. THAT MEANS YOU, SIMMONS.
JUST WHAT ARE YOU IMPLYING?
MR. BRAZOS!
PROCURED YOUR INFORMATION, WITWICKY.
FANTASTIC, THANKS, SEE YA LATER—
HANG ON. THERE WAS A CONDITION, BY WHICH I DO NOT SUE YOU. LEMME SEE ONE.
WELL? WHAT'S IT SAY?
DUTCH, GO EASY ON THE MAN, LET HIM CATCH HIS BREATH.
IF YOU'RE GONNA STAY ON AS MY ASSISTANT, YOU'RE GONNA HAVE TO REALIZE THAT YOU GOTTA TAKE TIME AND—
—HEYYY, NICE BUNNY.
RRRRR?
FREAKIN' AWESOME... REAL LIVE ALIENS!
OKAY, LUNAR RECONNAISSANCE ORBITER—NASA LAUNCHED IT IN 2009. BRAZOS' DATA SHOWS WANG MAY HAVE MESSED WITH THE CODE, PREVENTING IT FROM MAPPING A SECTION OF THE FAR SIDE.
HOT DAMN. THEY INFILTRATE US, COERCE US TO DO THEIR DIRTY WORK. AND ONCE THEY'RE DONE?
BA-DOOSH! DOUBLE-TAP TO THE CEREBELLUM!
KID, THIS AIN'T ABOUT THE DECEPTICONS FINDING SOMETHING ON THE MOON. IT'S ABOUT SOMETHING THEY'VE WANTED TO—
KLAK

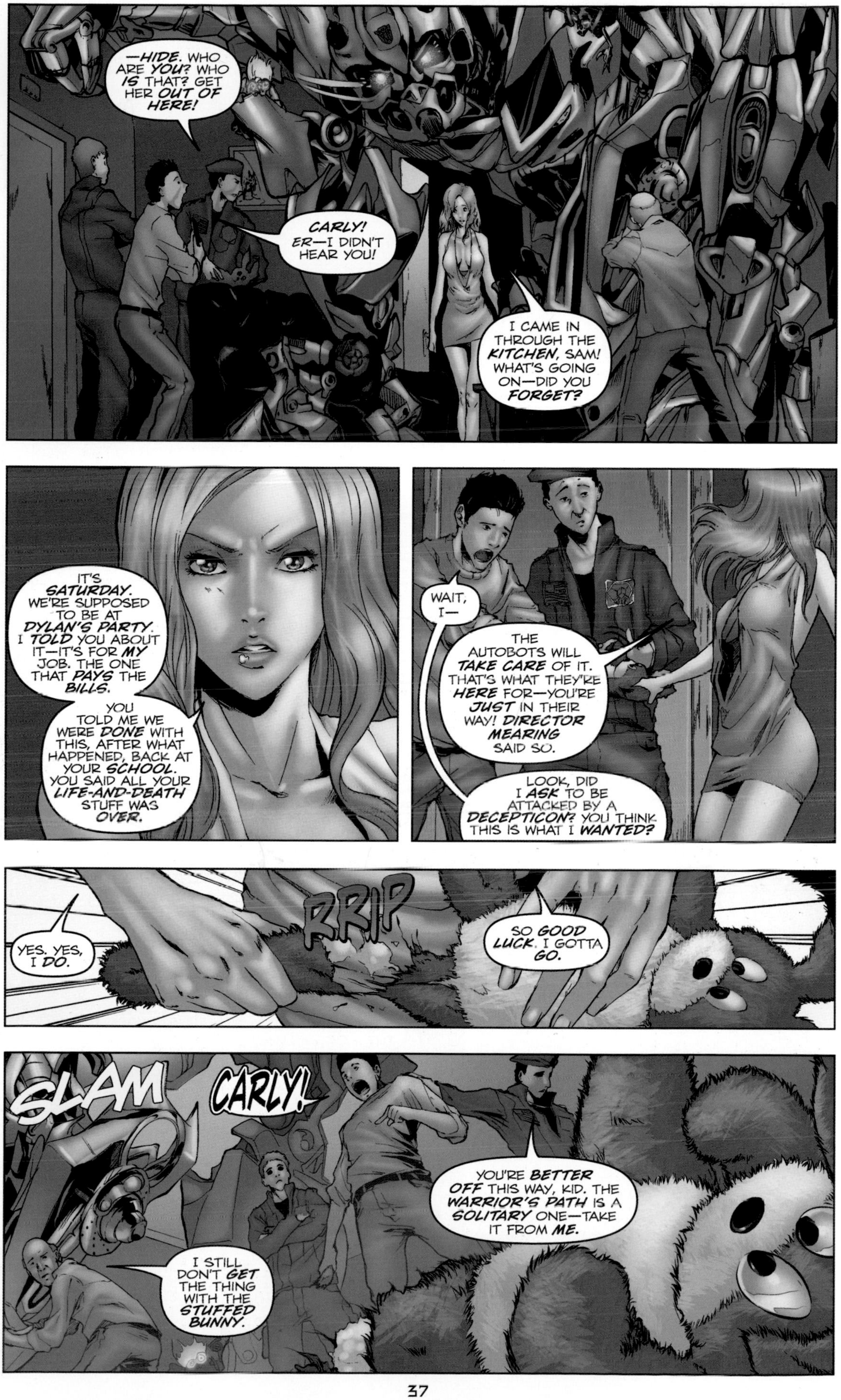
—HIDE. WHO ARE YOU? WHO IS THAT? GET HER OUT OF HERE!
CARLY! ER—I DIDN'T HEAR YOU!
I CAME IN THROUGH THE KITCHEN, SAM! WHAT'S GOING ON—DID YOU FORGET?
IT'S SATURDAY. WE'RE SUPPOSED TO BE AT DYLAN'S PARTY. I TOLD YOU ABOUT IT—IT'S FOR MY JOB. THE ONE THAT PAYS THE BILLS.
YOU TOLD ME WE WERE DONE WITH THIS, AFTER WHAT HAPPENED, BACK AT YOUR SCHOOL. YOU SAID ALL YOUR LIFE-AND-DEATH STUFF WAS OVER.
WAIT, I—
THE AUTOBOTS WILL TAKE CARE OF IT. THAT'S WHAT THEY'RE HERE FOR—YOU'RE JUST IN THEIR WAY! DIRECTOR MEARING SAID SO.
LOOK, DID I ASK TO BE ATTACKED BY A DECEPTICON? YOU THINK THIS IS WHAT I WANTED?
YES. YES, I DO.
RRIP
SO GOOD LUCK. I GOTTA GO.
SLAM
CARLY!
YOU'RE BETTER OFF THIS WAY, KID. THE WARRIOR'S PATH IS A SOLITARY ONE—TAKE IT FROM ME.
I STILL DON'T GET THE THING WITH THE STUFFED BUNNY.

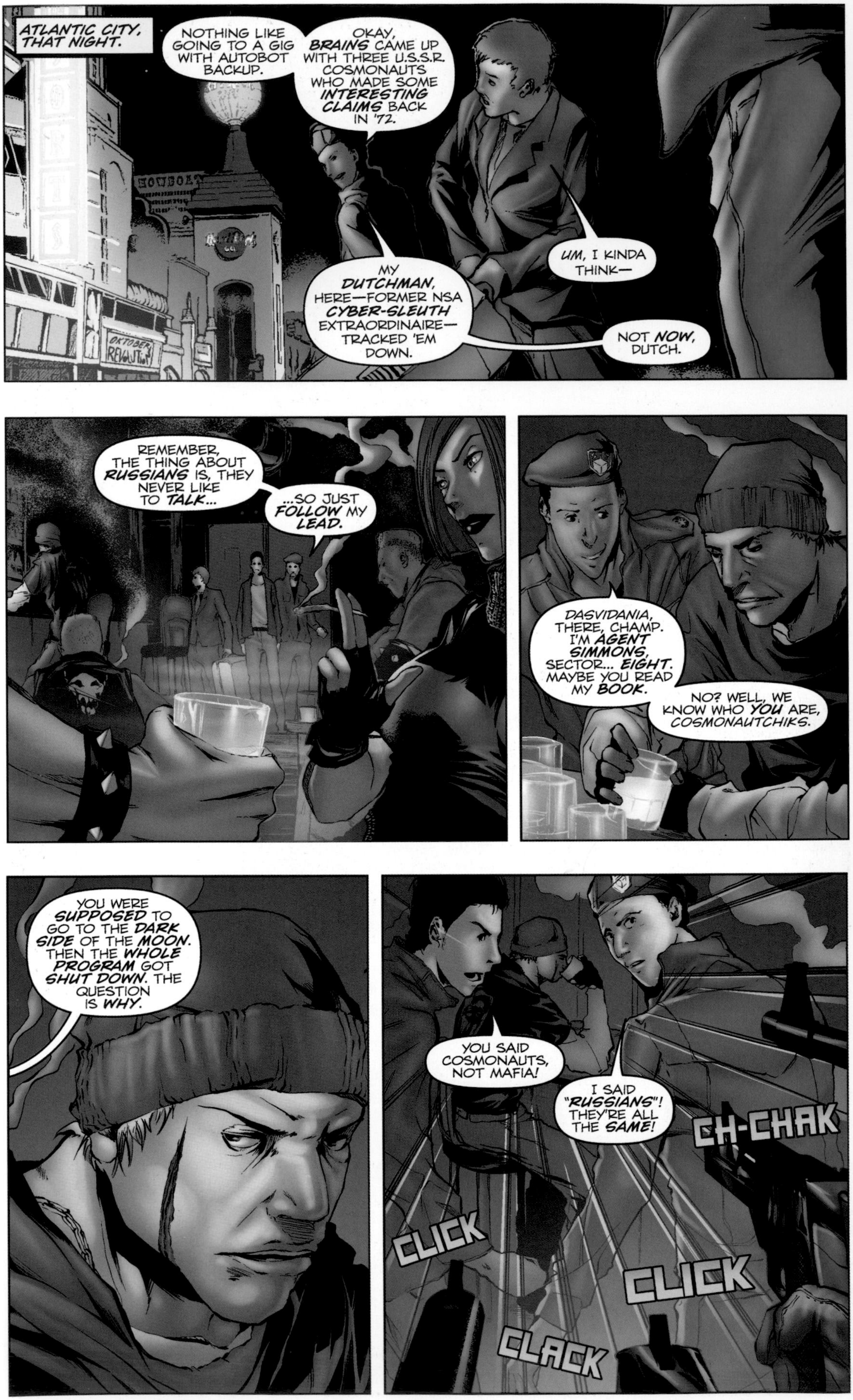
ATLANTIC CITY, THAT NIGHT.
NOTHING LIKE GOING TO A GIG WITH AUTOBOT BACKUP.
OKAY, BRAINS CAME UP WITH THREE U.S.S.R. COSMONAUTS WHO MADE SOME INTERESTING CLAIMS BACK IN '72.
MY DUTCHMAN, HERE—FORMER NSA CYBER-SLEUTH EXTRAORDINAIRE—TRACKED 'EM DOWN.
UM, I KINDA THINK—
NOT NOW, DUTCH.
OKTOBER REVOLUTION
REMEMBER, THE THING ABOUT RUSSIANS IS, THEY NEVER LIKE TO TALK...
...SO JUST FOLLOW MY LEAD.
DASVIDANIA, THERE, CHAMP. I'M AGENT SIMMONS, SECTOR... EIGHT. MAYBE YOU READ MY BOOK.
NO? WELL, WE KNOW WHO YOU ARE, COSMONAUTCHIKS.
YOU WERE SUPPOSED TO GO TO THE DARK SIDE OF THE MOON. THEN THE WHOLE PROGRAM GOT SHUT DOWN. THE QUESTION IS WHY.
YOU SAID COSMONAUTS, NOT MAFIA!
I SAID "RUSSIANS"! THEY'RE ALL THE SAME!
CH-CHAK
CLICK
CLICK
CLACK

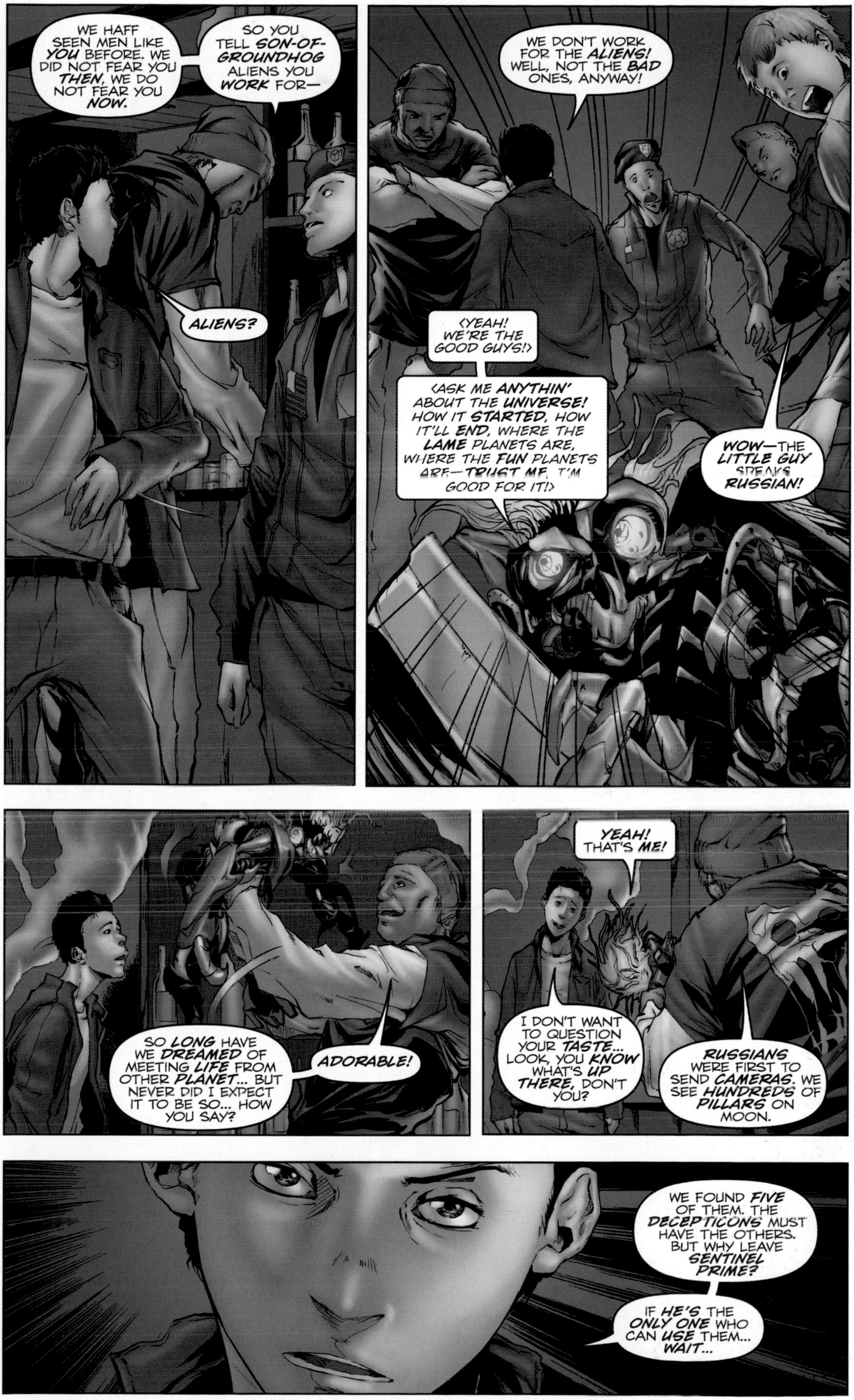
WE HAFF SEEN MEN LIKE YOU BEFORE. WE DID NOT FEAR YOU THEN, WE DO NOT FEAR YOU NOW.
SO YOU TELL SON-OF-GROUNDHOG ALIENS YOU WORK FOR—
ALIENS?
WE DON'T WORK FOR THE ALIENS! WELL, NOT THE BAD ONES, ANYWAY!
<YEAH! WE'RE THE GOOD GUYS!>
<ASK ME ANYTHIN' ABOUT THE UNIVERSE! HOW IT STARTED, HOW IT'LL END, WHERE THE LAME PLANETS ARE, WHERE THE FUN PLANETS ARE—TRUST ME, I'M GOOD FOR IT!>
WOW—THE LITTLE GUY SPEAKS RUSSIAN!
SO LONG HAVE WE DREAMED OF MEETING LIFE FROM OTHER PLANET... BUT NEVER DID I EXPECT IT TO BE SO... HOW YOU SAY?
ADORABLE!
YEAH! THAT'S ME!
I DON'T WANT TO QUESTION YOUR TASTE... LOOK, YOU KNOW WHAT'S UP THERE, DON'T YOU?
RUSSIANS WERE FIRST TO SEND CAMERAS. WE SEE HUNDREDS OF PILLARS ON MOON.
WE FOUND FIVE OF THEM. THE DECEPTICONS MUST HAVE THE OTHERS. BUT WHY LEAVE SENTINEL PRIME?
IF HE'S THE ONLY ONE WHO CAN USE THEM... WAIT...

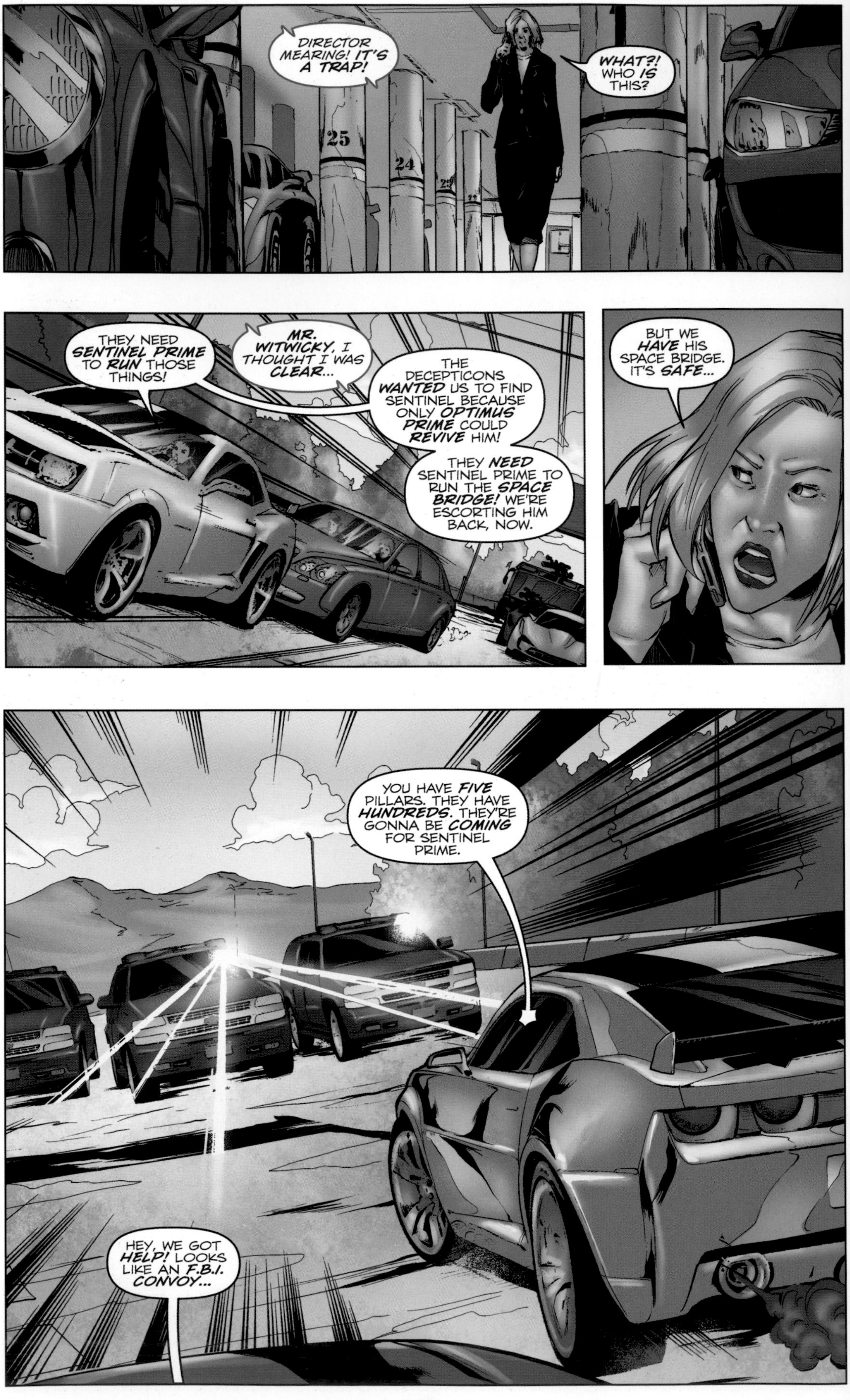
DIRECTOR MEARING! IT'S A TRAP!
WHAT?! WHO IS THIS?
25
24
THEY NEED SENTINEL PRIME TO RUN THOSE THINGS!
MR. WITWICKY, I THOUGHT I WAS CLEAR...
THE DECEPTICONS WANTED US TO FIND SENTINEL BECAUSE ONLY OPTIMUS PRIME COULD REVIVE HIM!
THEY NEED SENTINEL PRIME TO RUN THE SPACE BRIDGE! WE'RE ESCORTING HIM BACK, NOW.
BUT WE HAVE HIS SPACE BRIDGE. IT'S SAFE...
YOU HAVE FIVE PILLARS. THEY HAVE HUNDREDS. THEY'RE GONNA BE COMING FOR SENTINEL PRIME.
HEY, WE GOT HELP! LOOKS LIKE AN F.B.I. CONVOY...

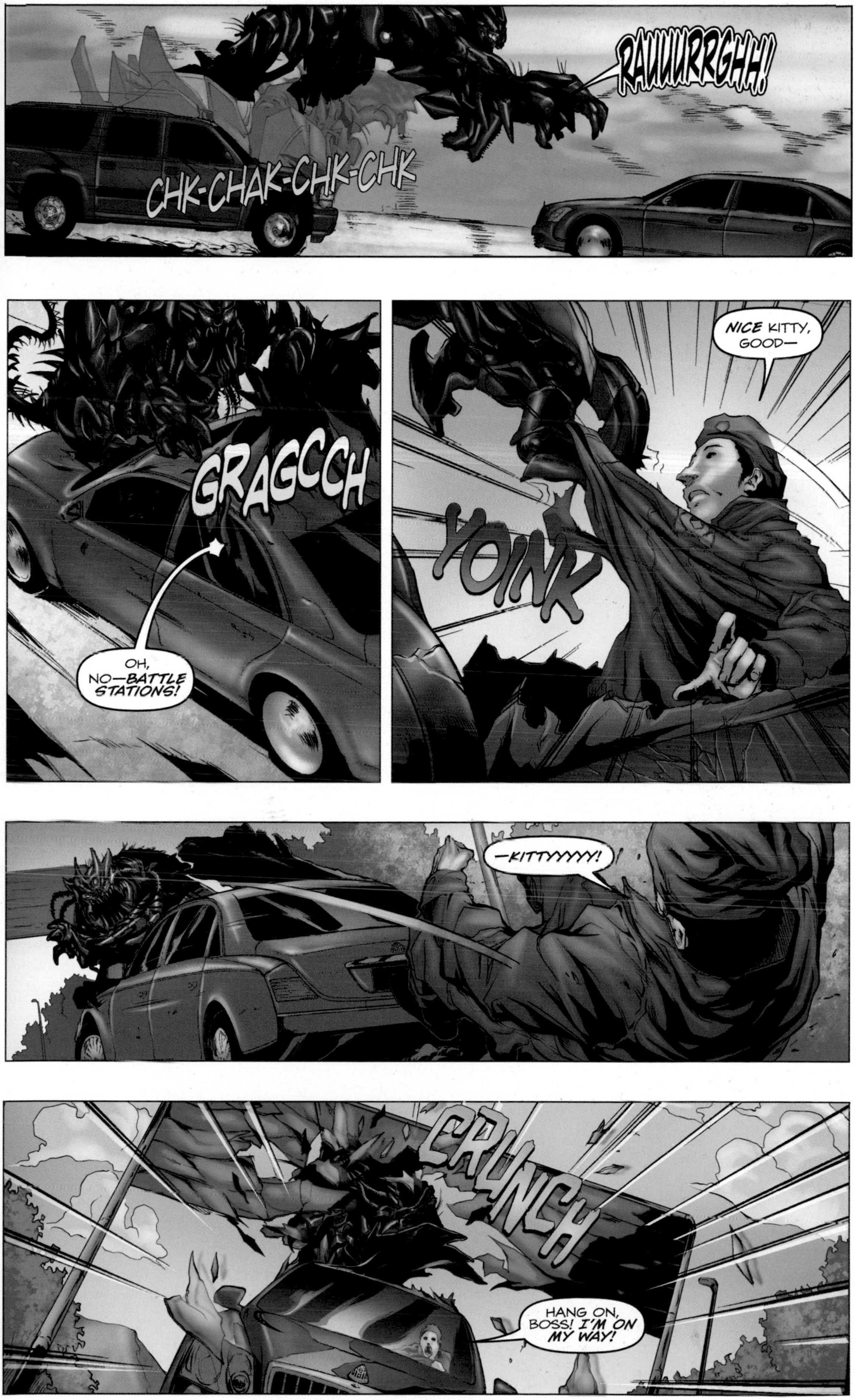
RAUUURRGHH!
CHK-CHAK-CHK-CHK
GRAGCCH
OH, NO—BATTLE STATIONS!
NICE KITTY, GOOD—
YOINK
—KITTYYYYY!
CRUNCH
HANG ON, BOSS! I'M ON MY WAY!

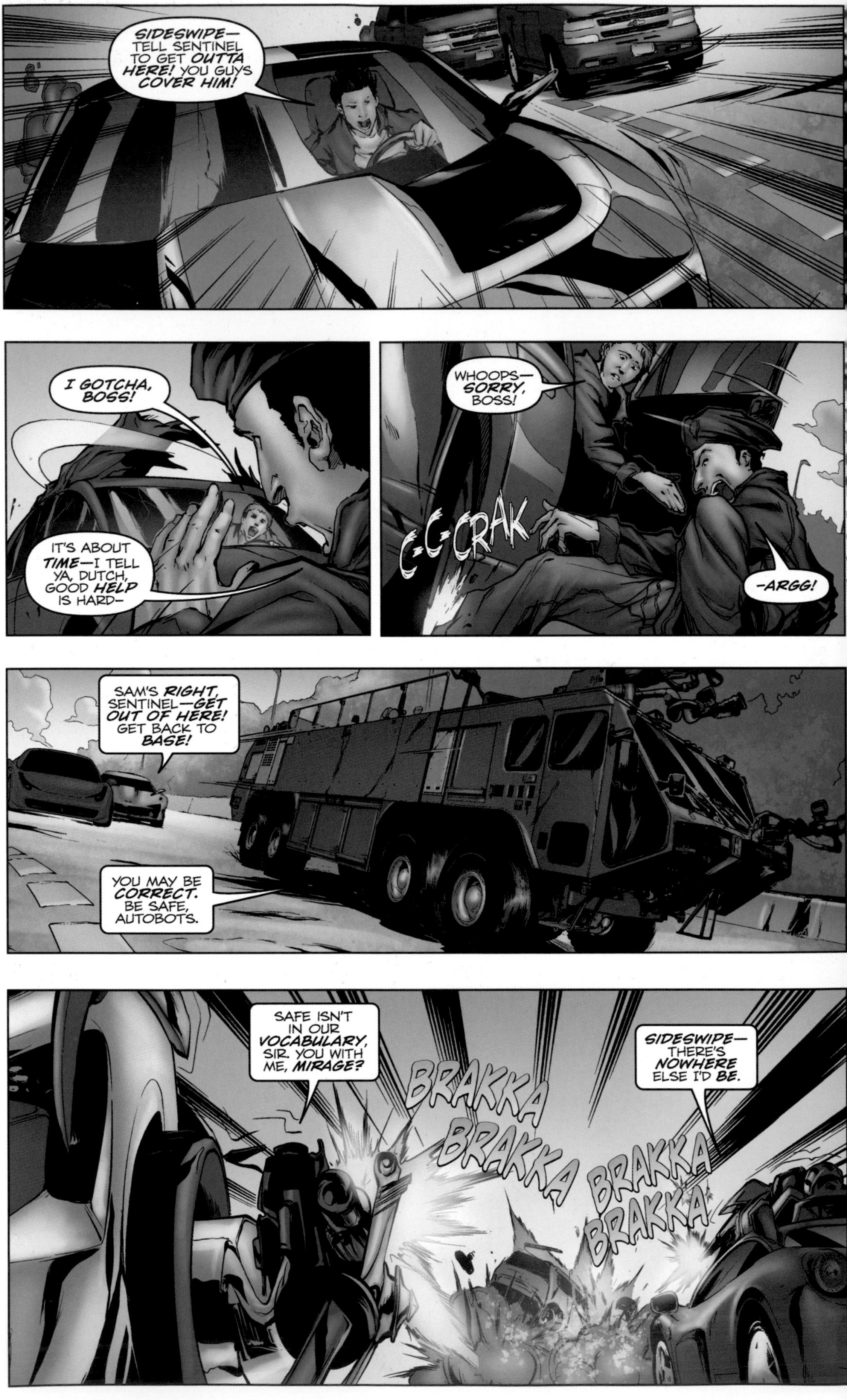
SIDESWIPE— TELL SENTINEL TO GET OUTTA HERE! YOU GUYS COVER HIM!
I GOTCHA, BOSS!
IT'S ABOUT TIME—I TELL YA, DUTCH, GOOD HELP IS HARD–
WHOOPS— SORRY, BOSS!
C-C-CRAK
–ARGG!
SAM'S RIGHT, SENTINEL—GET OUT OF HERE! GET BACK TO BASE!
YOU MAY BE CORRECT. BE SAFE, AUTOBOTS.
SAFE ISN'T IN OUR VOCABULARY, SIR. YOU WITH ME, MIRAGE?
BRAKKA BRAKKA BRAKKA BRAKKA
SIDESWIPE— THERE'S NOWHERE ELSE I'D BE.

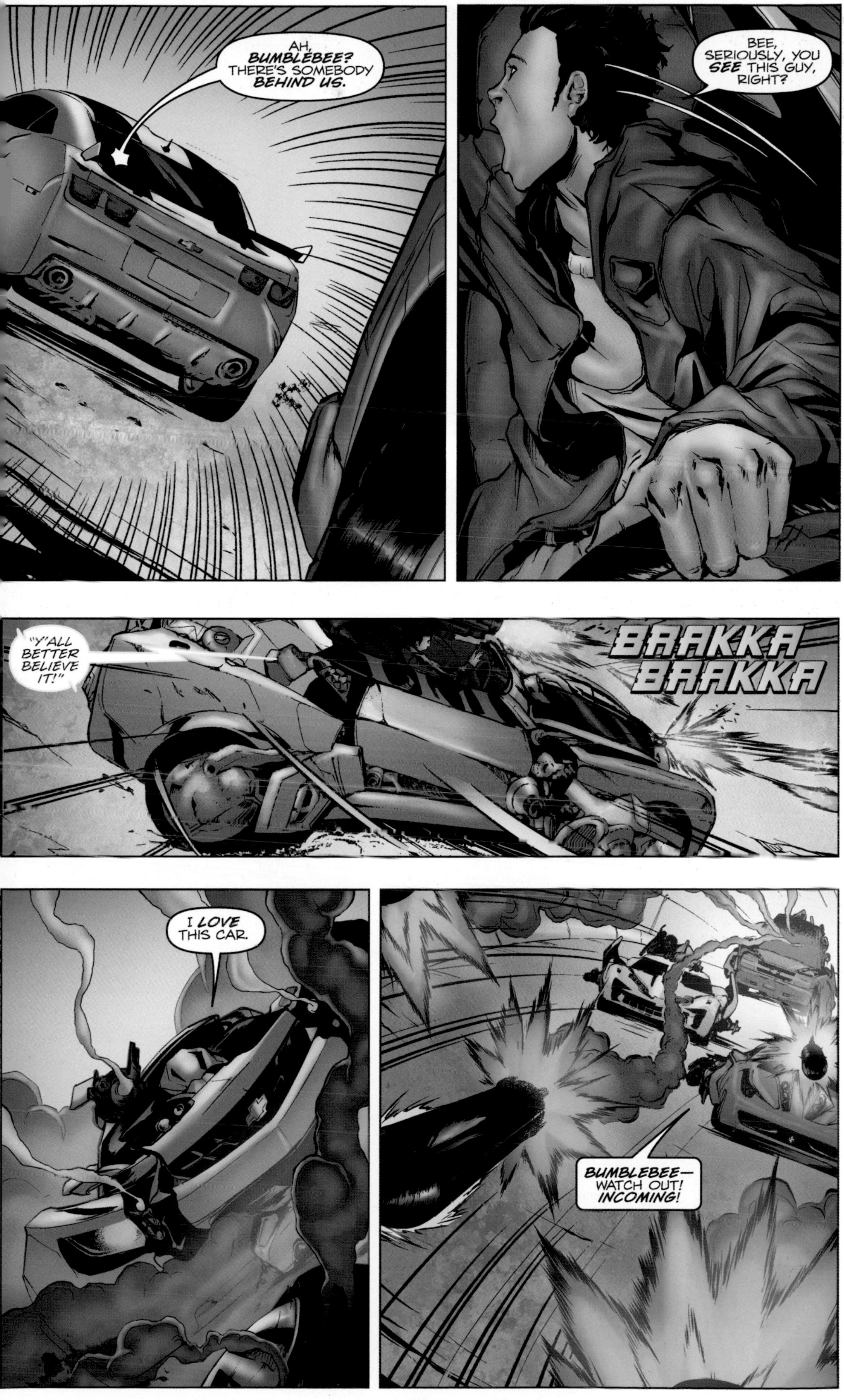
AH, BUMBLEBEE? THERE'S SOMEBODY BEHIND US.
BEE, SERIOUSLY, YOU SEE THIS GUY, RIGHT?
"Y'ALL BETTER BELIEVE IT!"
BRAKKA BRAKKA
I LOVE THIS CAR.
BUMBLEBEE— WATCH OUT! INCOMING!

BEE—

—DO—

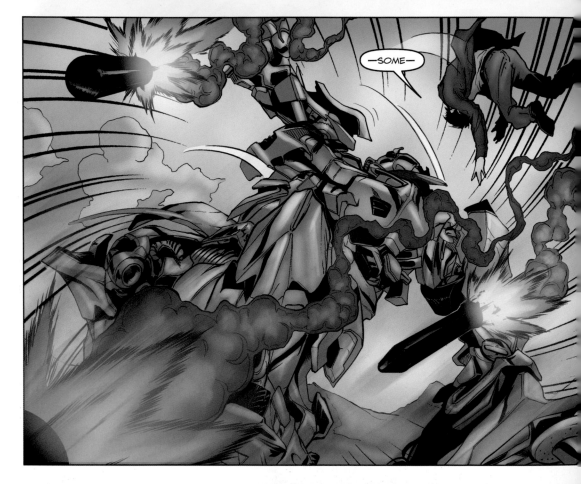

—SOME—

—THING!

WHEW. PLEASE DON'T EVER DO *THAT* AGAIN.

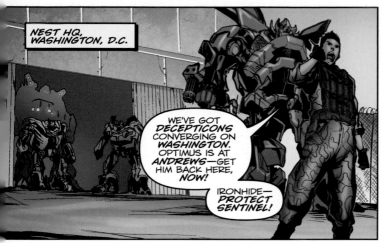

NEST HQ, WASHINGTON, D.C.

WE'VE GOT *DECEPTICONS* ON *WASHINGTON.* OPTIMUS IS AT *ANDREWS*—GET HIM BACK HERE, *NOW!*

IRONHIDE—*PROTECT SENTINEL!*

FRIENDS ARE *SUPPOSED* TO HELP YOU WHEN YOU'RE DOWN.

OR SO I'M *TOLD.*

OF COURSE, COLONEL LENNOX...

...THAT'S WHAT I'M *HERE* FOR.

KA-SMASH

BUT I'VE LEARNED THAT WITH *FRIENDSHIP* COMES *TRUST,* AND WITH *TRUST* COME *LIES.*

BUT WHAT DO *I* HAVE TO *LIE* ABOUT?

KEEP HIM GUARDED! *HE'S THE KEY!*

THAT'S RIGHT, IRONHIDE.

MY MOTIVES, MY *OBJECTIVES,* ARE A MATTER OF *RECORD:* I *FIGHT* FOR *CYBERTRON.*

CHOOF

WHAT USE WOULD *MEGATRON* HAVE...

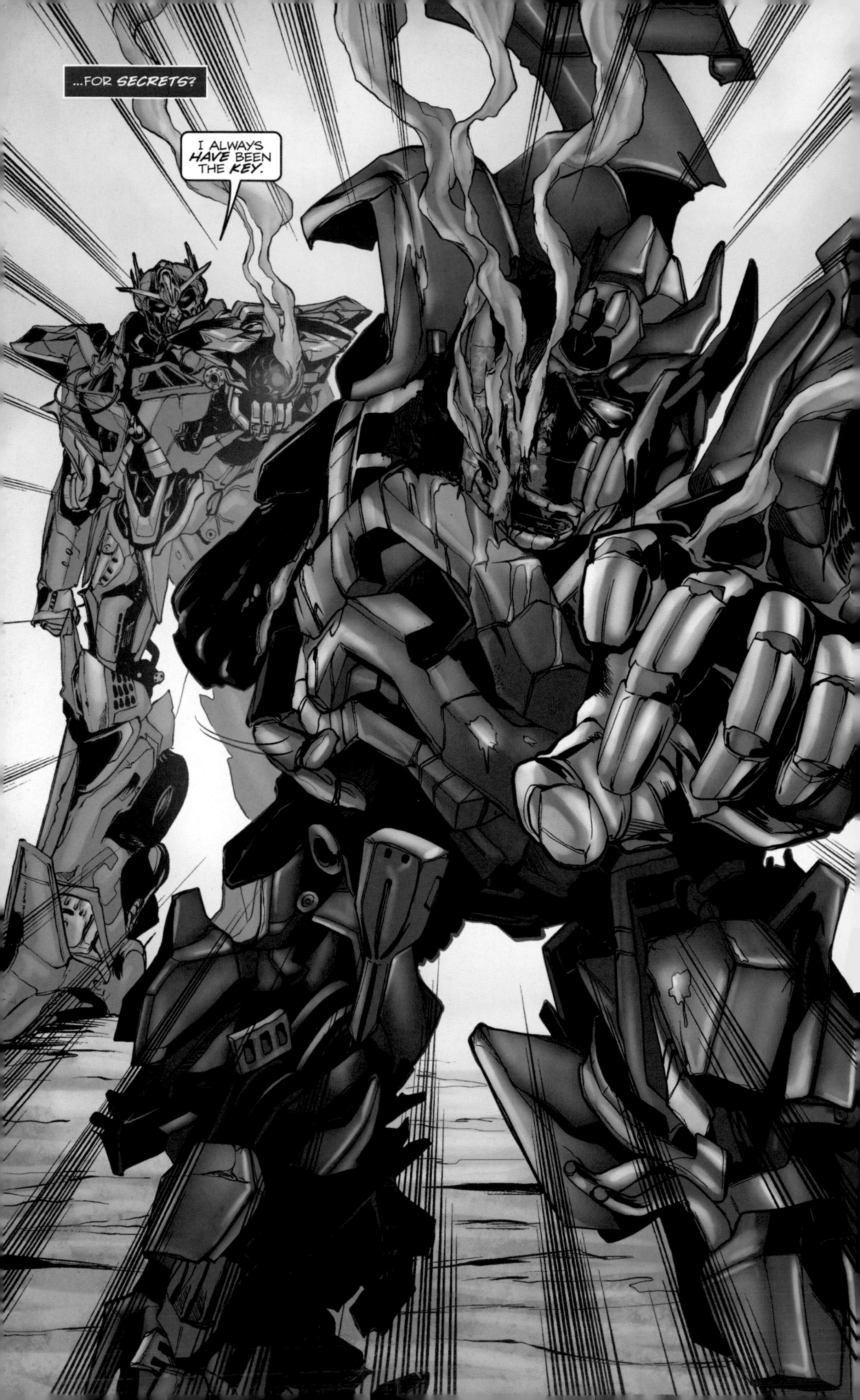
...FOR SECRETS?
I ALWAYS HAVE BEEN THE KEY.

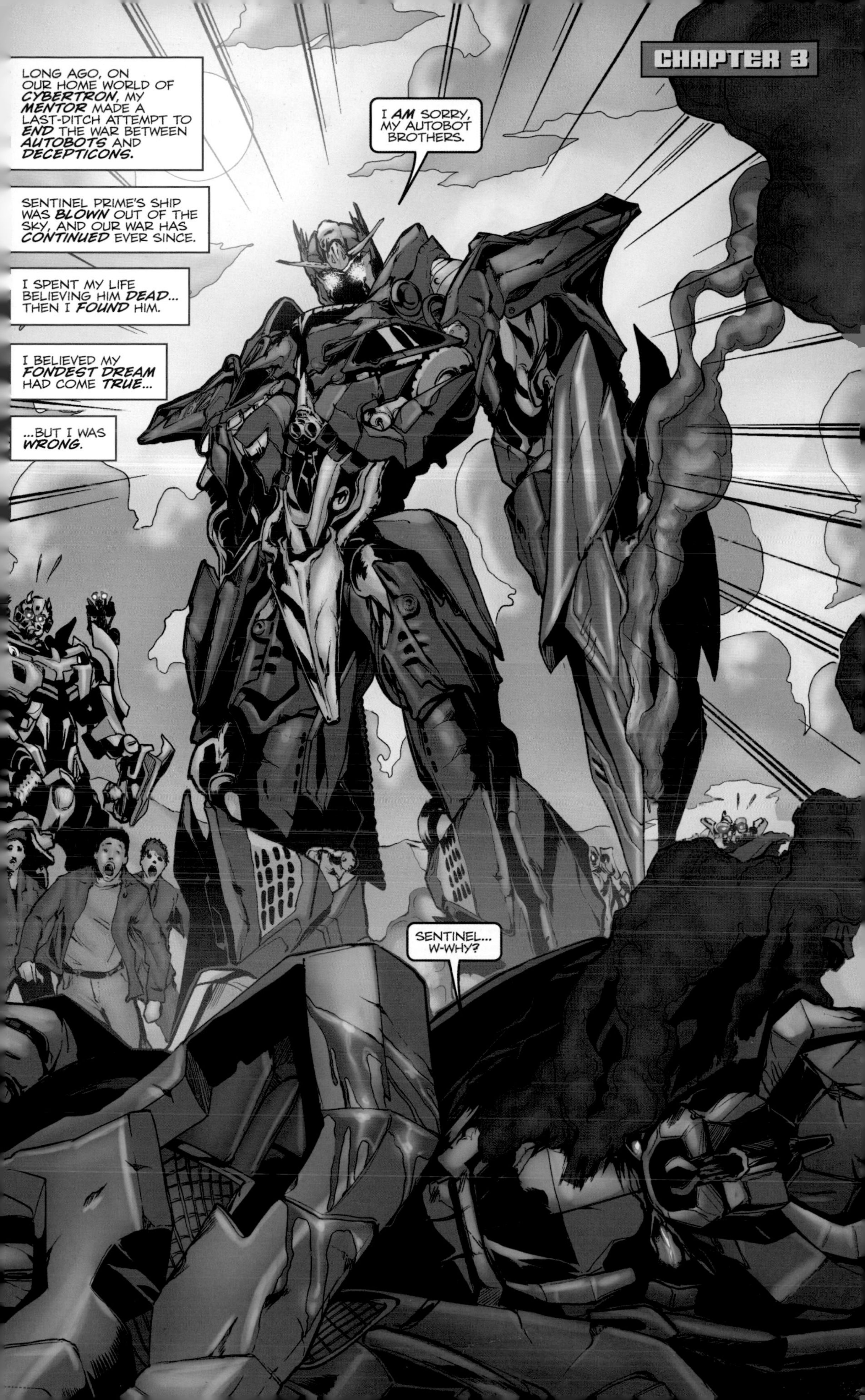

CHAPTER 3
LONG AGO, ON OUR HOME WORLD OF CYBERTRON, MY MENTOR MADE A LAST-DITCH ATTEMPT TO END THE WAR BETWEEN AUTOBOTS AND DECEPTICONS.
I AM SORRY, MY AUTOBOT BROTHERS.
SENTINEL PRIME'S SHIP WAS BLOWN OUT OF THE SKY, AND OUR WAR HAS CONTINUED EVER SINCE.
I SPENT MY LIFE BELIEVING HIM DEAD... THEN I FOUND HIM.
I BELIEVED MY FONDEST DREAM HAD COME TRUE...
...BUT I WAS WRONG.
SENTINEL... W-WHY?

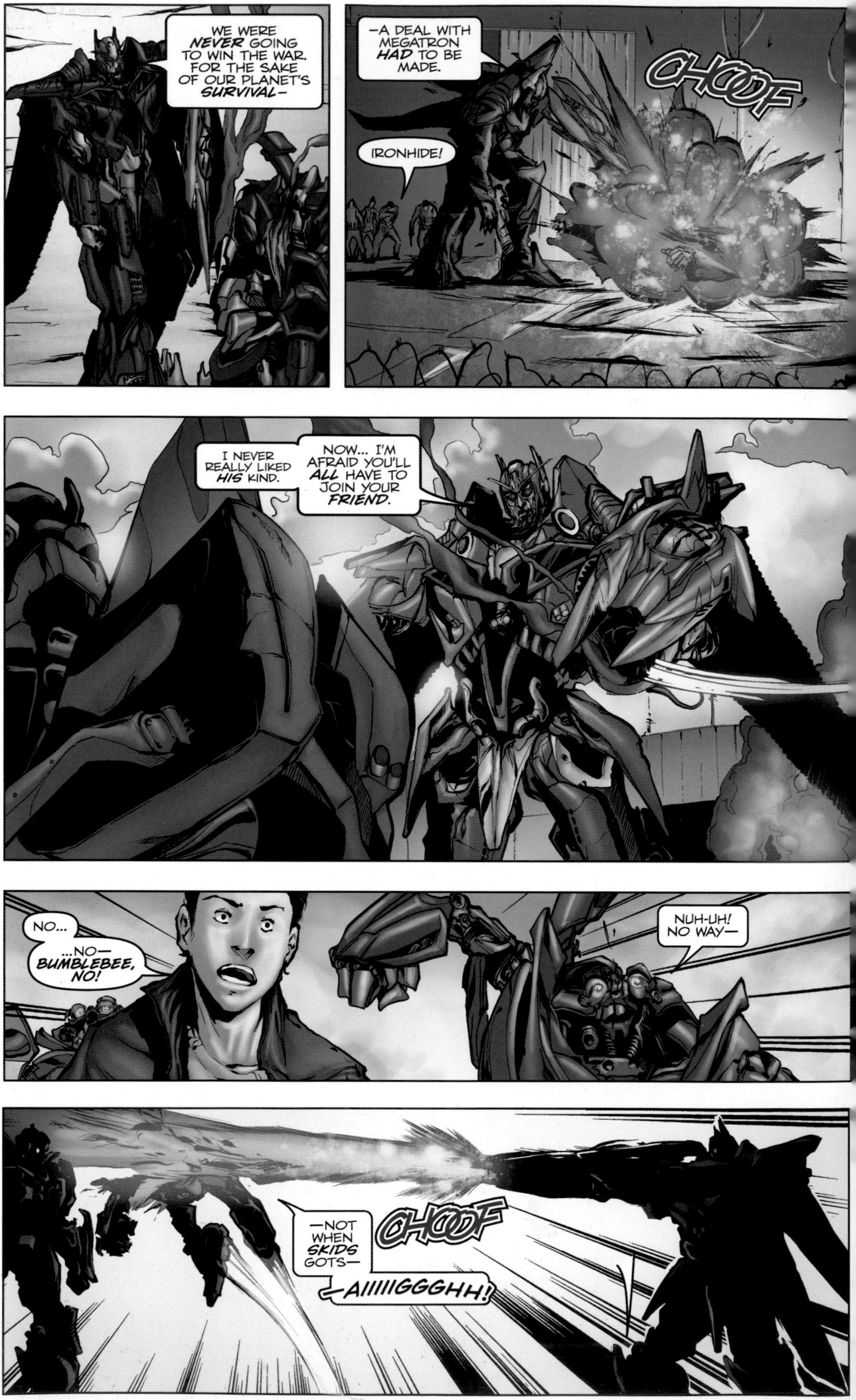
WE WERE NEVER GOING TO WIN THE WAR. FOR THE SAKE OF OUR PLANET'S SURVIVAL—
—A DEAL WITH MEGATRON HAD TO BE MADE.
CHOOF
IRONHIDE!
I NEVER REALLY LIKED HIS KIND.
NOW... I'M AFRAID YOU'LL ALL HAVE TO JOIN YOUR FRIEND.
NO...
...NO—
BUMBLEBEE, NO!
NUH-UH! NO WAY—
—NOT WHEN SKIDS GOTS—
CHOOF
—AIIIIGGGHH!

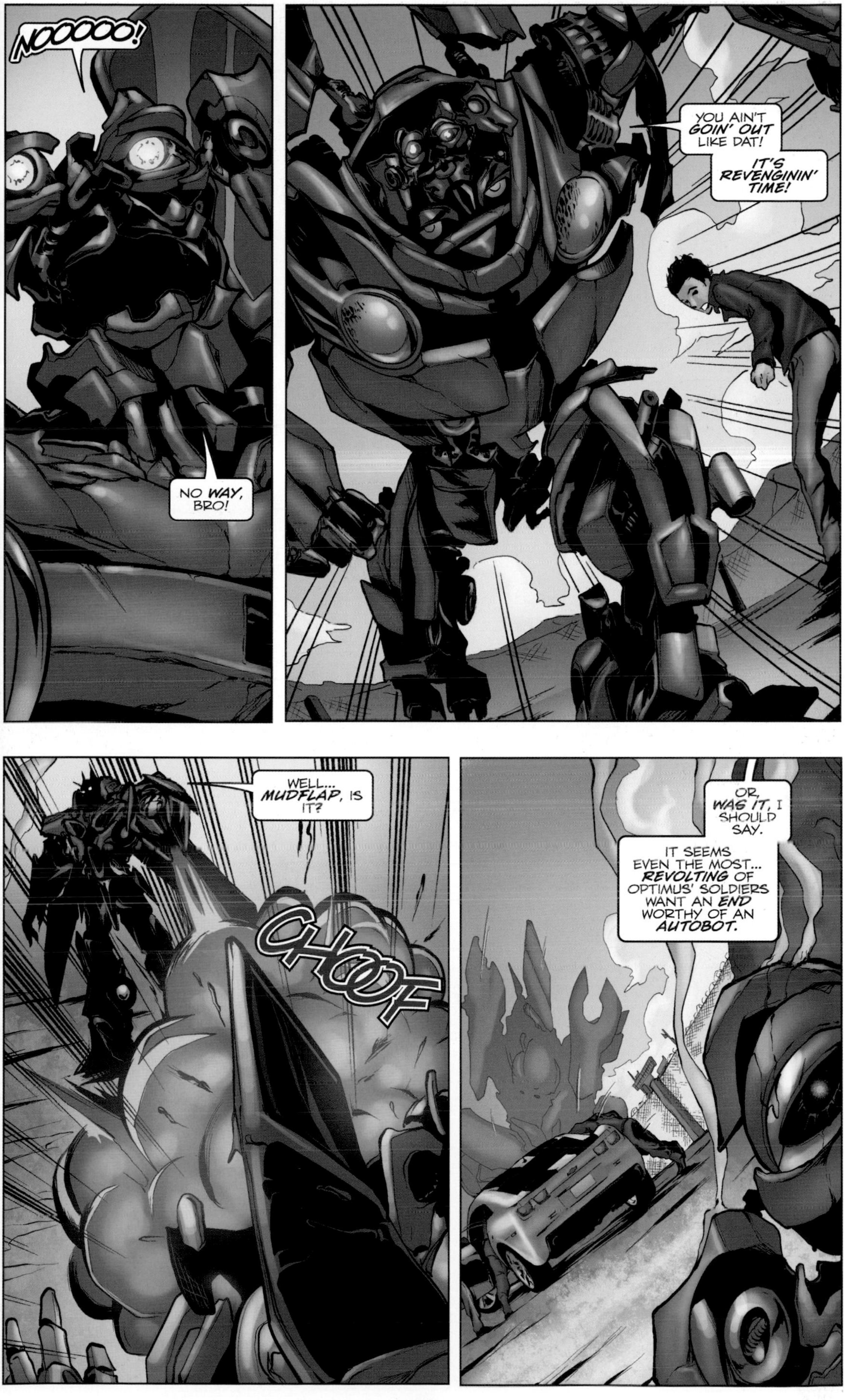
NOOOOO!
NO WAY, BRO!
YOU AIN'T GOIN' OUT LIKE DAT!
IT'S REVENGININ' TIME!
WELL... MUDFLAP, IS IT?
CHOOF
OR, WAS IT, I SHOULD SAY.
IT SEEMS EVEN THE MOST... REVOLTING OF OPTIMUS' SOLDIERS WANT AN END WORTHY OF AN AUTOBOT.

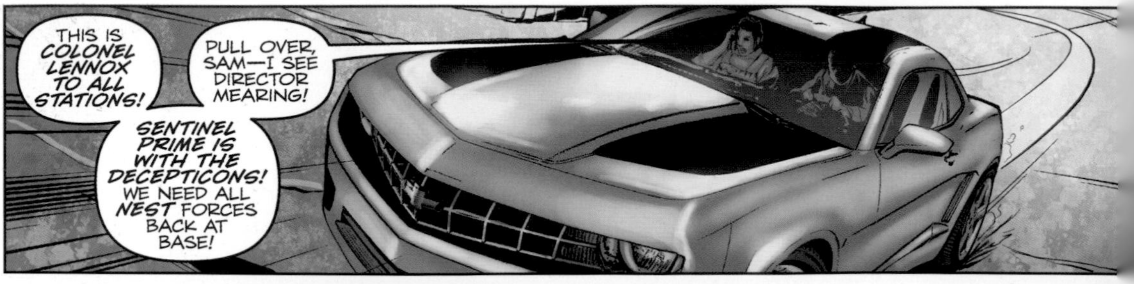
THIS IS COLONEL LENNOX TO ALL STATIONS!
PULL OVER, SAM—I SEE DIRECTOR MEARING!
SENTINEL PRIME IS WITH THE DECEPTICONS! WE NEED ALL NEST FORCES BACK AT BASE!

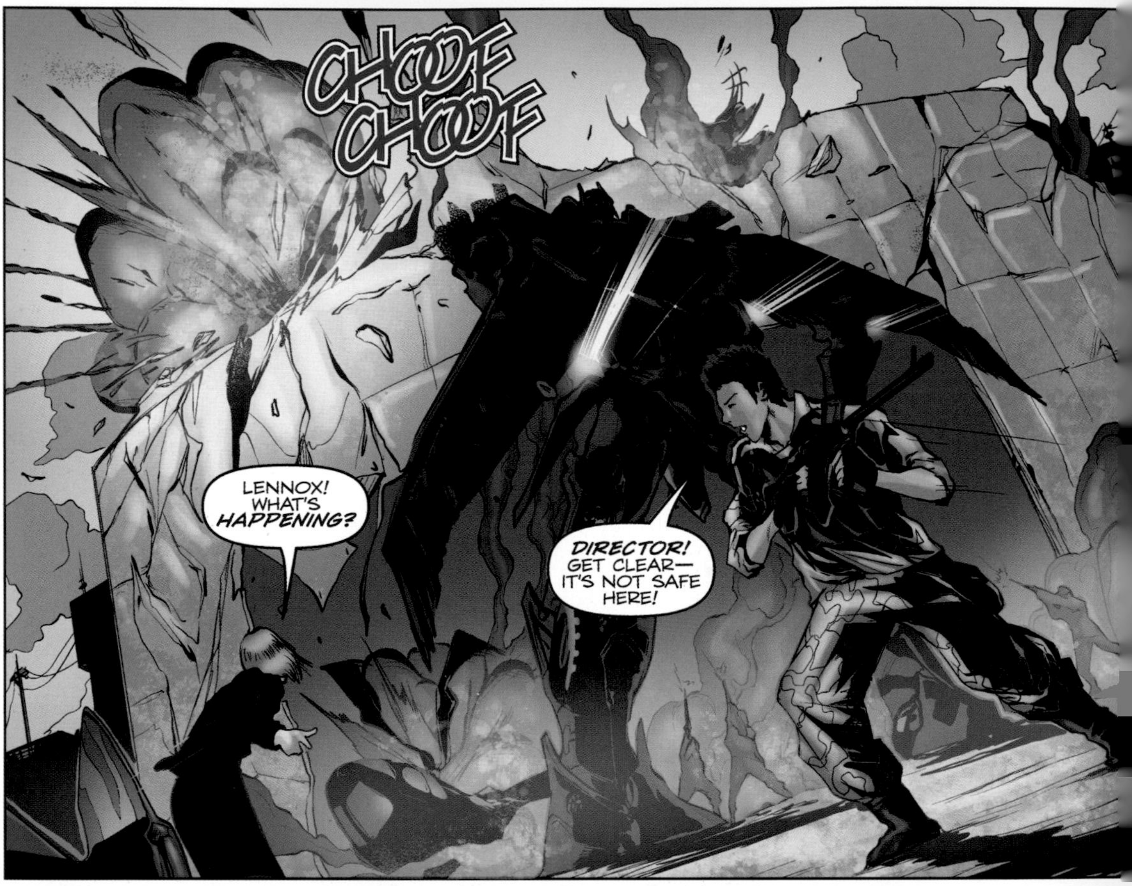
CHOOF CHOOF
LENNOX! WHAT'S HAPPENING?
DIRECTOR! GET CLEAR— IT'S NOT SAFE HERE!

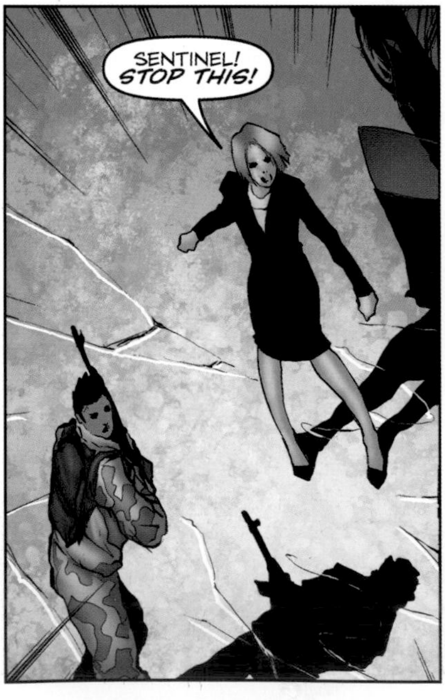
SENTINEL! STOP THIS!

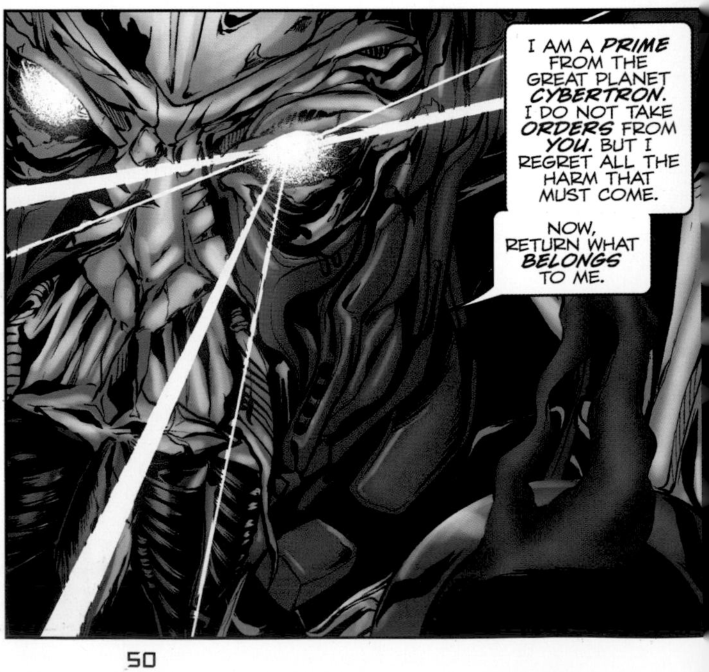
I AM A PRIME FROM THE GREAT PLANET CYBERTRON. I DO NOT TAKE ORDERS FROM YOU. BUT I REGRET ALL THE HARM THAT MUST COME.
NOW, RETURN WHAT BELONGS TO ME.

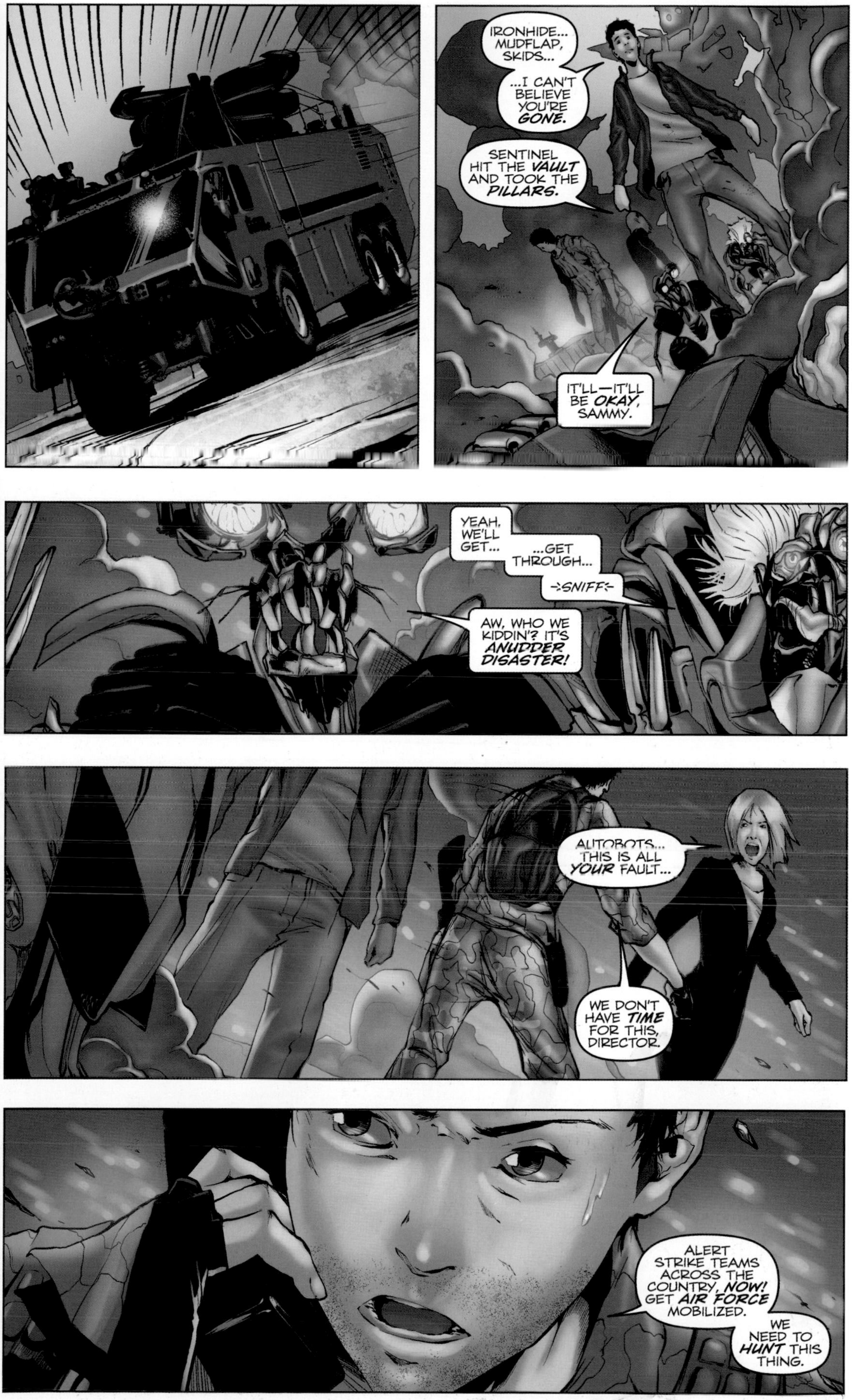
IRONHIDE... MUDFLAP, SKIDS...
...I CAN'T BELIEVE YOU'RE GONE.
SENTINEL HIT THE VAULT AND TOOK THE PILLARS.
IT'LL—IT'LL BE OKAY, SAMMY.
YEAH, WE'LL GET...
...GET THROUGH...
-SNIFF-
AW, WHO WE KIDDIN'? IT'S ANUDDER DISASTER!
AUTOBOTS... THIS IS ALL YOUR FAULT...
WE DON'T HAVE TIME FOR THIS, DIRECTOR.
ALERT STRIKE TEAMS ACROSS THE COUNTRY, NOW! GET AIR FORCE MOBILIZED.
WE NEED TO HUNT THIS THING.

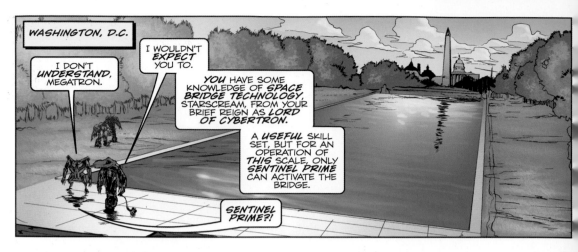

WASHINGTON, D.C.

I DON'T UNDERSTAND, MEGATRON.

I WOULDN'T EXPECT YOU TO.

YOU HAVE SOME KNOWLEDGE OF SPACE BRIDGE TECHNOLOGY, STARSCREAM, FROM YOUR BRIEF REIGN AS LORD OF CYBERTRON.

A USEFUL SKILL SET, BUT FOR AN OPERATION OF THIS SCALE, ONLY SENTINEL PRIME CAN ACTIVATE THE BRIDGE.

SENTINEL PRIME?!

CALM YOURSELF. HE'S WORKING FOR ME.

DON'T OVERSTATE THE REALITY OF YOUR SITUATION, MEGATRON.

SENTINEL—I—

WAIT—WHAT IS HE DOING ALIVE? I... ER, SAW YOU DIE ON CYBERTRON!

ON THAT DAY, IT WAS MY INTENTION TO LEAVE OUR HOMEWORLD—TO PROTECT THE CYBERTRONIAN RACE...

...WHATEVER THE COST.

SENTINEL WAS TO SEEK OUT THE LAST STAR HARVESTER—TO FUEL OUR EMPIRE'S EXPANSION—THEN RENDEZVOUS WITH ME.

BUT FATE WAYLAID US BOTH, BEFORE DRAWING US ALL TOGETHER—TO EARTH.

CHUFF

KARUNCH

TO ACTIVATE THE SPACE BRIDGE, WE NEED SENTINEL—AND TO REVIVE SENTINEL, WE NEEDED THE MATRIX...

NICE CHAIR.

OPTIMUS PRIME NEVER KNEW...

SPEAK OF THE DEVIL.

SENTINEL?

PRIME— THEY *USED* US... AND NOW HE'S *OPENING* THE SPACE BRIDGE!

BUT TO *WHERE*...

YOU WERE *ALWAYS* WEAK, OPTIMUS... MY ONLY REGRET IS THAT IT TOOK ME SO LONG TO *REALIZE*.

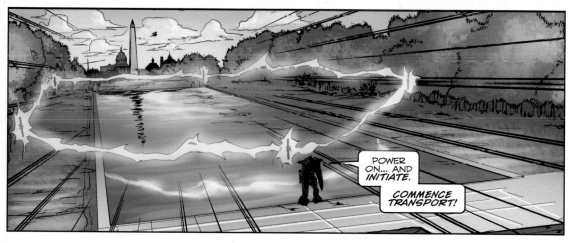

POWER ON... AND *INITIATE*.

COMMENCE TRANSPORT!

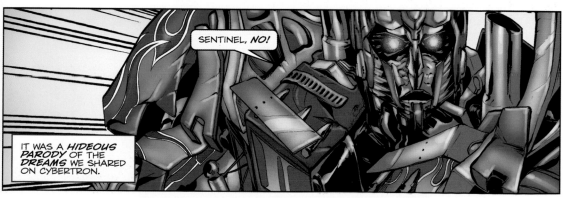

SENTINEL, *NO!*

IT WAS A *HIDEOUS PARODY* OF THE *DREAMS* WE SHARED ON CYBERTRON.

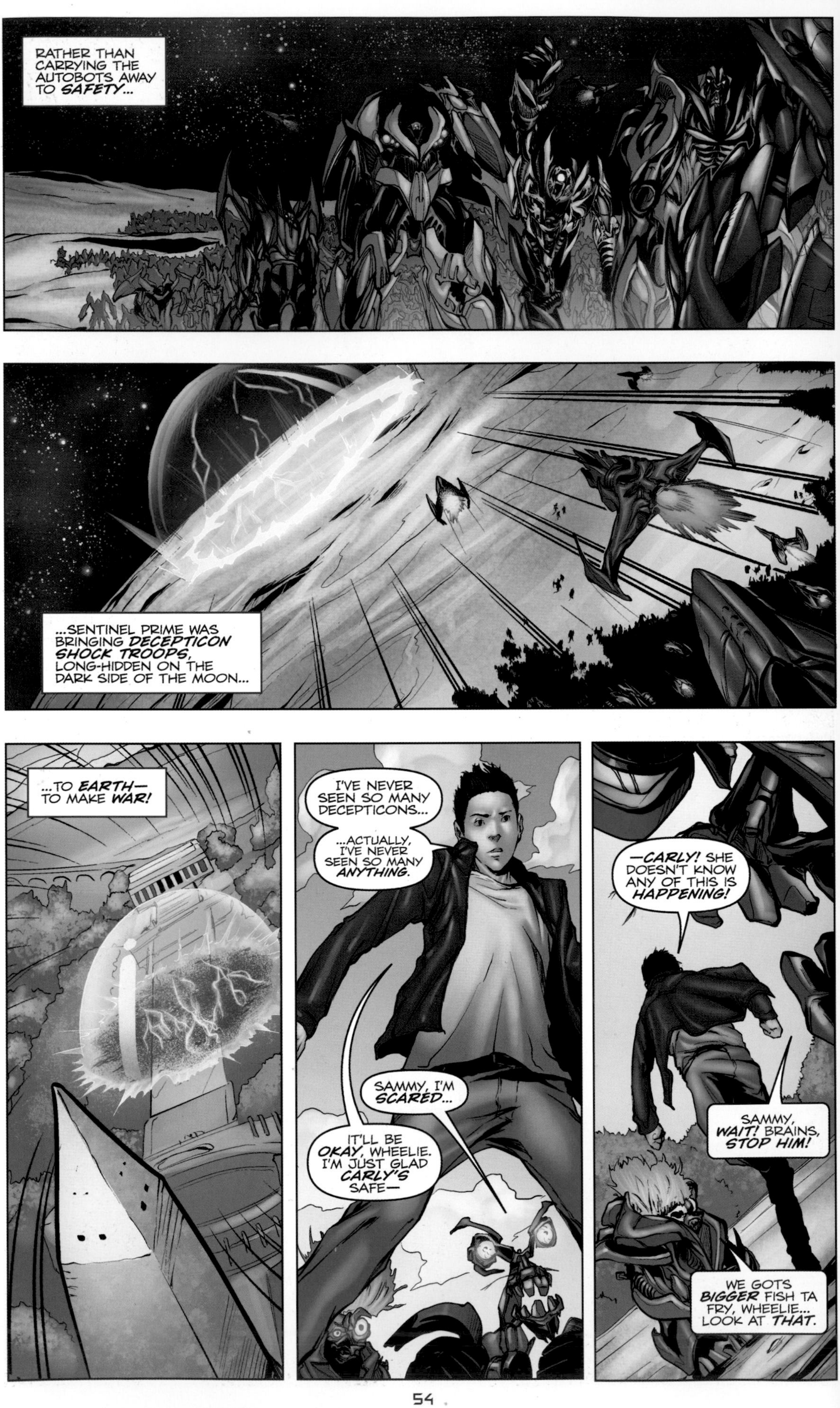
RATHER THAN CARRYING THE AUTOBOTS AWAY TO SAFETY...
...SENTINEL PRIME WAS BRINGING DECEPTICON SHOCK TROOPS, LONG-HIDDEN ON THE DARK SIDE OF THE MOON...
...TO EARTH— TO MAKE WAR!
I'VE NEVER SEEN SO MANY DECEPTICONS...
...ACTUALLY, I'VE NEVER SEEN SO MANY ANYTHING.
SAMMY, I'M SCARED...
IT'LL BE OKAY, WHEELIE. I'M JUST GLAD CARLY'S SAFE—
—CARLY! SHE DOESN'T KNOW ANY OF THIS IS HAPPENING!
SAMMY, WAIT! BRAINS, STOP HIM!
WE GOTS BIGGER FISH TA FRY, WHEELIE... LOOK AT THAT.

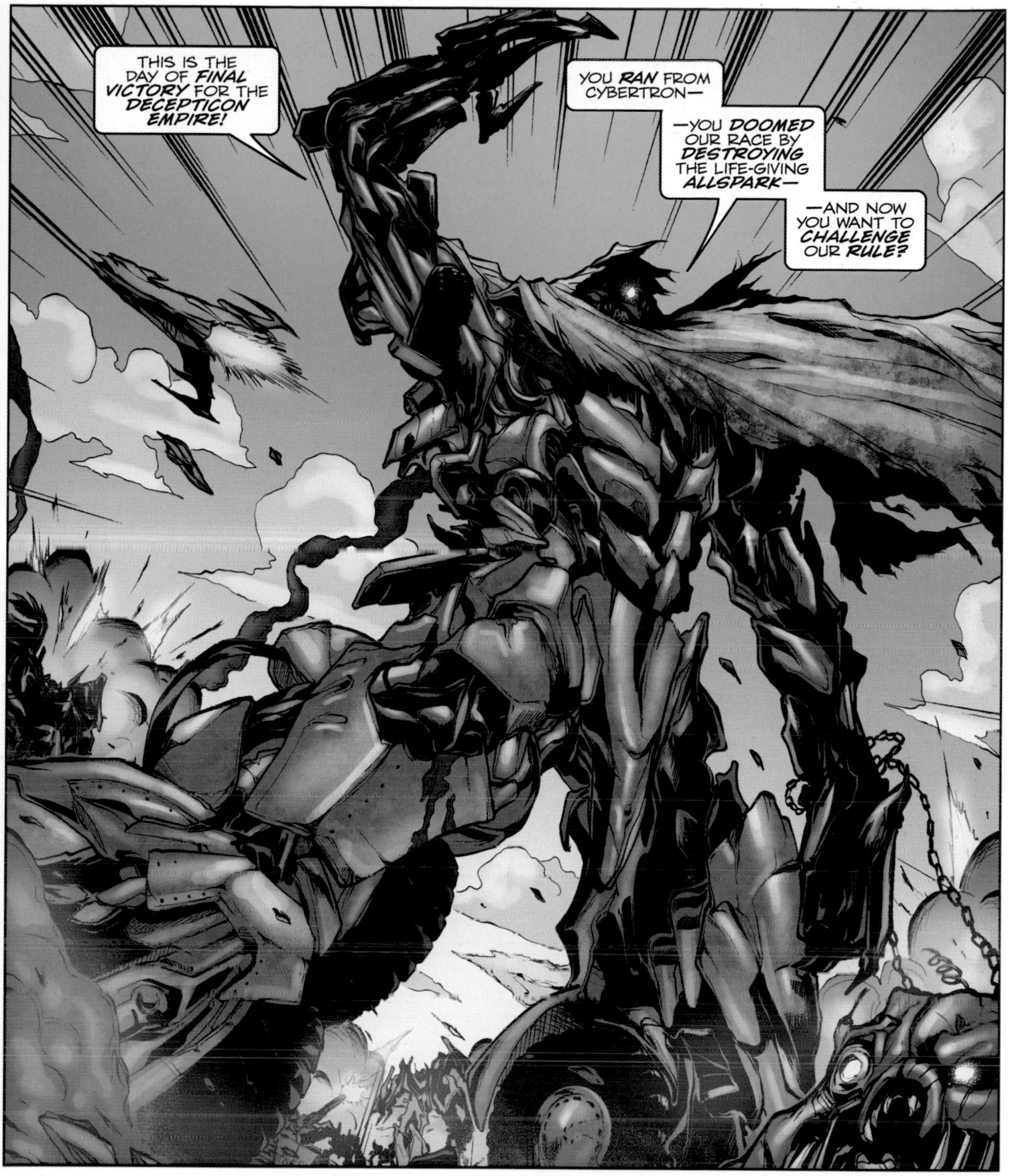
THIS IS THE DAY OF FINAL VICTORY FOR THE DECEPTICON EMPIRE!
YOU RAN FROM CYBERTRON—
—YOU DOOMED OUR RACE BY DESTROYING THE LIFE-GIVING ALLSPARK—
—AND NOW YOU WANT TO CHALLENGE OUR RULE?

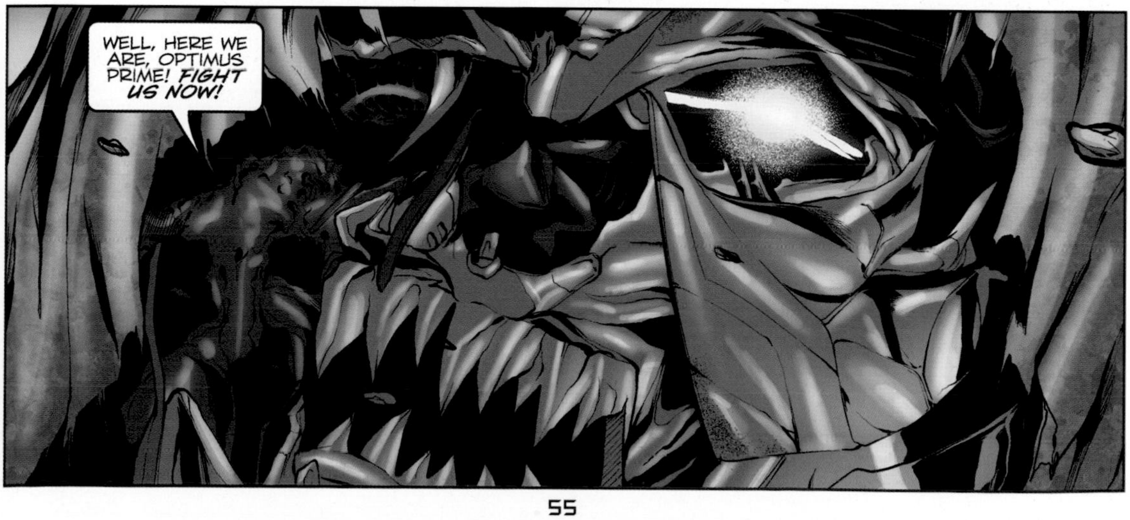
WELL, HERE WE ARE, OPTIMUS PRIME! FIGHT US NOW!

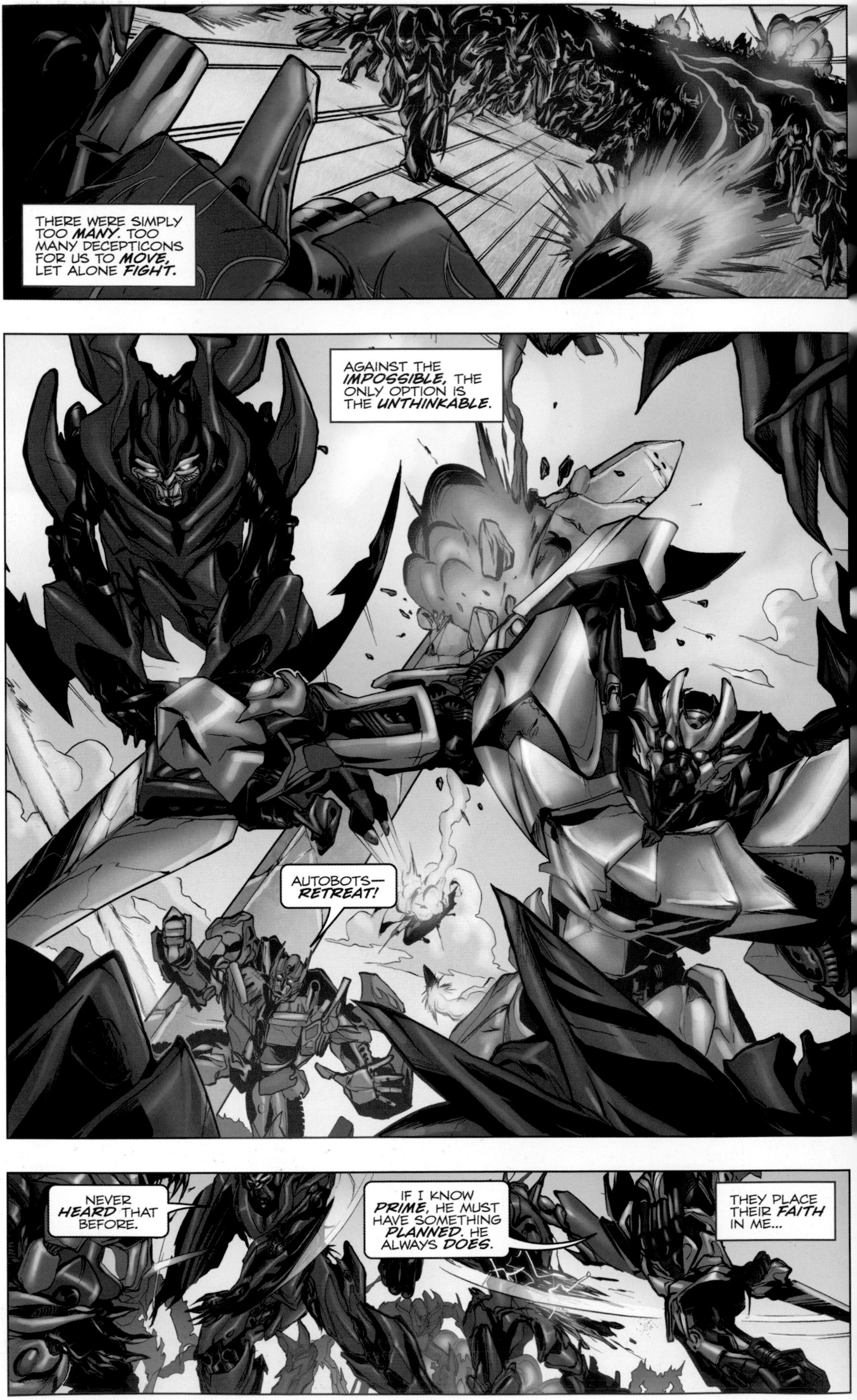
THERE WERE SIMPLY TOO MANY. TOO MANY DECEPTICONS FOR US TO MOVE, LET ALONE FIGHT.
AGAINST THE IMPOSSIBLE, THE ONLY OPTION IS THE UNTHINKABLE.
AUTOBOTS— RETREAT!
NEVER HEARD THAT BEFORE.
IF I KNOW PRIME, HE MUST HAVE SOMETHING PLANNED. HE ALWAYS DOES.
THEY PLACE THEIR FAITH IN ME...

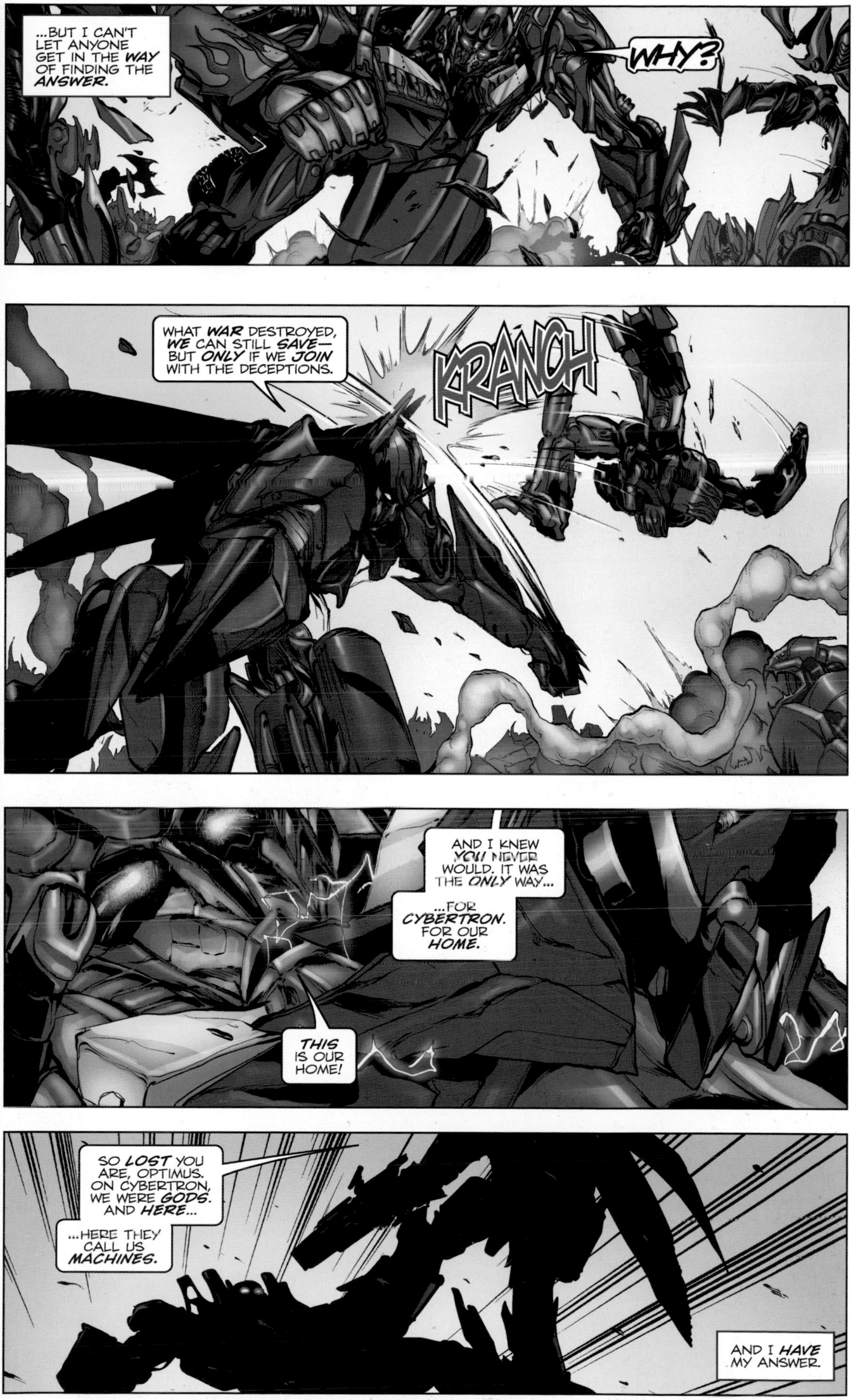
...BUT I CAN'T LET ANYONE GET IN THE WAY OF FINDING THE ANSWER.
WHY?
WHAT WAR DESTROYED, WE CAN STILL SAVE— BUT ONLY IF WE JOIN WITH THE DECEPTIONS.
KRANCH
AND I KNEW YOU NEVER WOULD. IT WAS THE ONLY WAY...
...FOR CYBERTRON. FOR OUR HOME.
THIS IS OUR HOME!
SO LOST YOU ARE, OPTIMUS. ON CYBERTRON, WE WERE GODS. AND HERE...
...HERE THEY CALL US MACHINES.
AND I HAVE MY ANSWER.

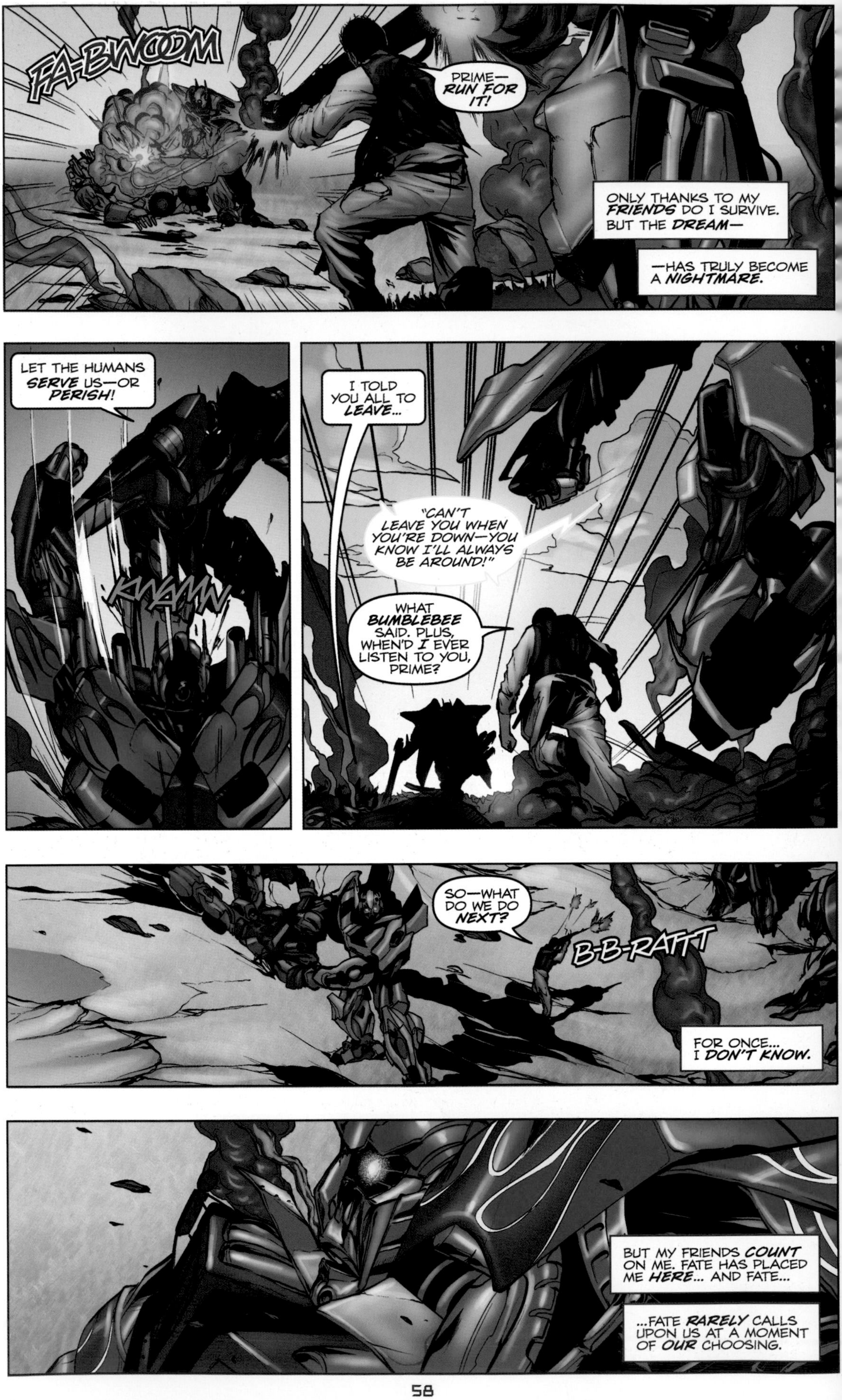
FA-BWOOM
PRIME— RUN FOR IT!
ONLY THANKS TO MY FRIENDS DO I SURVIVE. BUT THE DREAM—
—HAS TRULY BECOME A NIGHTMARE.
LET THE HUMANS SERVE US—OR PERISH!
KWAMM
I TOLD YOU ALL TO LEAVE...
"CAN'T LEAVE YOU WHEN YOU'RE DOWN—YOU KNOW I'LL ALWAYS BE AROUND!"
WHAT BUMBLEBEE SAID. PLUS, WHEN'D I EVER LISTEN TO YOU, PRIME?
SO—WHAT DO WE DO NEXT?
B-B-RATTT
FOR ONCE... I DON'T KNOW.
BUT MY FRIENDS COUNT ON ME. FATE HAS PLACED ME HERE... AND FATE...
...FATE RARELY CALLS UPON US AT A MOMENT OF OUR CHOOSING.

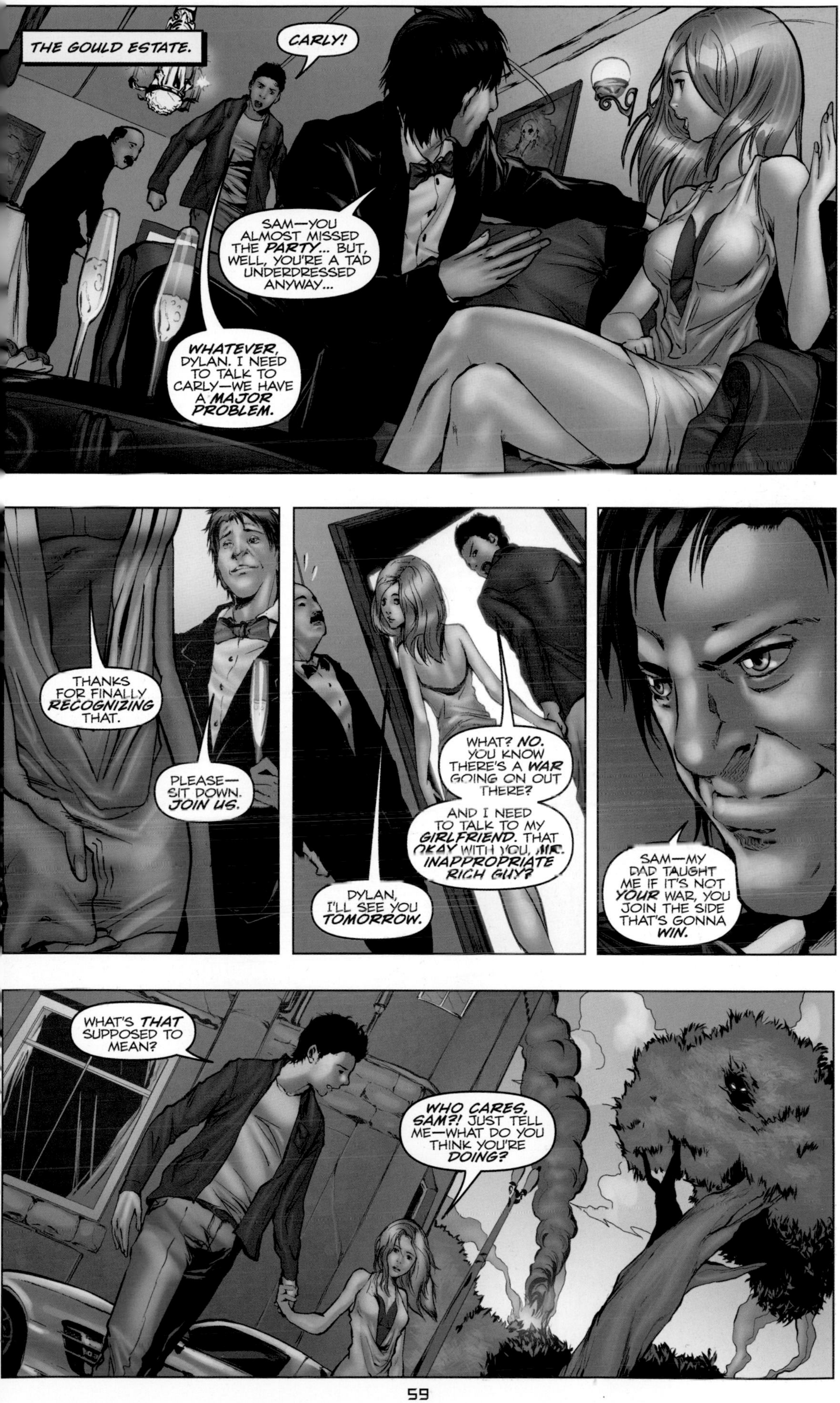
THE GOULD ESTATE.
CARLY!
SAM—YOU ALMOST MISSED THE PARTY... BUT, WELL, YOU'RE A TAD UNDERDRESSED ANYWAY...
WHATEVER, DYLAN. I NEED TO TALK TO CARLY—WE HAVE A MAJOR PROBLEM.
THANKS FOR FINALLY RECOGNIZING THAT.
PLEASE—SIT DOWN. JOIN US.
WHAT? NO. YOU KNOW THERE'S A WAR GOING ON OUT THERE?
AND I NEED TO TALK TO MY GIRLFRIEND. THAT OKAY WITH YOU, MR. INAPPROPRIATE RICH GUY?
DYLAN, I'LL SEE YOU TOMORROW.
SAM—MY DAD TAUGHT ME IF IT'S NOT YOUR WAR, YOU JOIN THE SIDE THAT'S GONNA WIN.
WHAT'S THAT SUPPOSED TO MEAN?
WHO CARES, SAM?! JUST TELL ME—WHAT DO YOU THINK YOU'RE DOING?

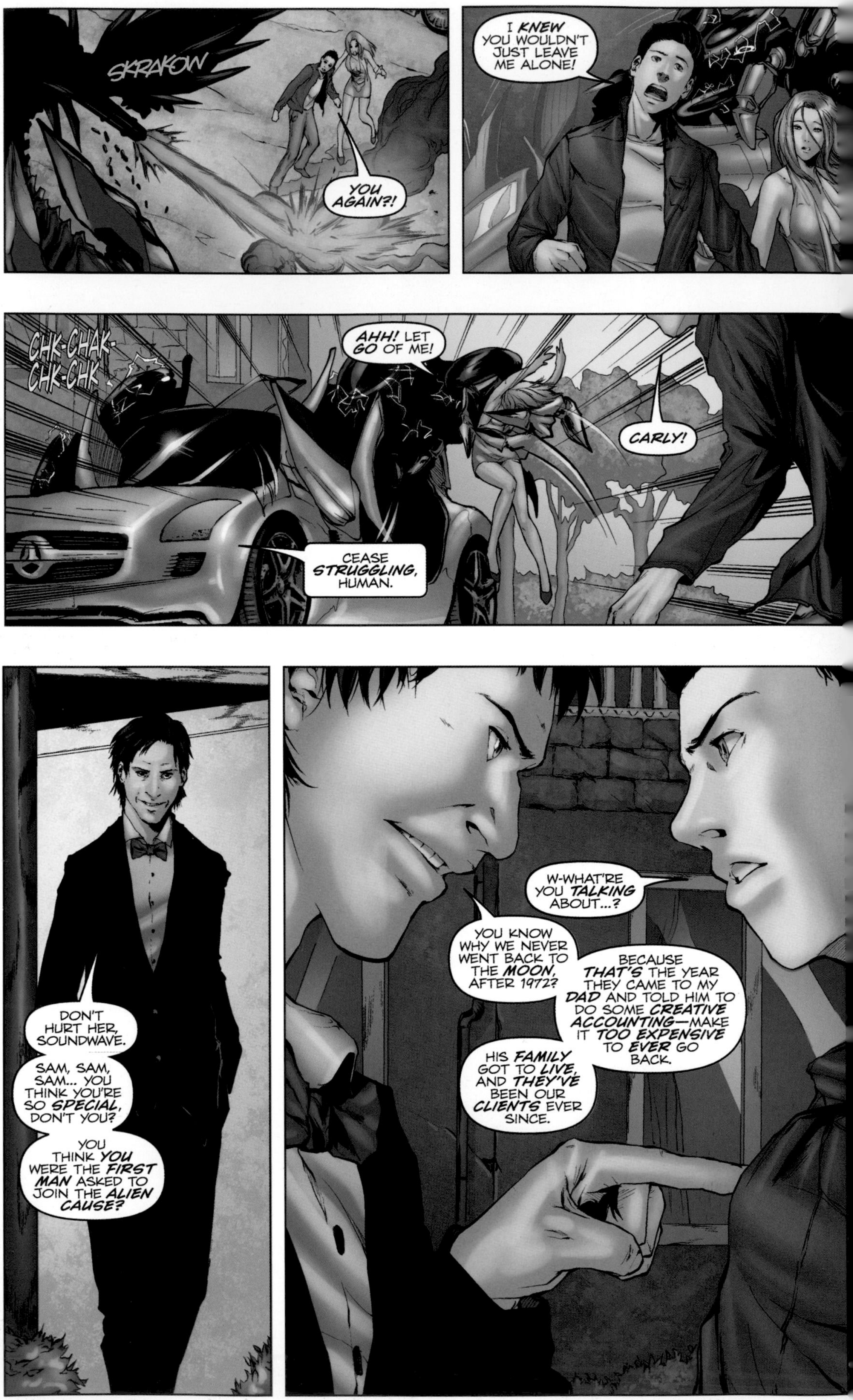
SKRAKOW
YOU AGAIN?!
I KNEW YOU WOULDN'T JUST LEAVE ME ALONE!
CHK-CHAK-CHK-CHK
AHH! LET GO OF ME!
CARLY!
CEASE STRUGGLING, HUMAN.
DON'T HURT HER, SOUNDWAVE.
SAM, SAM, SAM... YOU THINK YOU'RE SO SPECIAL, DON'T YOU?
YOU THINK YOU WERE THE FIRST MAN ASKED TO JOIN THE ALIEN CAUSE?
W-WHAT'RE YOU TALKING ABOUT...?
YOU KNOW WHY WE NEVER WENT BACK TO THE MOON, AFTER 1972?
BECAUSE THAT'S THE YEAR THEY CAME TO MY DAD AND TOLD HIM TO DO SOME CREATIVE ACCOUNTING—MAKE IT TOO EXPENSIVE TO EVER GO BACK.
HIS FAMILY GOT TO LIVE, AND THEY'VE BEEN OUR CLIENTS EVER SINCE.

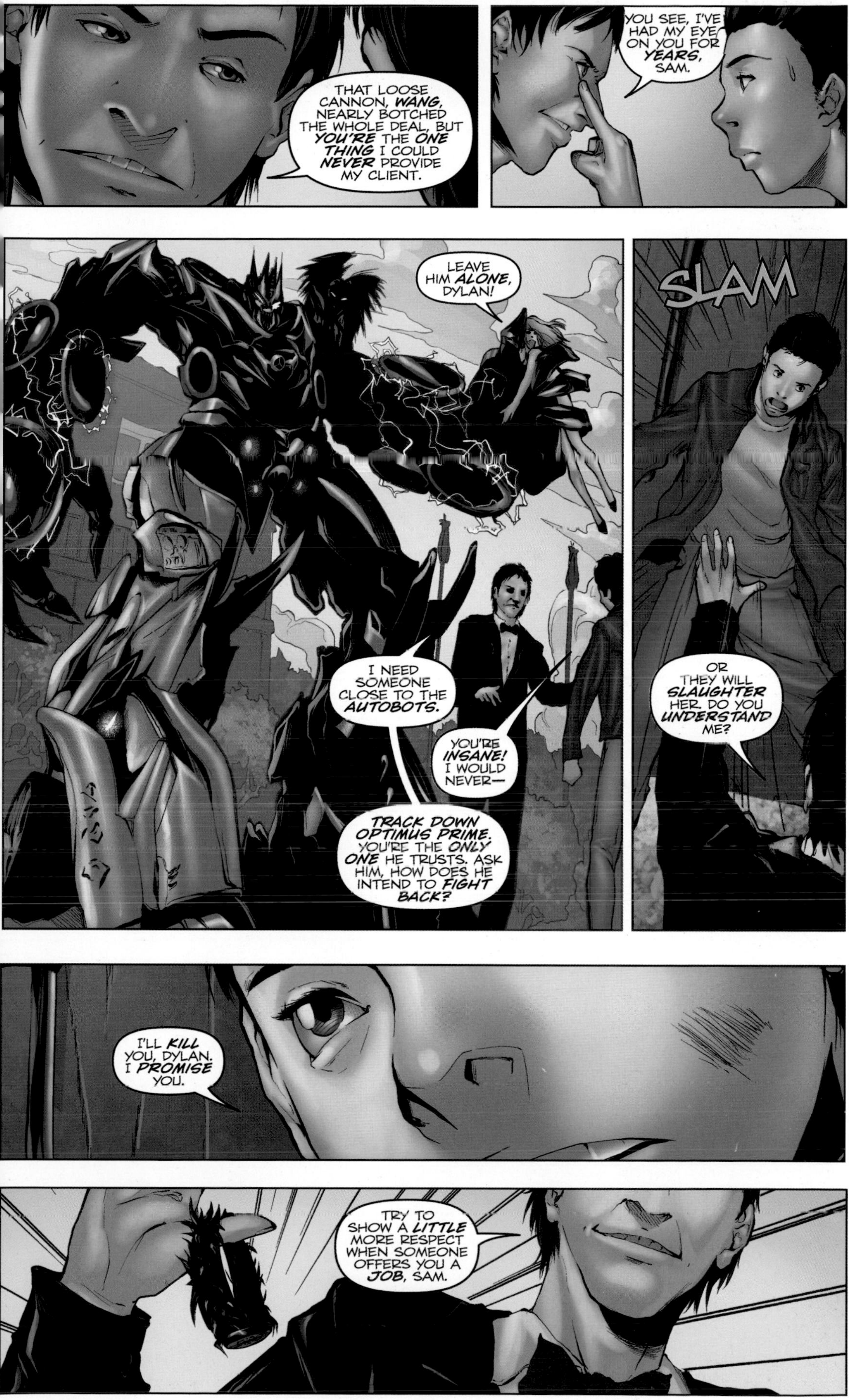
THAT LOOSE CANNON, WANG, NEARLY BOTCHED THE WHOLE DEAL, BUT YOU'RE THE ONE THING I COULD NEVER PROVIDE MY CLIENT.
YOU SEE, I'VE HAD MY EYE ON YOU FOR YEARS, SAM.
LEAVE HIM ALONE, DYLAN!
I NEED SOMEONE CLOSE TO THE AUTOBOTS.
YOU'RE INSANE! I WOULD NEVER—
TRACK DOWN OPTIMUS PRIME. YOU'RE THE ONLY ONE HE TRUSTS. ASK HIM, HOW DOES HE INTEND TO FIGHT BACK?
SLAM
OR THEY WILL SLAUGHTER HER. DO YOU UNDERSTAND ME?
I'LL KILL YOU, DYLAN. I PROMISE YOU.
TRY TO SHOW A LITTLE MORE RESPECT WHEN SOMEONE OFFERS YOU A JOB, SAM.

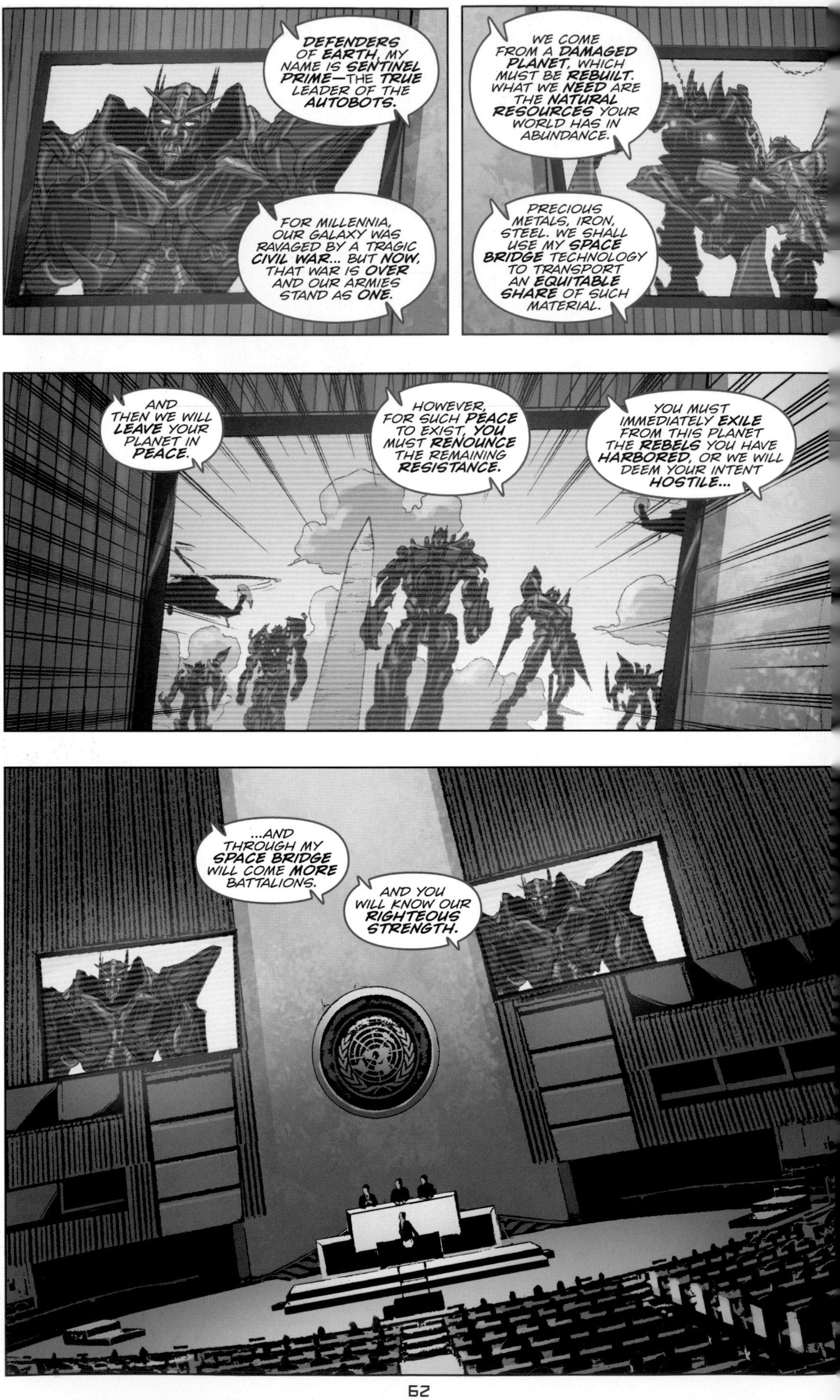
DEFENDERS OF EARTH, MY NAME IS SENTINEL PRIME—THE TRUE LEADER OF THE AUTOBOTS.
FOR MILLENNIA, OUR GALAXY WAS RAVAGED BY A TRAGIC CIVIL WAR... BUT NOW, THAT WAR IS OVER AND OUR ARMIES STAND AS ONE.
WE COME FROM A DAMAGED PLANET, WHICH MUST BE REBUILT. WHAT WE NEED ARE THE NATURAL RESOURCES YOUR WORLD HAS IN ABUNDANCE.
PRECIOUS METALS, IRON, STEEL. WE SHALL USE MY SPACE BRIDGE TECHNOLOGY TO TRANSPORT AN EQUITABLE SHARE OF SUCH MATERIAL.
AND THEN WE WILL LEAVE YOUR PLANET IN PEACE.
HOWEVER, FOR SUCH PEACE TO EXIST, YOU MUST RENOUNCE THE REMAINING RESISTANCE.
YOU MUST IMMEDIATELY EXILE FROM THIS PLANET THE REBELS YOU HAVE HARBORED, OR WE WILL DEEM YOUR INTENT HOSTILE...
...AND THROUGH MY SPACE BRIDGE WILL COME MORE BATTALIONS.
AND YOU WILL KNOW OUR RIGHTEOUS STRENGTH.

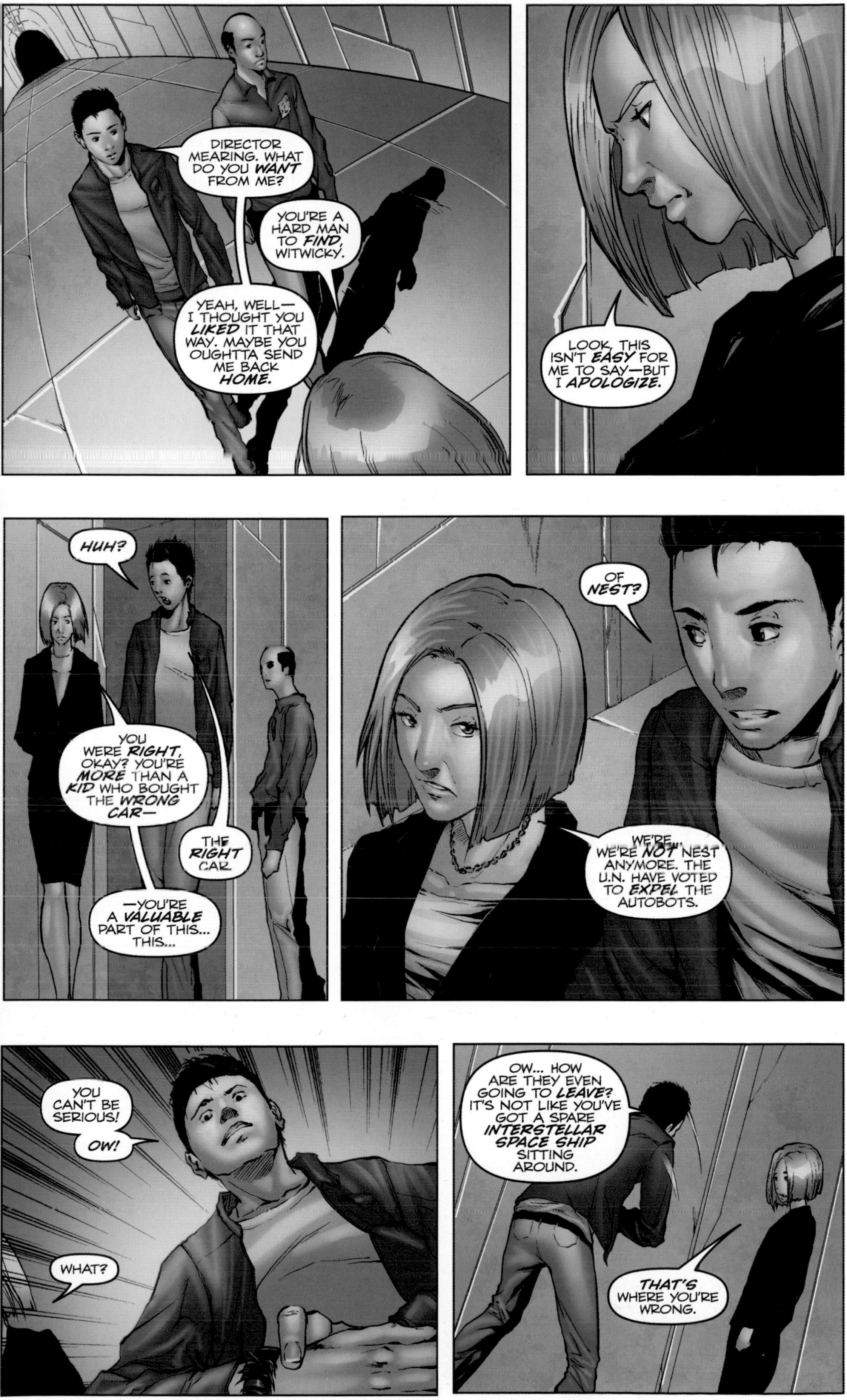
DIRECTOR MEARING. WHAT DO YOU WANT FROM ME?
YOU'RE A HARD MAN TO FIND, WITWICKY.
YEAH, WELL— I THOUGHT YOU LIKED IT THAT WAY. MAYBE YOU OUGHTTA SEND ME BACK HOME.
LOOK, THIS ISN'T EASY FOR ME TO SAY—BUT I APOLOGIZE.
HUH?
YOU WERE RIGHT, OKAY? YOU'RE MORE THAN A KID WHO BOUGHT THE WRONG CAR—
THE RIGHT CAR.
—YOU'RE A VALUABLE PART OF THIS... THIS...
OF NEST?
WE'RE... WE'RE NOT NEST ANYMORE. THE U.N. HAVE VOTED TO EXPEL THE AUTOBOTS.
YOU CAN'T BE SERIOUS!
OW!
WHAT?
OW... HOW ARE THEY EVEN GOING TO LEAVE? IT'S NOT LIKE YOU'VE GOT A SPARE INTERSTELLAR SPACE SHIP SITTING AROUND.
THAT'S WHERE YOU'RE WRONG.

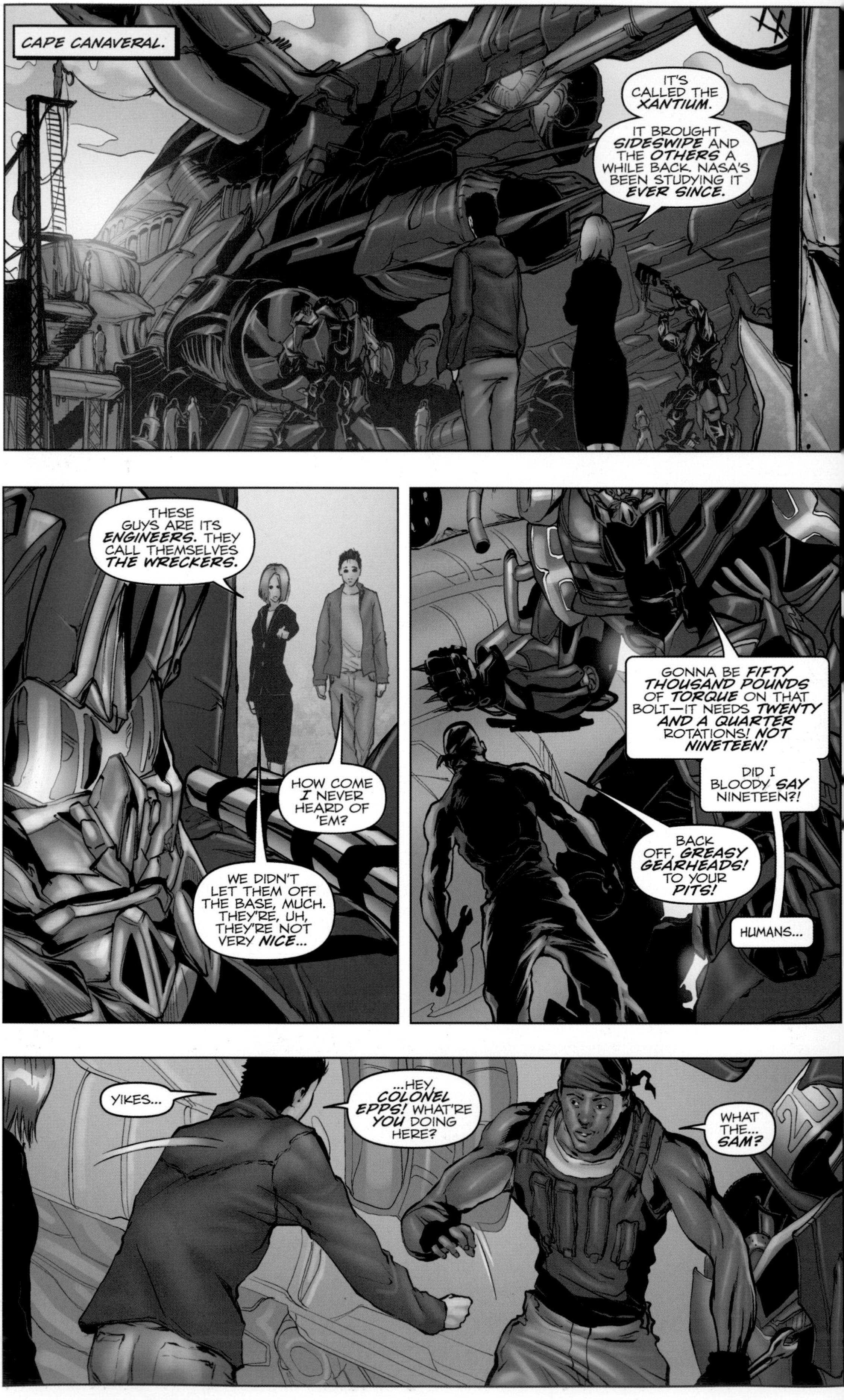
CAPE CANAVERAL.
IT'S CALLED THE XANTIUM.
IT BROUGHT SIDESWIPE AND THE OTHERS A WHILE BACK. NASA'S BEEN STUDYING IT EVER SINCE.
THESE GUYS ARE ITS ENGINEERS. THEY CALL THEMSELVES THE WRECKERS.
HOW COME I NEVER HEARD OF 'EM?
WE DIDN'T LET THEM OFF THE BASE, MUCH. THEY'RE, UH, THEY'RE NOT VERY NICE...
GONNA BE FIFTY THOUSAND POUNDS OF TORQUE ON THAT BOLT—IT NEEDS TWENTY AND A QUARTER ROTATIONS! NOT NINETEEN!
DID I BLOODY SAY NINETEEN?!
BACK OFF, GREASY GEARHEADS! TO YOUR PITS!
HUMANS...
YIKES...
...HEY, COLONEL EPPS! WHAT'RE YOU DOING HERE?
WHAT THE... SAM?

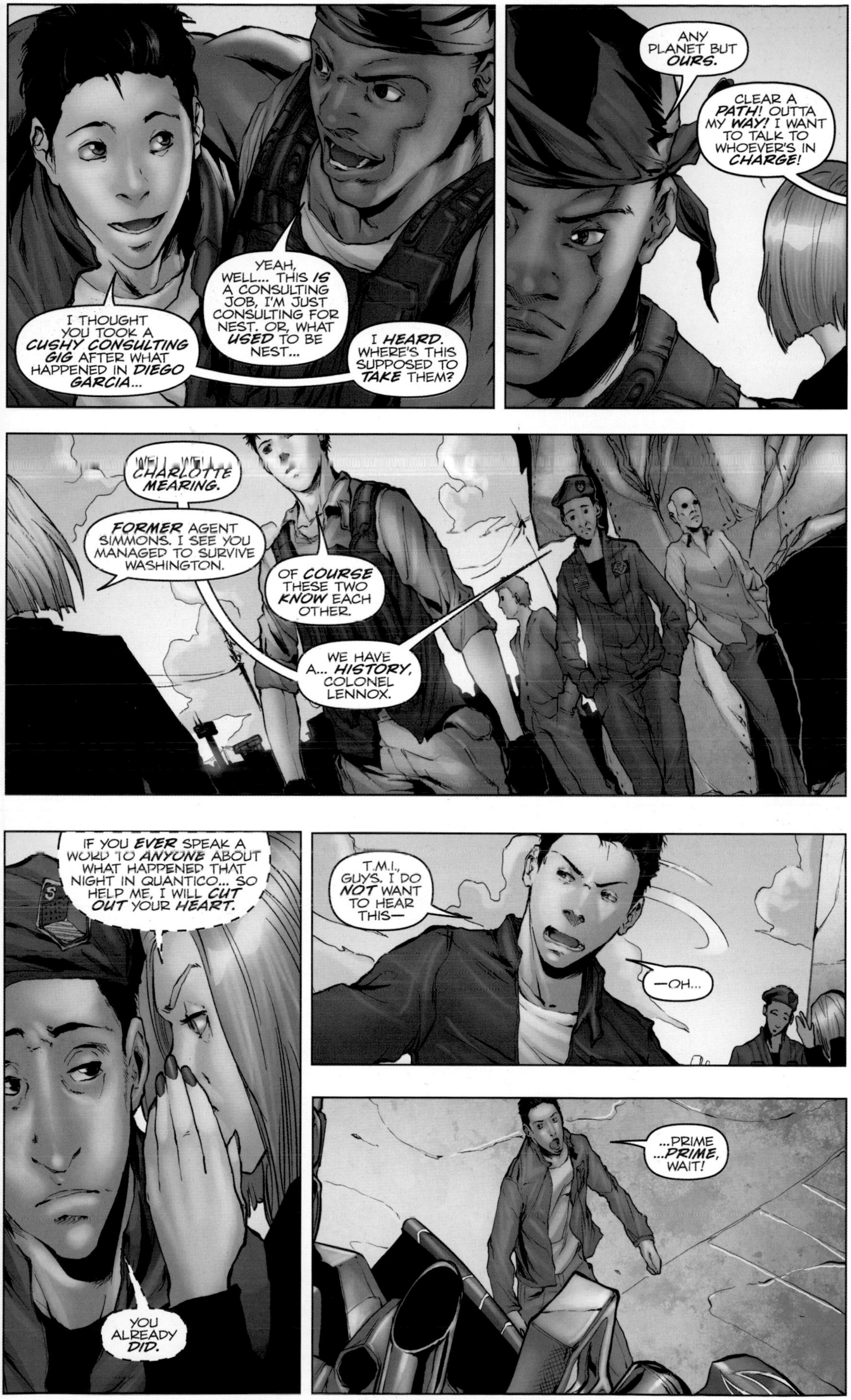
I THOUGHT YOU TOOK A CUSHY CONSULTING GIG AFTER WHAT HAPPENED IN DIEGO GARCIA...
YEAH, WELL... THIS IS A CONSULTING JOB, I'M JUST CONSULTING FOR NEST. OR, WHAT USED TO BE NEST...
I HEARD. WHERE'S THIS SUPPOSED TO TAKE THEM?
ANY PLANET BUT OURS.
CLEAR A PATH! OUTTA MY WAY! I WANT TO TALK TO WHOEVER'S IN CHARGE!
WELL, WELL... CHARLOTTE MEARING.
FORMER AGENT SIMMONS. I SEE YOU MANAGED TO SURVIVE WASHINGTON.
OF COURSE THESE TWO KNOW EACH OTHER.
WE HAVE A... HISTORY, COLONEL LENNOX.
IF YOU EVER SPEAK A WORD TO ANYONE ABOUT WHAT HAPPENED THAT NIGHT IN QUANTICO... SO HELP ME, I WILL CUT OUT YOUR HEART.
YOU ALREADY DID.
T.M.I., GUYS. I DO NOT WANT TO HEAR THIS—
—OH...
...PRIME ...PRIME, WAIT!

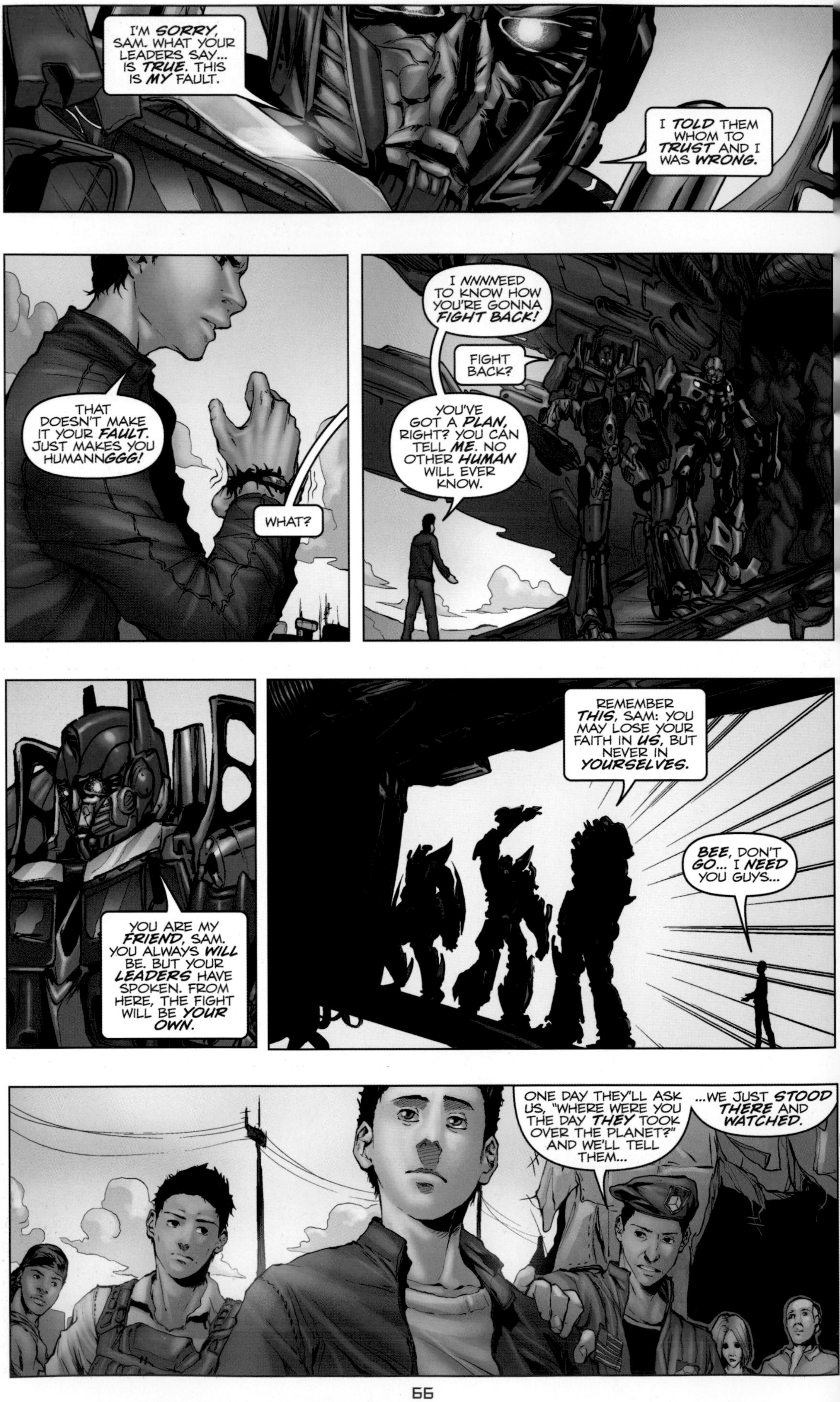
I'M SORRY, SAM. WHAT YOUR LEADERS SAY... IS TRUE. THIS IS MY FAULT.
I TOLD THEM WHOM TO TRUST AND I WAS WRONG.
THAT DOESN'T MAKE IT YOUR FAULT. JUST MAKES YOU HUMANNGGG!
WHAT?
I NNNNEED TO KNOW HOW YOU'RE GONNA FIGHT BACK!
FIGHT BACK?
YOU'VE GOT A PLAN, RIGHT? YOU CAN TELL ME. NO OTHER HUMAN WILL EVER KNOW.
YOU ARE MY FRIEND, SAM. YOU ALWAYS WILL BE. BUT YOUR LEADERS HAVE SPOKEN. FROM HERE, THE FIGHT WILL BE YOUR OWN.
REMEMBER THIS, SAM: YOU MAY LOSE YOUR FAITH IN US, BUT NEVER IN YOURSELVES.
BEE, DON'T GO... I NEED YOU GUYS...
ONE DAY THEY'LL ASK US, "WHERE WERE YOU THE DAY THEY TOOK OVER THE PLANET?" AND WE'LL TELL THEM...
...WE JUST STOOD THERE AND WATCHED.

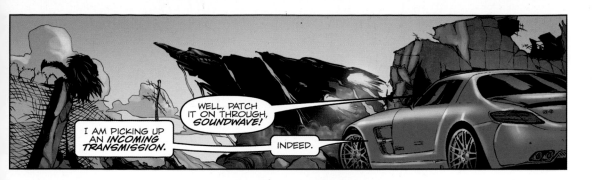

WELL, PATCH IT ON THROUGH, *SOUNDWAVE!*

I AM PICKING UP AN *INCOMING TRANSMISSION.*

INDEED.

THIS'LL BE OUR LITTLE *MOLE.* BE SURE TO SAY *"HI,"* CARLY.

YOU'RE A *COWARD,* RYLAN.

IT'S JUST *BUSINESS.*

SAM— HOW'VE YOU *BEEN?* WHAT'S *NEW?*

LET HER *GO,* DYLAN. THERE'S *NO PLAN.* THE AUTOBOTS ARE JUST *LEAVING.*

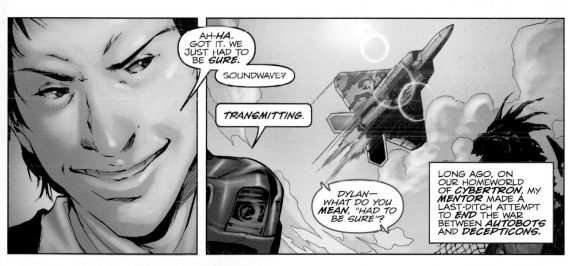

AH-*HA.* GOT IT. WE JUST HAD TO BE *SURE.*

SOUNDWAVE?

TRANSMITTING.

DYLAN— WHAT DO YOU *MEAN,* *"HAD TO BE SURE"?*

LONG AGO, ON OUR HOMEWORLD OF *CYBERTRON,* MY *MENTOR* MADE A LAST-DITCH ATTEMPT TO *END* THE WAR BETWEEN *AUTOBOTS* AND *DECEPTICONS.*

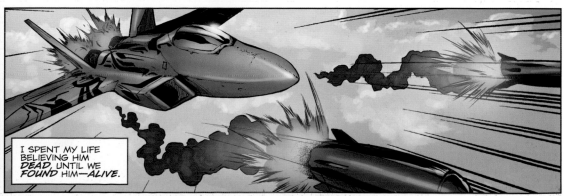

I SPENT MY LIFE BELIEVING HIM *DEAD,* UNTIL WE *FOUND* HIM—*ALIVE.*

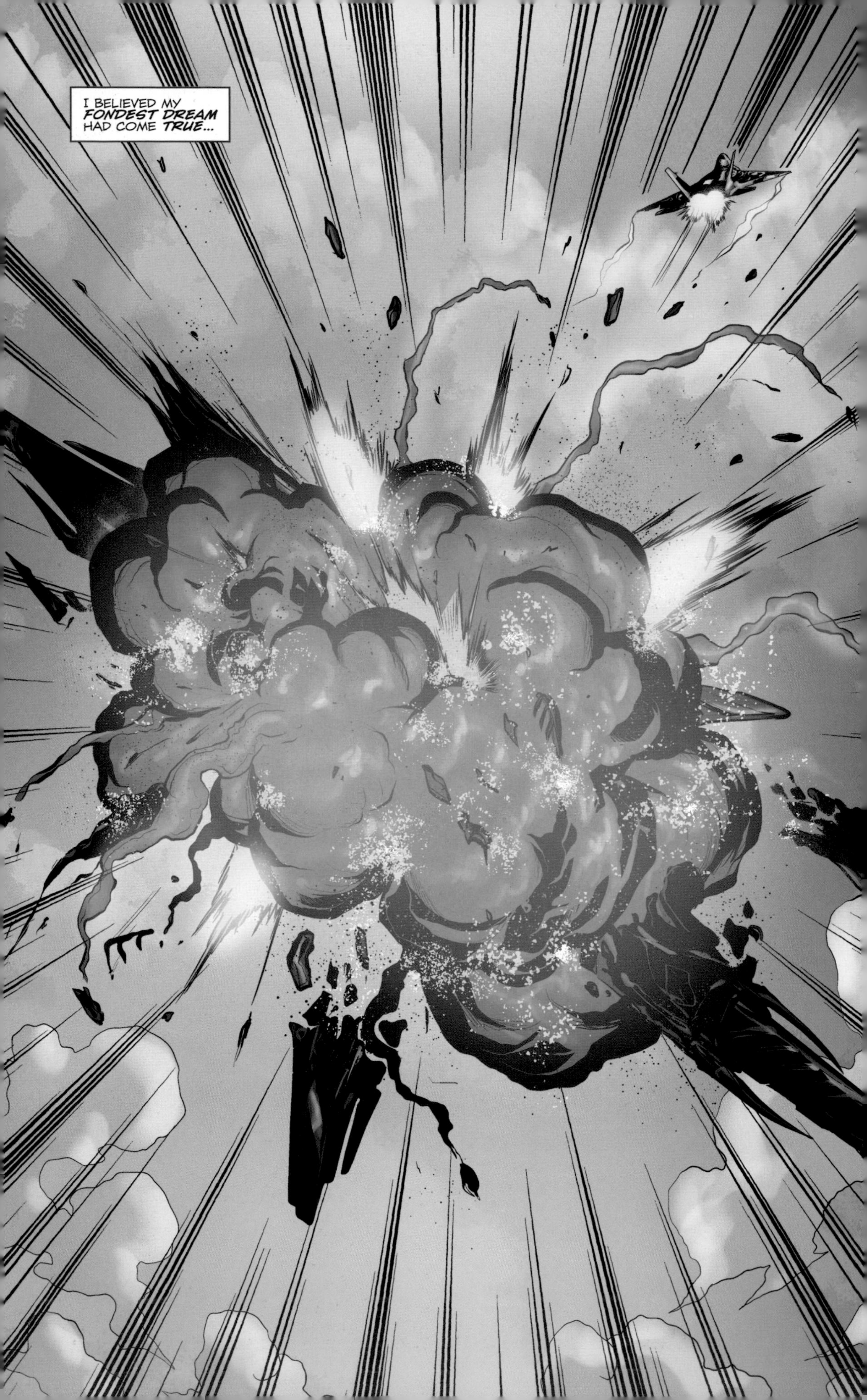
I BELIEVED MY FONDEST DREAM HAD COME TRUE...

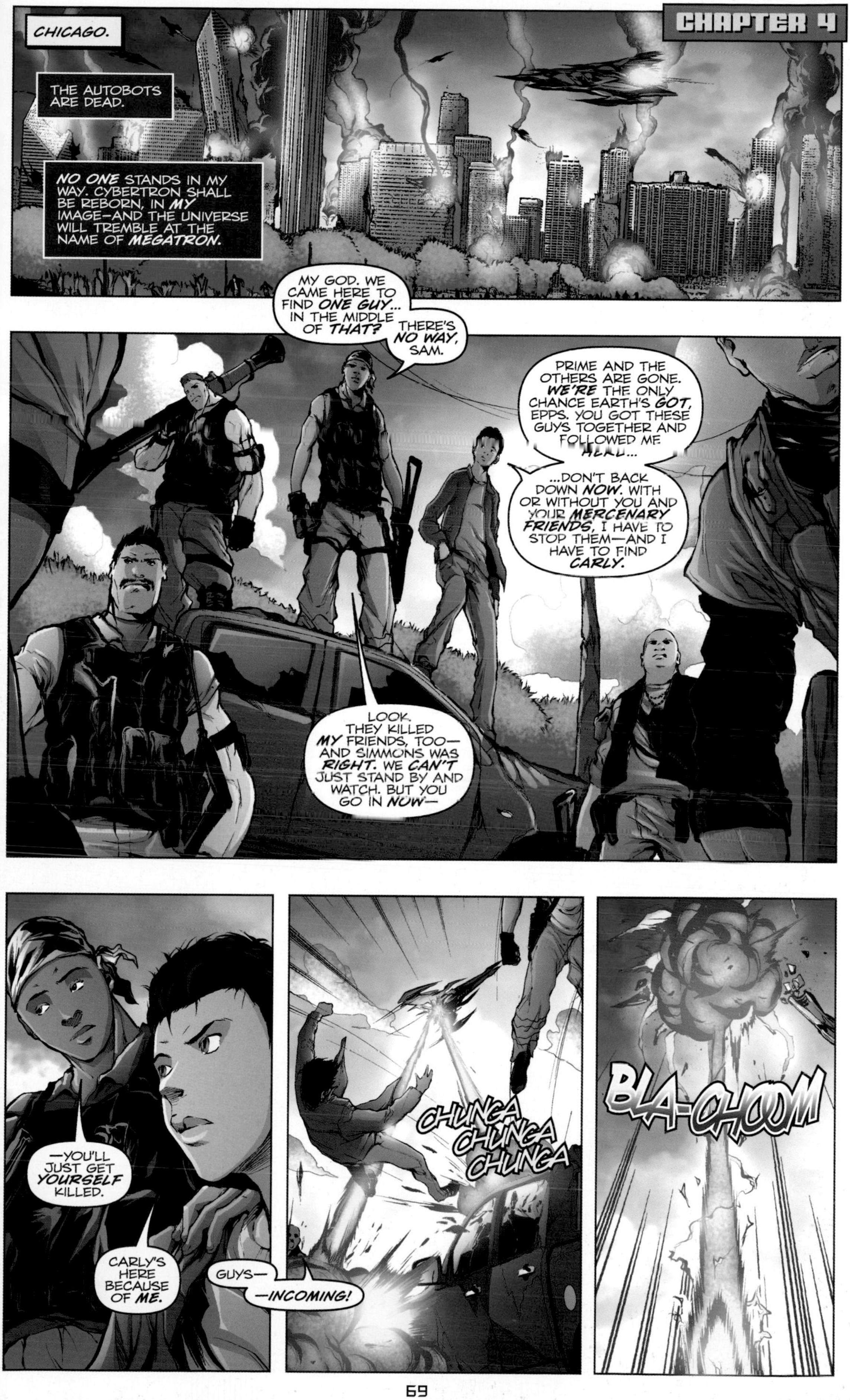
CHAPTER 4
CHICAGO.
THE AUTOBOTS ARE DEAD.
NO ONE STANDS IN MY WAY. CYBERTRON SHALL BE REBORN, IN MY IMAGE—AND THE UNIVERSE WILL TREMBLE AT THE NAME OF MEGATRON.
MY GOD. WE CAME HERE TO FIND ONE GUY... IN THE MIDDLE OF THAT?
THERE'S NO WAY, SAM.
PRIME AND THE OTHERS ARE GONE. WE'RE THE ONLY CHANCE EARTH'S GOT, EPPS. YOU GOT THESE GUYS TOGETHER AND FOLLOWED ME HERE...
...DON'T BACK DOWN NOW. WITH OR WITHOUT YOU AND YOUR MERCENARY FRIENDS, I HAVE TO STOP THEM—AND I HAVE TO FIND CARLY.
LOOK. THEY KILLED MY FRIENDS, TOO—AND SIMMONS WAS RIGHT. WE CAN'T JUST STAND BY AND WATCH. BUT YOU GO IN NOW—
—YOU'LL JUST GET YOURSELF KILLED.
CARLY'S HERE BECAUSE OF ME.
GUYS—
—INCOMING!
CHUNGA CHUNGA CHUNGA
BLA-CHOOM

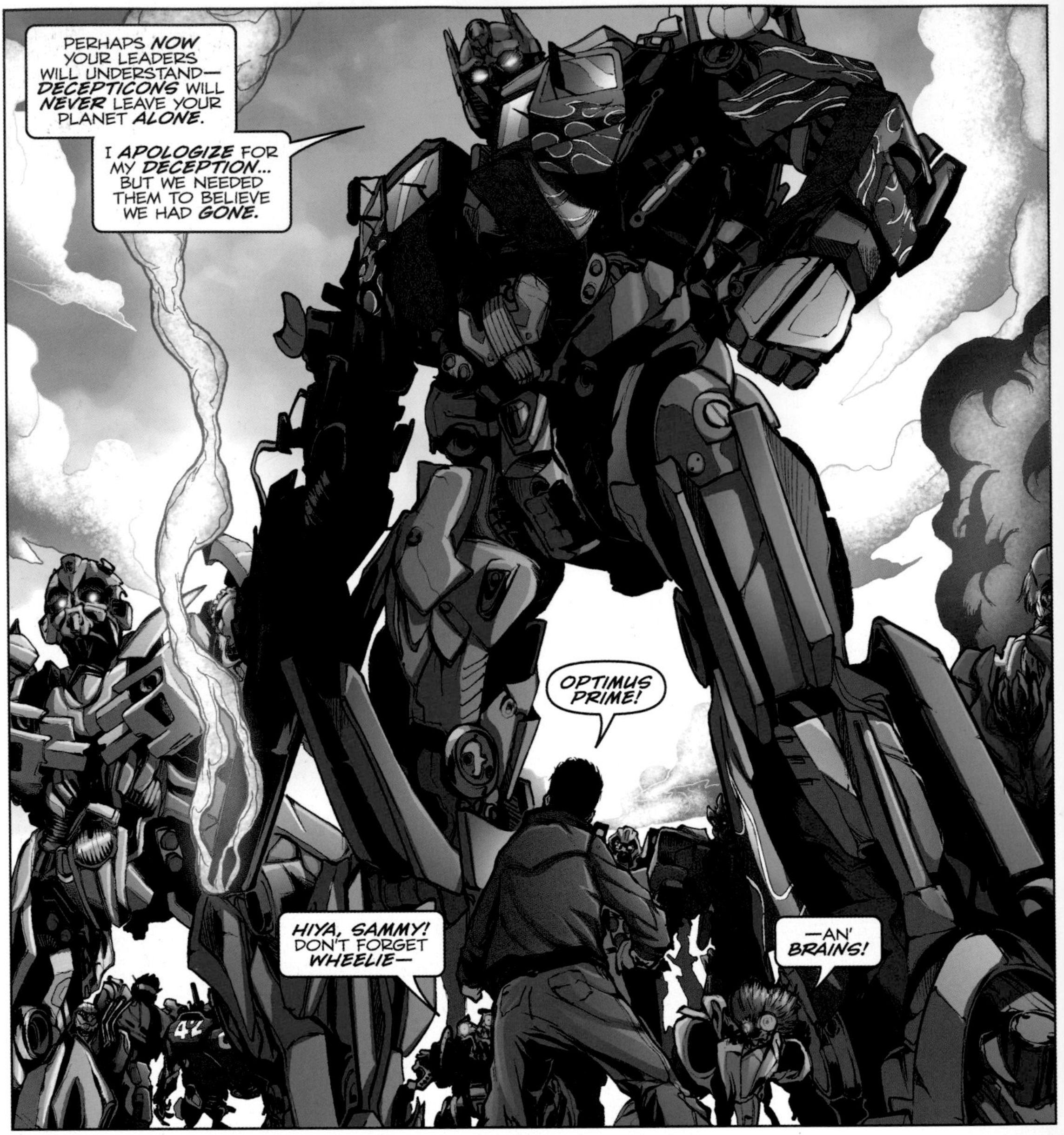
PERHAPS NOW YOUR LEADERS WILL UNDERSTAND— DECEPTICONS WILL NEVER LEAVE YOUR PLANET ALONE.
I APOLOGIZE FOR MY DECEPTION... BUT WE NEEDED THEM TO BELIEVE WE HAD GONE.
OPTIMUS PRIME!
HIYA, SAMMY! DON'T FORGET WHEELIE—
—AN' BRAINS!

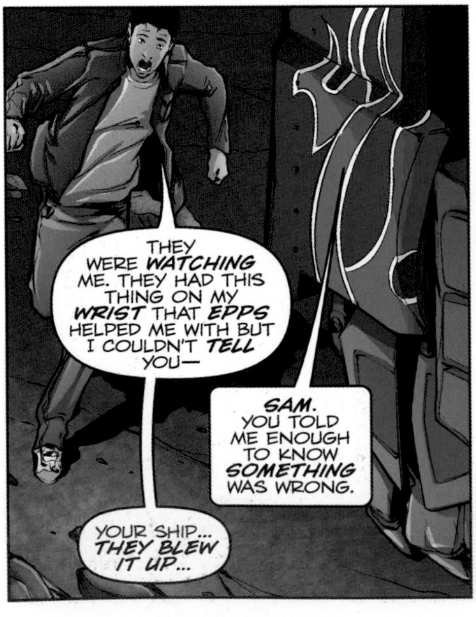
THEY WERE WATCHING ME. THEY HAD THIS THING ON MY WRIST THAT EPPS HELPED ME WITH BUT I COULDN'T TELL YOU—
SAM. YOU TOLD ME ENOUGH TO KNOW SOMETHING WAS WRONG.
YOUR SHIP... THEY BLEW IT UP...

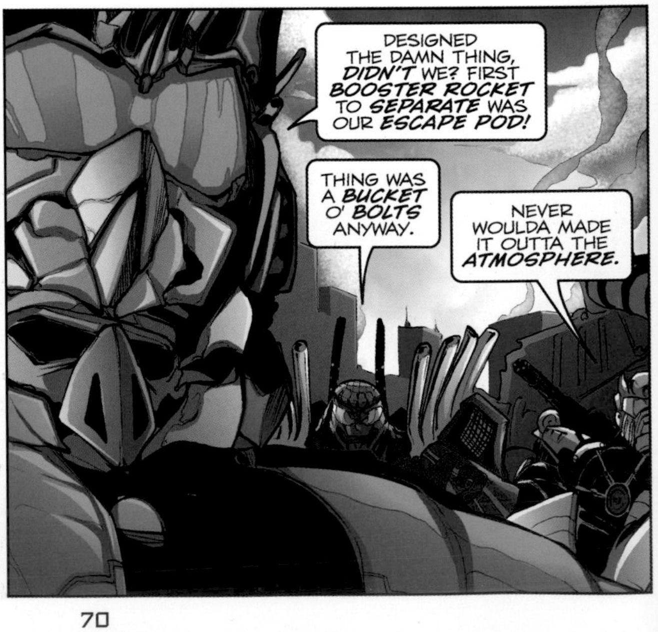
DESIGNED THE DAMN THING, DIDN'T WE? FIRST BOOSTER ROCKET TO SEPARATE WAS OUR ESCAPE POD!
THING WAS A BUCKET O' BOLTS ANYWAY.
NEVER WOULDA MADE IT OUTTA THE ATMOSPHERE.

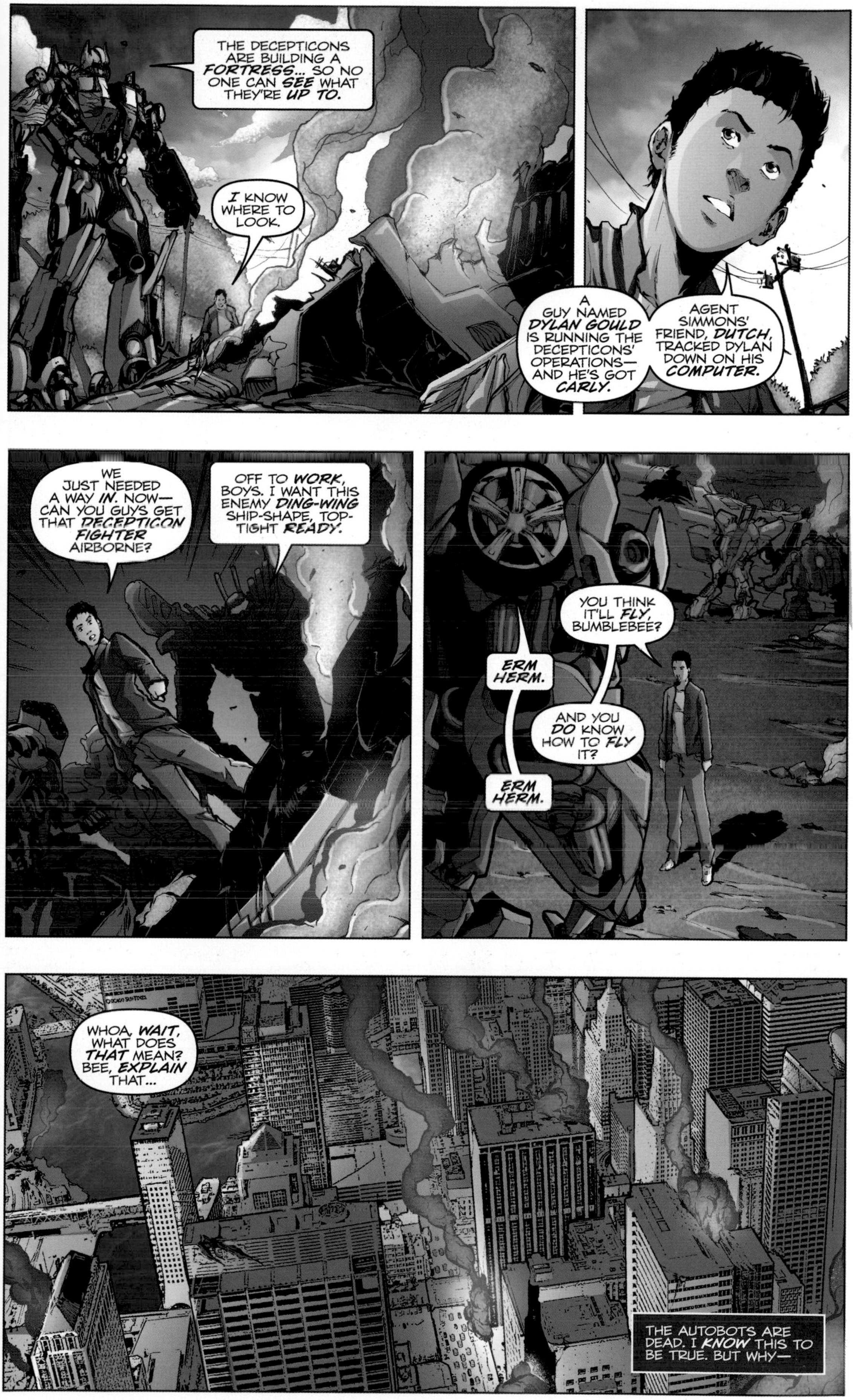
THE DECEPTICONS ARE BUILDING A FORTRESS... SO NO ONE CAN SEE WHAT THEY'RE UP TO.
I KNOW WHERE TO LOOK.
A GUY NAMED DYLAN GOULD IS RUNNING THE DECEPTICONS' OPERATIONS— AND HE'S GOT CARLY.
AGENT SIMMONS' FRIEND, DUTCH, TRACKED DYLAN DOWN ON HIS COMPUTER.
WE JUST NEEDED A WAY IN. NOW— CAN YOU GUYS GET THAT DECEPTICON FIGHTER AIRBORNE?
OFF TO WORK, BOYS. I WANT THIS ENEMY DING-WING SHIP-SHAPE, TOP-TIGHT READY.
YOU THINK IT'LL FLY, BUMBLEBEE?
ERM HERM.
AND YOU DO KNOW HOW TO FLY IT?
ERM HERM.
WHOA, WAIT, WHAT DOES THAT MEAN? BEE, EXPLAIN THAT...
THE AUTOBOTS ARE DEAD. I KNOW THIS TO BE TRUE. BUT WHY—

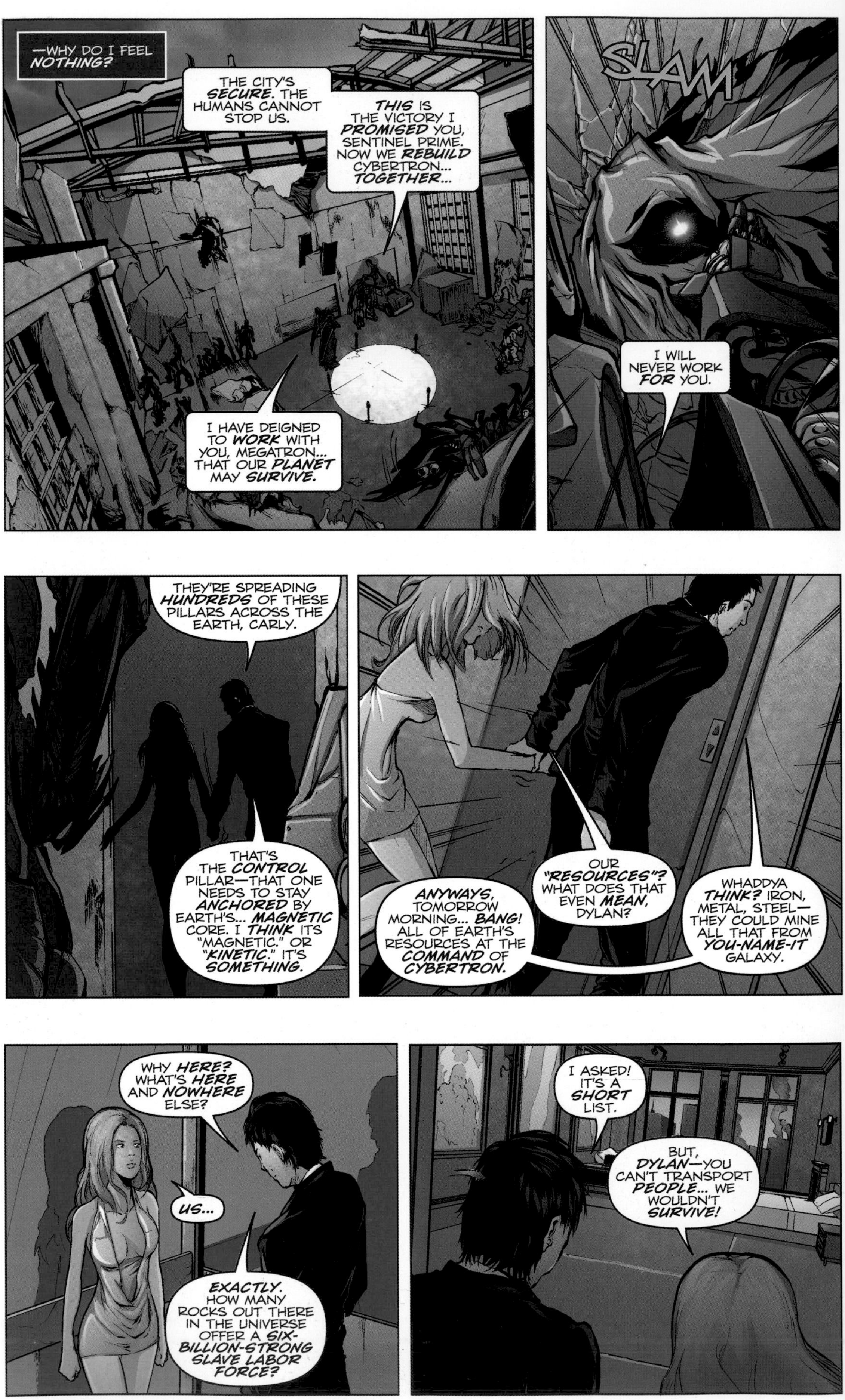
—WHY DO I FEEL NOTHING?
THE CITY'S SECURE. THE HUMANS CANNOT STOP US.
THIS IS THE VICTORY I PROMISED YOU, SENTINEL PRIME. NOW WE REBUILD CYBERTRON... TOGETHER...
I HAVE DEIGNED TO WORK WITH YOU, MEGATRON... THAT OUR PLANET MAY SURVIVE.
SLAM
I WILL NEVER WORK FOR YOU.
THEY'RE SPREADING HUNDREDS OF THESE PILLARS ACROSS THE EARTH, CARLY.
THAT'S THE CONTROL PILLAR—THAT ONE NEEDS TO STAY ANCHORED BY EARTH'S... MAGNETIC CORE. I THINK ITS "MAGNETIC." OR "KINETIC." IT'S SOMETHING.
ANYWAYS, TOMORROW MORNING... BANG! ALL OF EARTH'S RESOURCES AT THE COMMAND OF CYBERTRON.
OUR "RESOURCES"? WHAT DOES THAT EVEN MEAN, DYLAN?
WHADDYA THINK? IRON, METAL, STEEL—THEY COULD MINE ALL THAT FROM YOU-NAME-IT GALAXY.
WHY HERE? WHAT'S HERE AND NOWHERE ELSE?
US...
EXACTLY. HOW MANY ROCKS OUT THERE IN THE UNIVERSE OFFER A SIX-BILLION-STRONG SLAVE LABOR FORCE?
I ASKED! IT'S A SHORT LIST.
BUT, DYLAN—YOU CAN'T TRANSPORT PEOPLE... WE WOULDN'T SURVIVE!

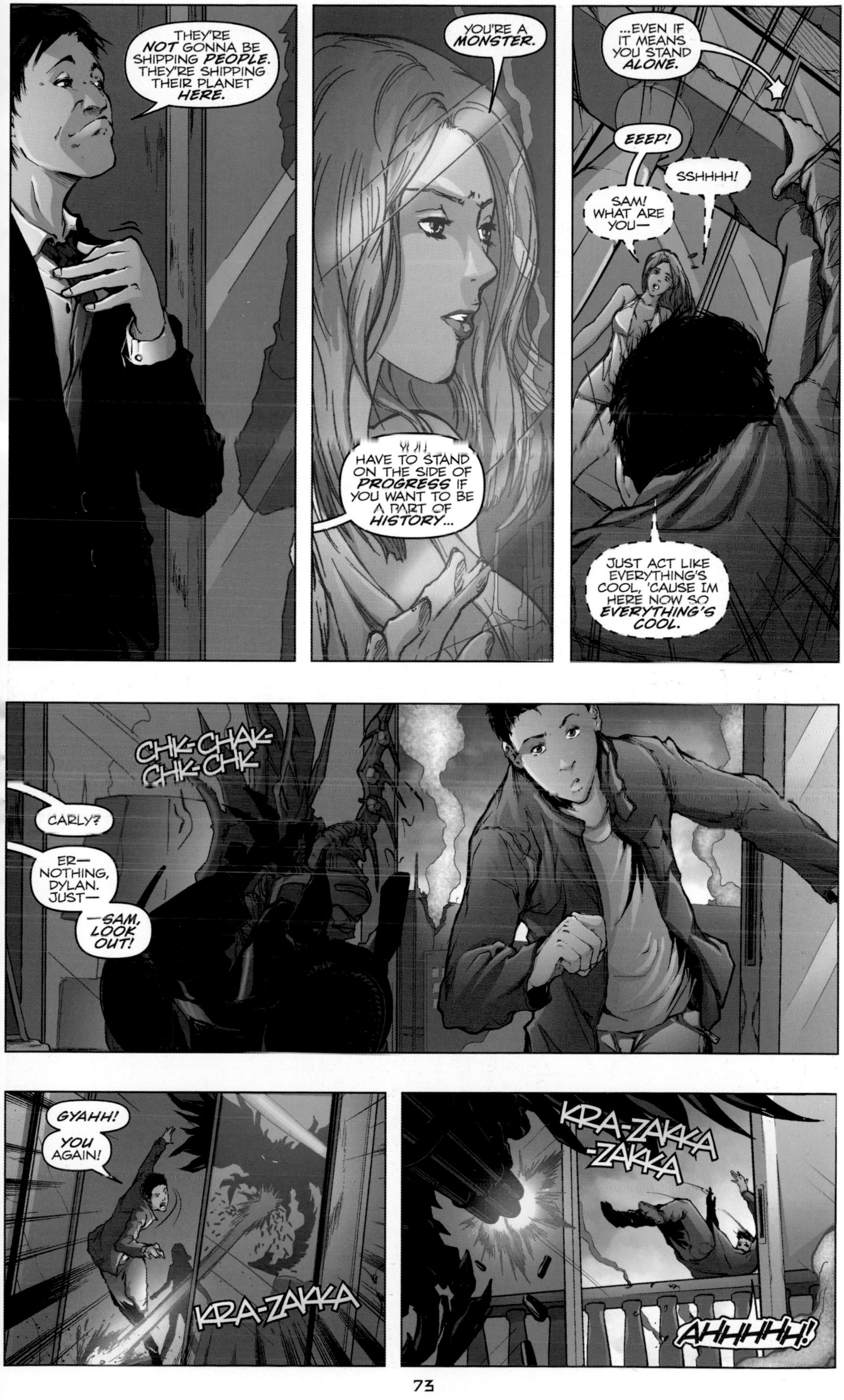
THEY'RE NOT GONNA BE SHIPPING PEOPLE. THEY'RE SHIPPING THEIR PLANET HERE.
YOU'RE A MONSTER.
HAVE TO STAND ON THE SIDE OF PROGRESS IF YOU WANT TO BE A PART OF HISTORY...
...EVEN IF IT MEANS YOU STAND ALONE.
EEEP!
SAM! WHAT ARE YOU—
SSHHHH!
JUST ACT LIKE EVERYTHING'S COOL, 'CAUSE IM HERE NOW SO EVERYTHING'S COOL.
CHK-CHAK-CHK-CHK
CARLY?
ER—NOTHING, DYLAN. JUST—
—SAM, LOOK OUT!
GYAHH!
YOU AGAIN!
KRA-ZAKKA
KRA-ZAKKA-ZAKKA
AHHHHH!

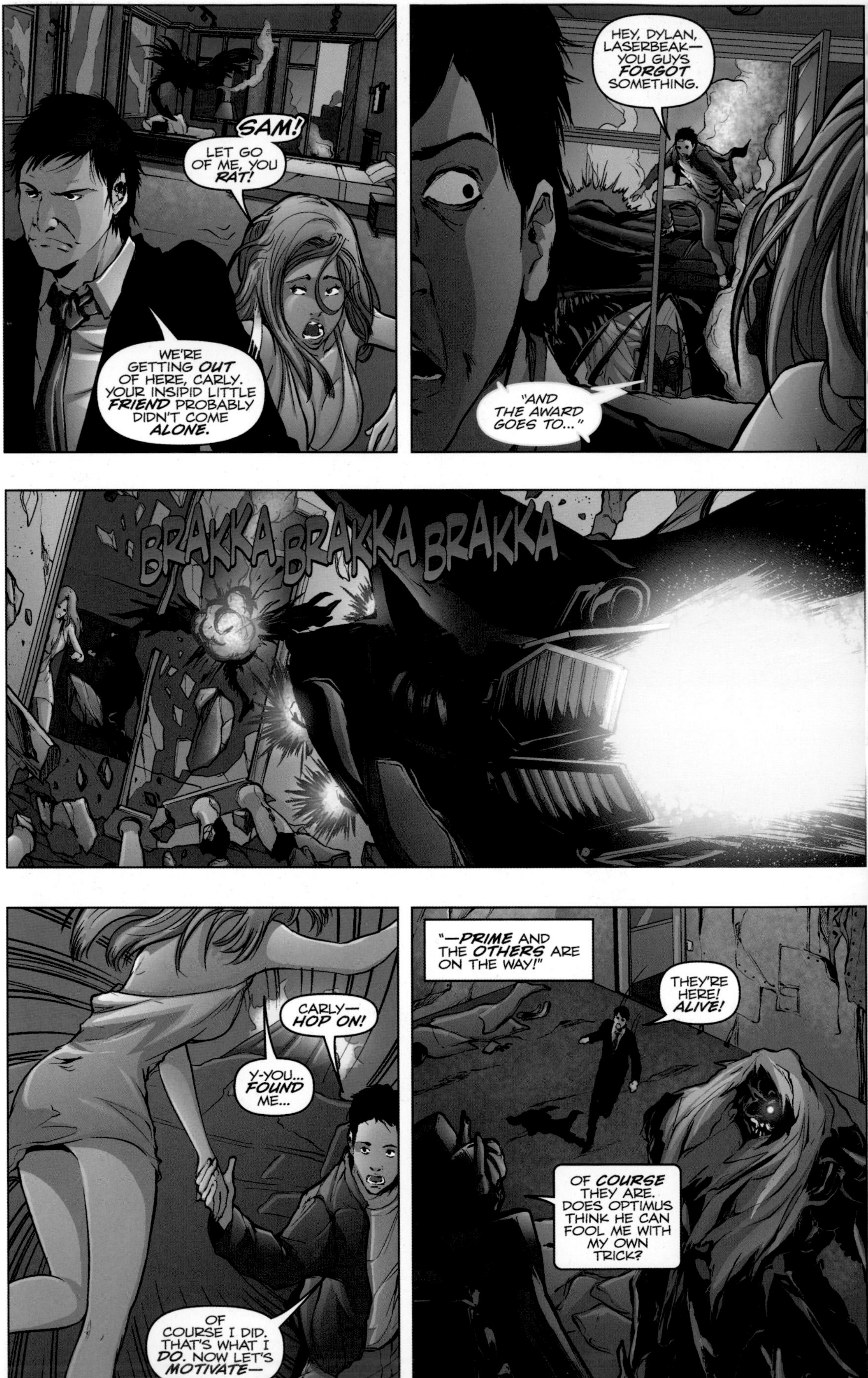
SAM!
LET GO OF ME, YOU RAT!
WE'RE GETTING OUT OF HERE, CARLY. YOUR INSIPID LITTLE FRIEND PROBABLY DIDN'T COME ALONE.
HEY, DYLAN, LASERBEAK— YOU GUYS FORGOT SOMETHING.
"AND THE AWARD GOES TO..."
BRAKKA BRAKKA BRAKKA
CARLY— HOP ON!
Y-YOU... FOUND ME...
OF COURSE I DID. THAT'S WHAT I DO. NOW LET'S MOTIVATE—
"—PRIME AND THE OTHERS ARE ON THE WAY!"
THEY'RE HERE! ALIVE!
OF COURSE THEY ARE. DOES OPTIMUS THINK HE CAN FOOL ME WITH MY OWN TRICK?

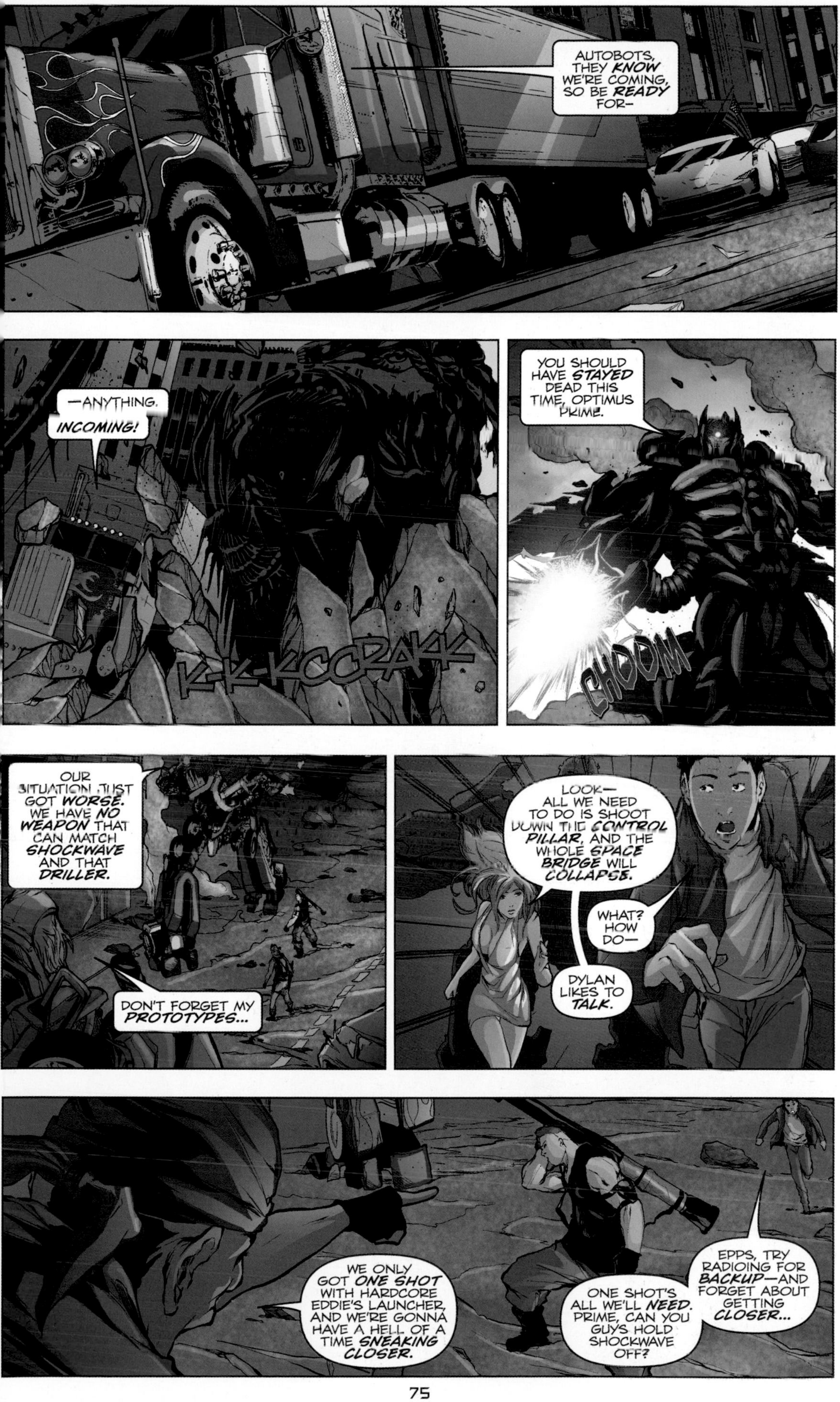
AUTOBOTS, THEY KNOW WE'RE COMING, SO BE READY FOR—
—ANYTHING.
INCOMING!
K-K-KCCRAKK
YOU SHOULD HAVE STAYED DEAD THIS TIME, OPTIMUS PRIME.
CHOOM
OUR SITUATION JUST GOT WORSE. WE HAVE NO WEAPON THAT CAN MATCH SHOCKWAVE AND THAT DRILLER.
DON'T FORGET MY PROTOTYPES...
LOOK— ALL WE NEED TO DO IS SHOOT DOWN THE CONTROL PILLAR, AND THE WHOLE SPACE BRIDGE WILL COLLAPSE.
WHAT? HOW DO—
DYLAN LIKES TO TALK.
WE ONLY GOT ONE SHOT WITH HARDCORE EDDIE'S LAUNCHER, AND WE'RE GONNA HAVE A HELL OF A TIME SNEAKING CLOSER.
ONE SHOT'S ALL WE'LL NEED. PRIME, CAN YOU GUYS HOLD SHOCKWAVE OFF?
EPPS, TRY RADIOING FOR BACKUP—AND FORGET ABOUT GETTING CLOSER...

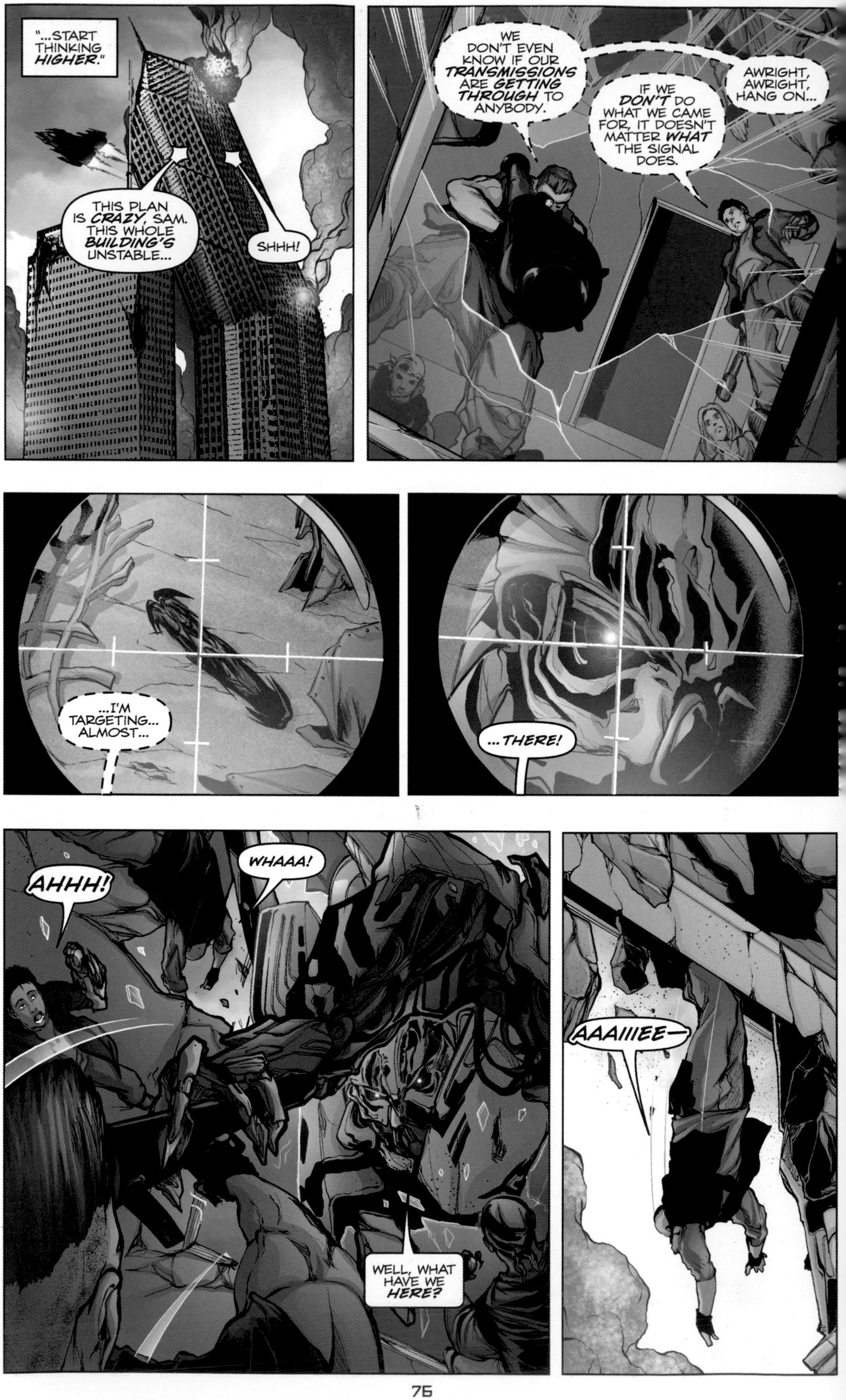
"...START THINKING HIGHER."
THIS PLAN IS CRAZY, SAM. THIS WHOLE BUILDING'S UNSTABLE...
SHHH!
WE DON'T EVEN KNOW IF OUR TRANSMISSIONS ARE GETTING THROUGH TO ANYBODY.
IF WE DON'T DO WHAT WE CAME FOR, IT DOESN'T MATTER WHAT THE SIGNAL DOES.
AWRIGHT, AWRIGHT, HANG ON...
...I'M TARGETING... ALMOST...
...THERE!
AHHH!
WHAAA!
WELL, WHAT HAVE WE HERE?
AAAIIIEE—

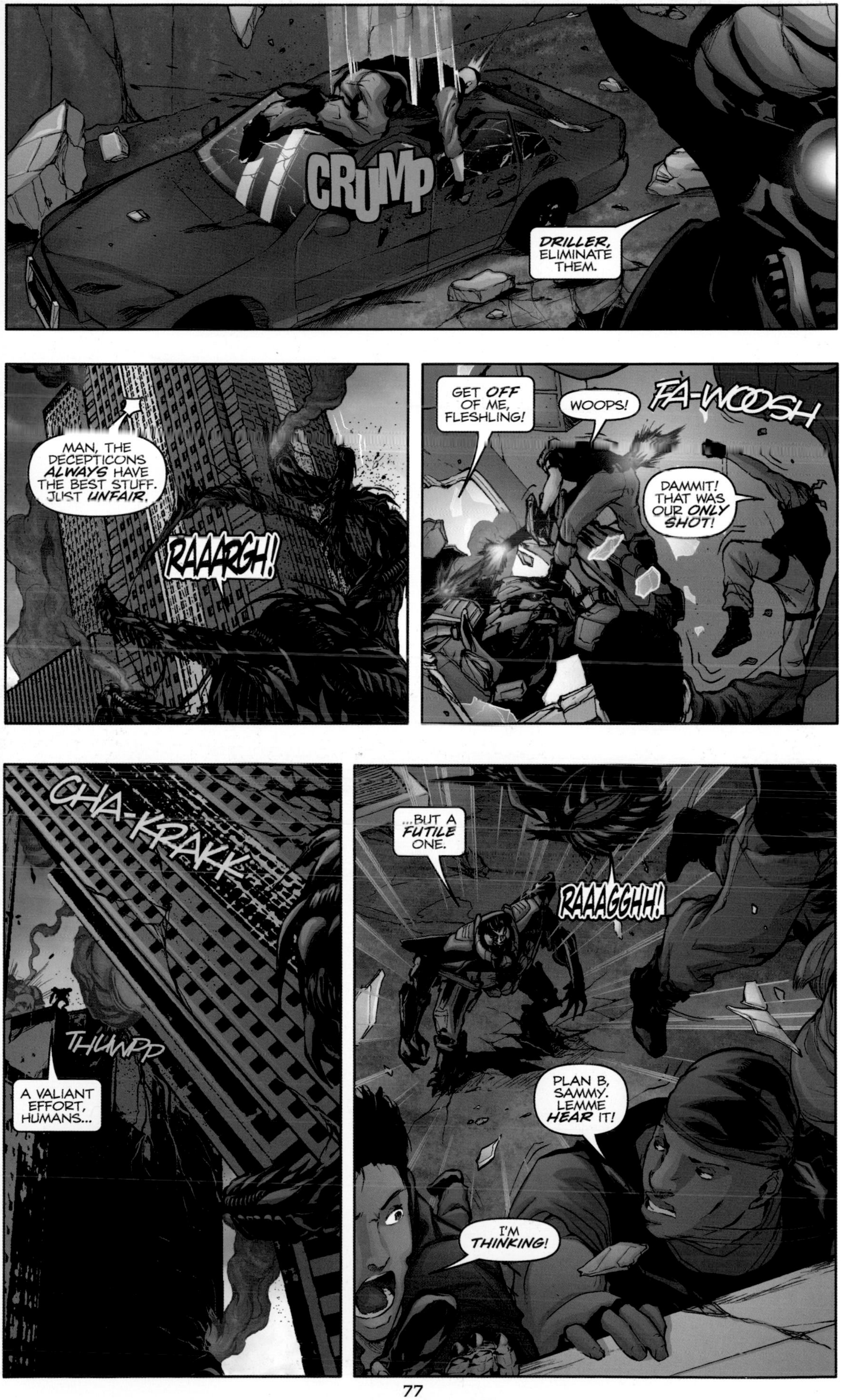
CRUMP
DRILLER, ELIMINATE THEM.
MAN, THE DECEPTICONS ALWAYS HAVE THE BEST STUFF. JUST UNFAIR.
RAAARGH!
GET OFF OF ME, FLESHLING!
WOOPS!
FA-WOOSH
DAMMIT! THAT WAS OUR ONLY SHOT!
CHA-KRAKK
THUMPP
A VALIANT EFFORT, HUMANS...
...BUT A FUTILE ONE.
RAAAGGHH!
PLAN B, SAMMY. LEMME HEAR IT!
I'M THINKING!

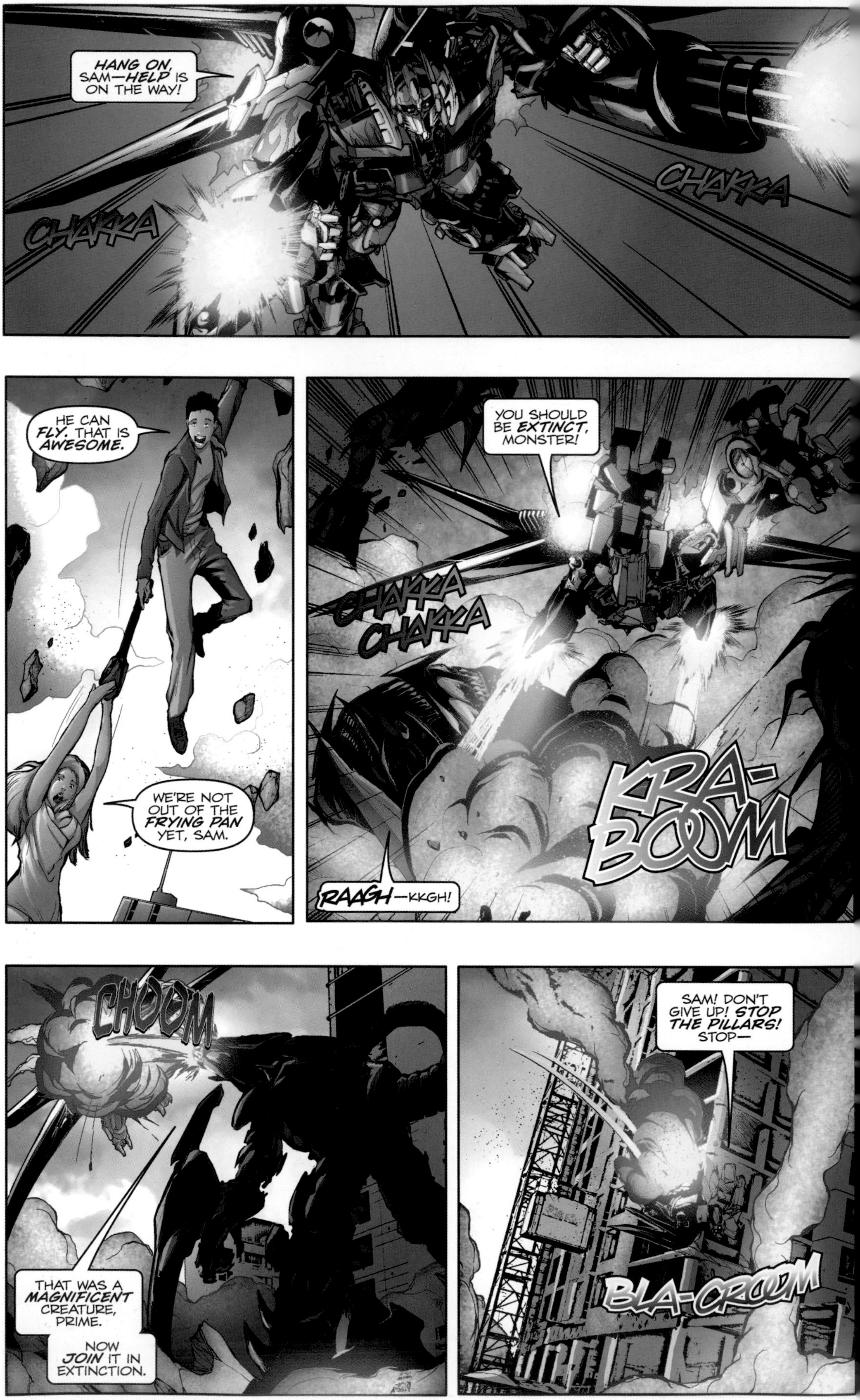
HANG ON, SAM—HELP IS ON THE WAY!
CHAKKA
CHAKKA
HE CAN FLY. THAT IS AWESOME.
WE'RE NOT OUT OF THE FRYING PAN YET, SAM.
YOU SHOULD BE EXTINCT, MONSTER!
CHAKKA CHAKKA
KRA-BOOM
RAAGH—KKGH!
CHOOM
THAT WAS A MAGNIFICENT CREATURE, PRIME.
NOW JOIN IT IN EXTINCTION.
SAM! DON'T GIVE UP! STOP THE PILLARS! STOP—
BLA-CROOM

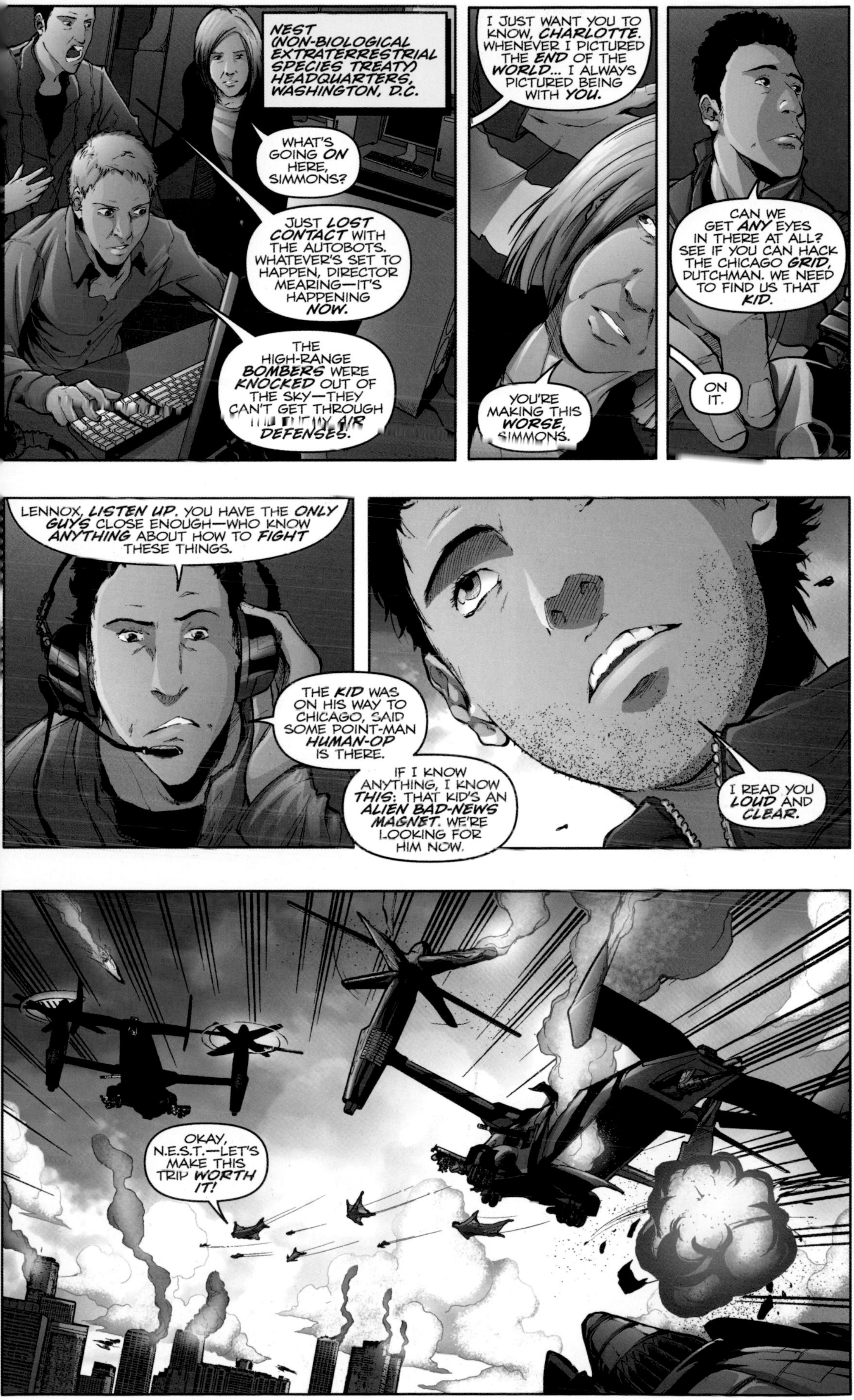
NEST (NON-BIOLOGICAL EXTRATERRESTRIAL SPECIES TREATY) HEADQUARTERS, WASHINGTON, D.C.
WHAT'S GOING ON HERE, SIMMONS?
JUST LOST CONTACT WITH THE AUTOBOTS. WHATEVER'S SET TO HAPPEN, DIRECTOR MEARING—IT'S HAPPENING NOW.
THE HIGH-RANGE BOMBERS WERE KNOCKED OUT OF THE SKY—THEY CAN'T GET THROUGH AIR DEFENSES.
I JUST WANT YOU TO KNOW, CHARLOTTE. WHENEVER I PICTURED THE END OF THE WORLD... I ALWAYS PICTURED BEING WITH YOU.
YOU'RE MAKING THIS WORSE, SIMMONS.
CAN WE GET ANY EYES IN THERE AT ALL? SEE IF YOU CAN HACK THE CHICAGO GRID, DUTCHMAN. WE NEED TO FIND US THAT KID.
ON IT.
LENNOX, LISTEN UP. YOU HAVE THE ONLY GUYS CLOSE ENOUGH—WHO KNOW ANYTHING ABOUT HOW TO FIGHT THESE THINGS.
THE KID WAS ON HIS WAY TO CHICAGO, SAID SOME POINT-MAN HUMAN-OP IS THERE.
IF I KNOW ANYTHING, I KNOW THIS: THAT KID'S AN ALIEN BAD-NEWS MAGNET. WE'RE LOOKING FOR HIM NOW.
I READ YOU LOUD AND CLEAR.
OKAY, N.E.S.T.—LET'S MAKE THIS TRIP WORTH IT!

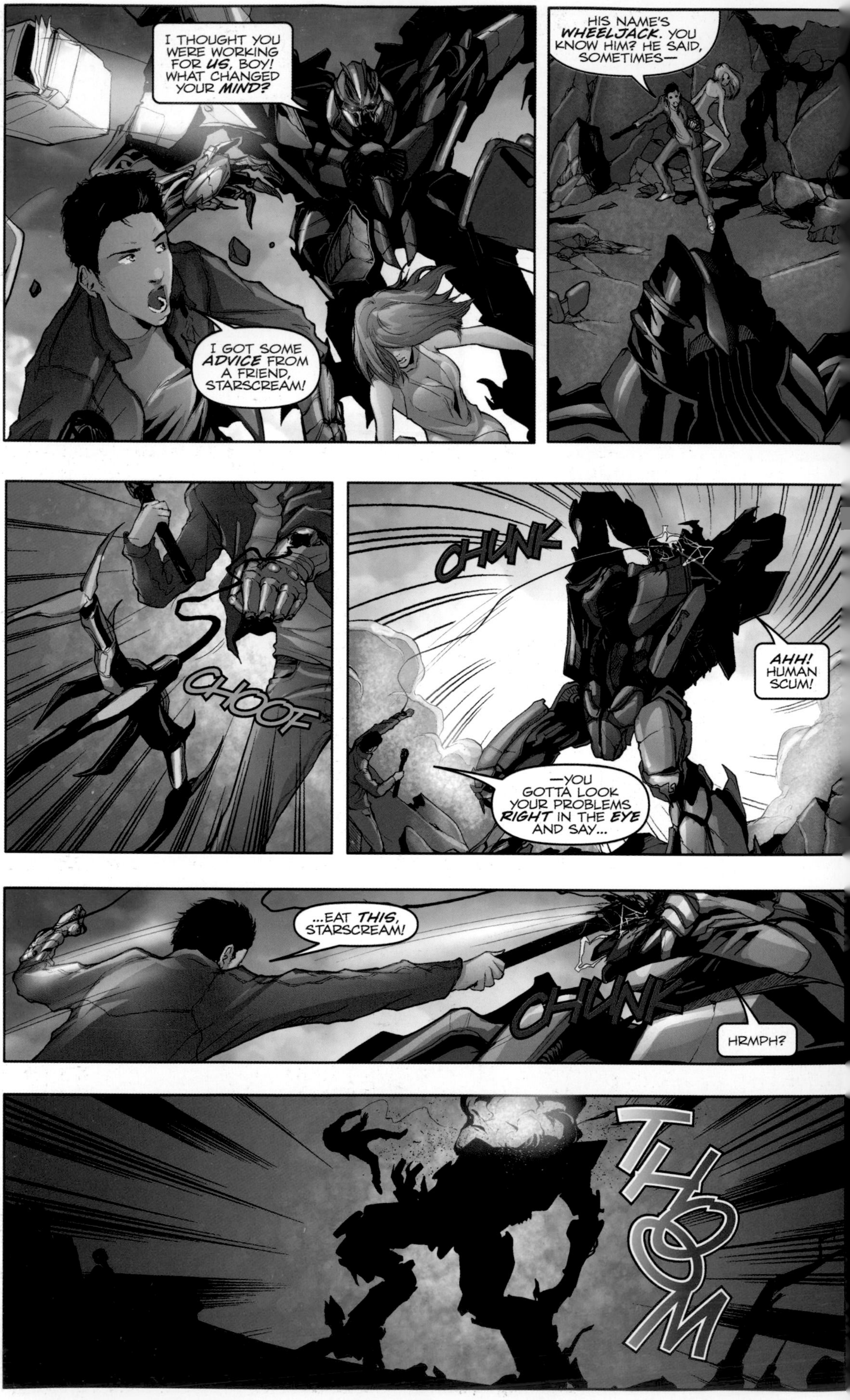
I THOUGHT YOU WERE WORKING FOR US, BOY! WHAT CHANGED YOUR MIND?
I GOT SOME ADVICE FROM A FRIEND, STARSCREAM!
HIS NAME'S WHEELJACK. YOU KNOW HIM? HE SAID, SOMETIMES—
CHOOF
CHUNK
AHH! HUMAN SCUM!
—YOU GOTTA LOOK YOUR PROBLEMS RIGHT IN THE EYE AND SAY...
...EAT THIS, STARSCREAM!
CHUNK
HRMPH?
THOOM

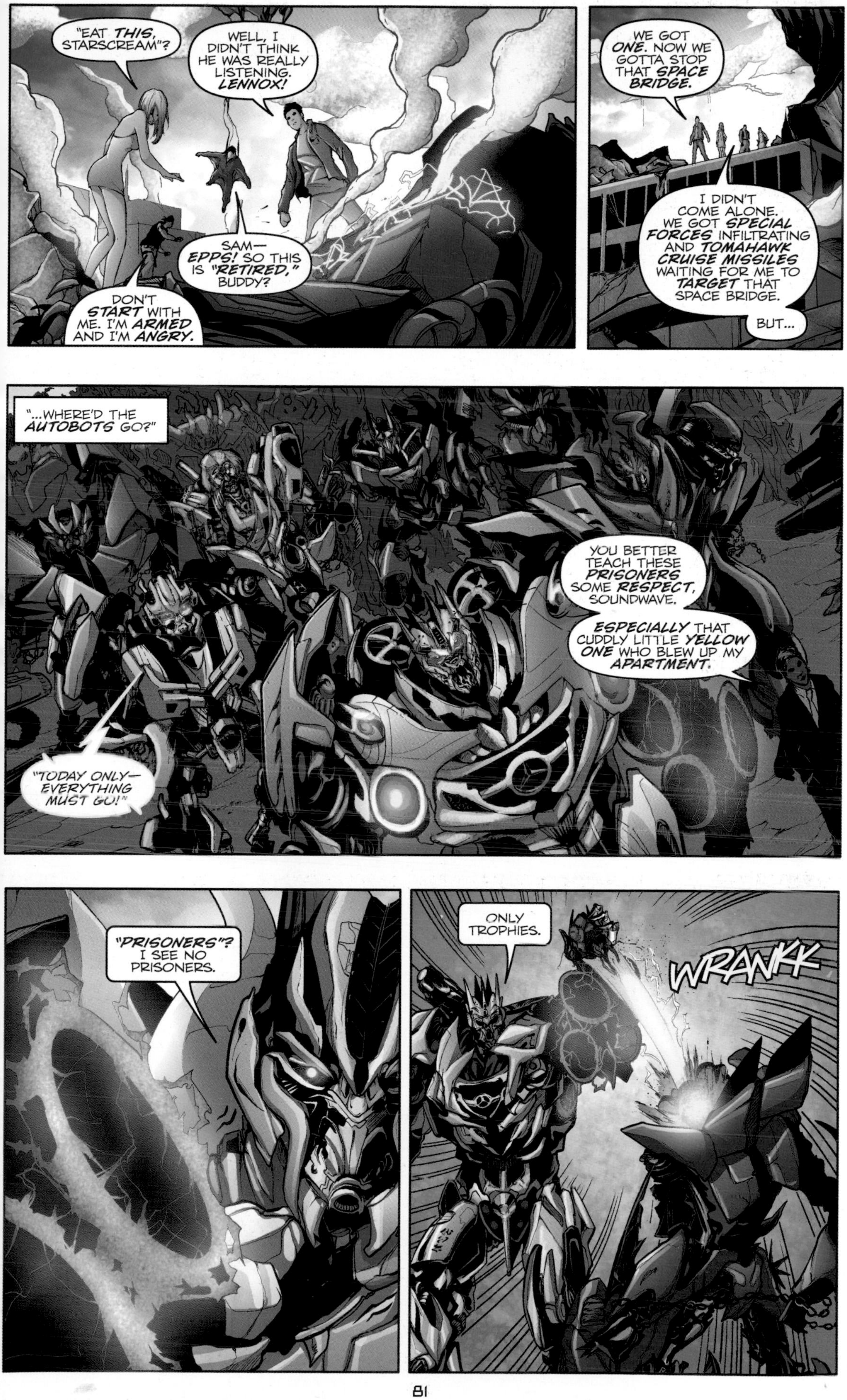
"EAT THIS, STARSCREAM"?
WELL, I DIDN'T THINK HE WAS REALLY LISTENING. LENNOX!
SAM— EPPS! SO THIS IS "RETIRED," BUDDY?
DON'T START WITH ME. I'M ARMED AND I'M ANGRY.
WE GOT ONE. NOW WE GOTTA STOP THAT SPACE BRIDGE.
I DIDN'T COME ALONE. WE GOT SPECIAL FORCES INFILTRATING AND TOMAHAWK CRUISE MISSILES WAITING FOR ME TO TARGET THAT SPACE BRIDGE.
BUT...
"...WHERE'D THE AUTOBOTS GO?"
YOU BETTER TEACH THESE PRISONERS SOME RESPECT, SOUNDWAVE.
ESPECIALLY THAT CUDDLY LITTLE YELLOW ONE WHO BLEW UP MY APARTMENT.
"TODAY ONLY— EVERYTHING MUST GO!"
"PRISONERS"? I SEE NO PRISONERS.
ONLY TROPHIES.
WRANKK

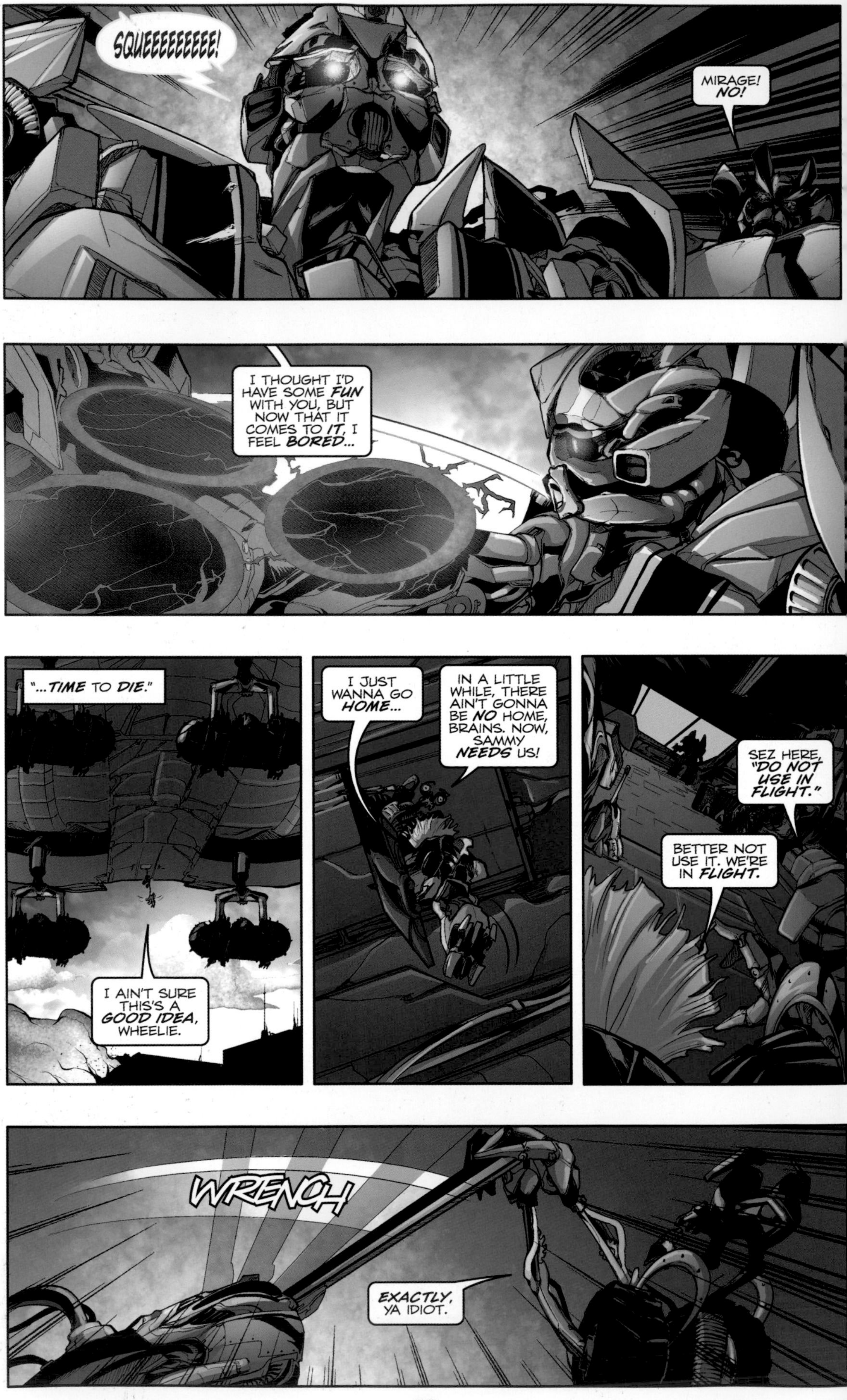
SQUEEEEEEEEEE!
MIRAGE! NO!
I THOUGHT I'D HAVE SOME FUN WITH YOU, BUT NOW THAT IT COMES TO IT, I FEEL BORED...
"...TIME TO DIE."
I AIN'T SURE THIS'S A GOOD IDEA, WHEELIE.
I JUST WANNA GO HOME...
IN A LITTLE WHILE, THERE AIN'T GONNA BE NO HOME, BRAINS. NOW, SAMMY NEEDS US!
SEZ HERE, "DO NOT USE IN FLIGHT."
BETTER NOT USE IT. WE'RE IN FLIGHT.
WRENCH
EXACTLY, YA IDIOT.

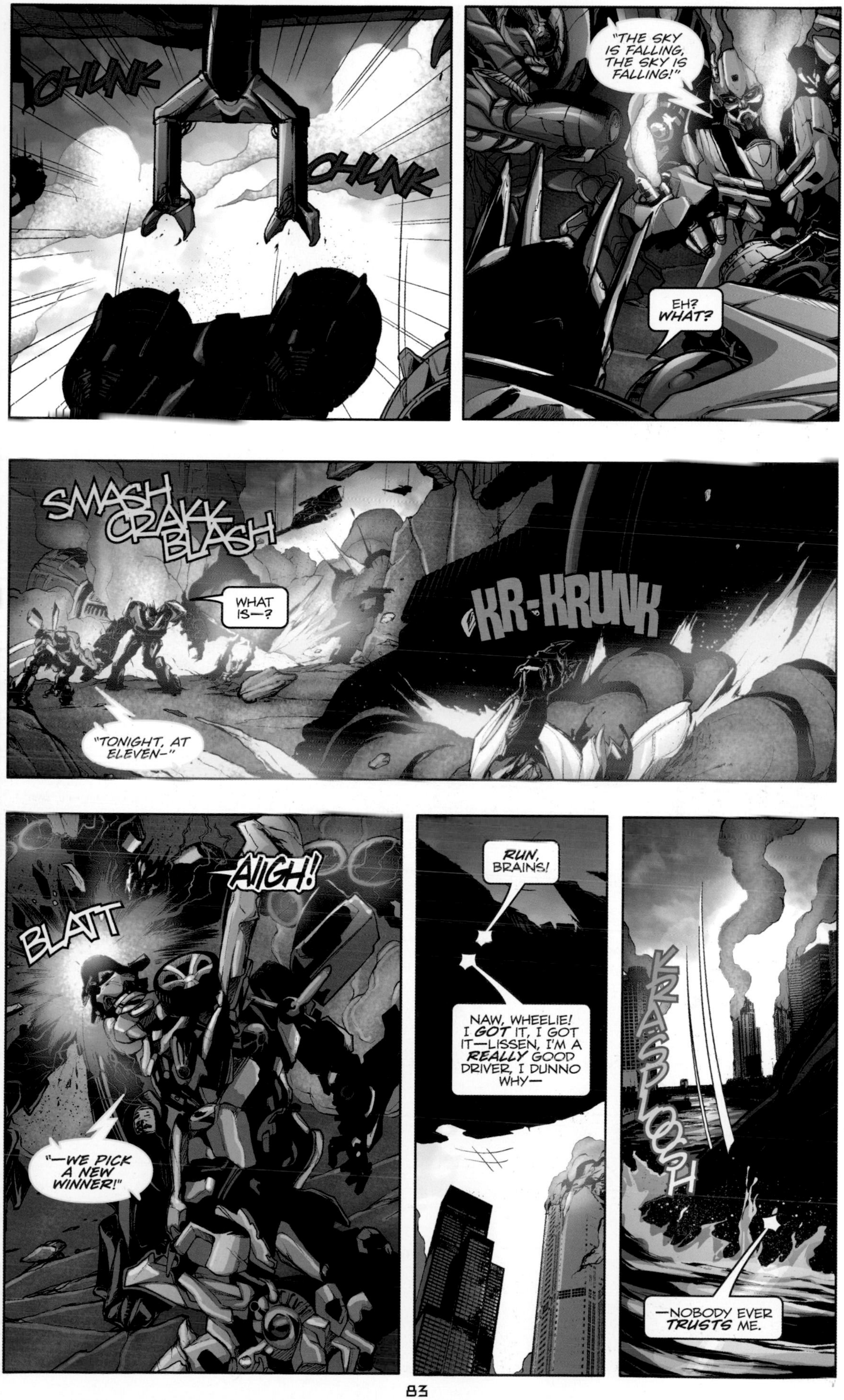
CHUNK
CHUNK
"THE SKY IS FALLING, THE SKY IS FALLING!"
EH? WHAT?
SMASH CRAKK BLASH
WHAT IS—?
KR-KRUNK
"TONIGHT, AT ELEVEN—"
AIIGH!
BLATT
"—WE PICK A NEW WINNER!"
RUN, BRAINS!
NAW, WHEELIE! I GOT IT, I GOT IT—LISSEN, I'M A REALLY GOOD DRIVER, I DUNNO WHY—
KRASPLOOSH
—NOBODY EVER TRUSTS ME.

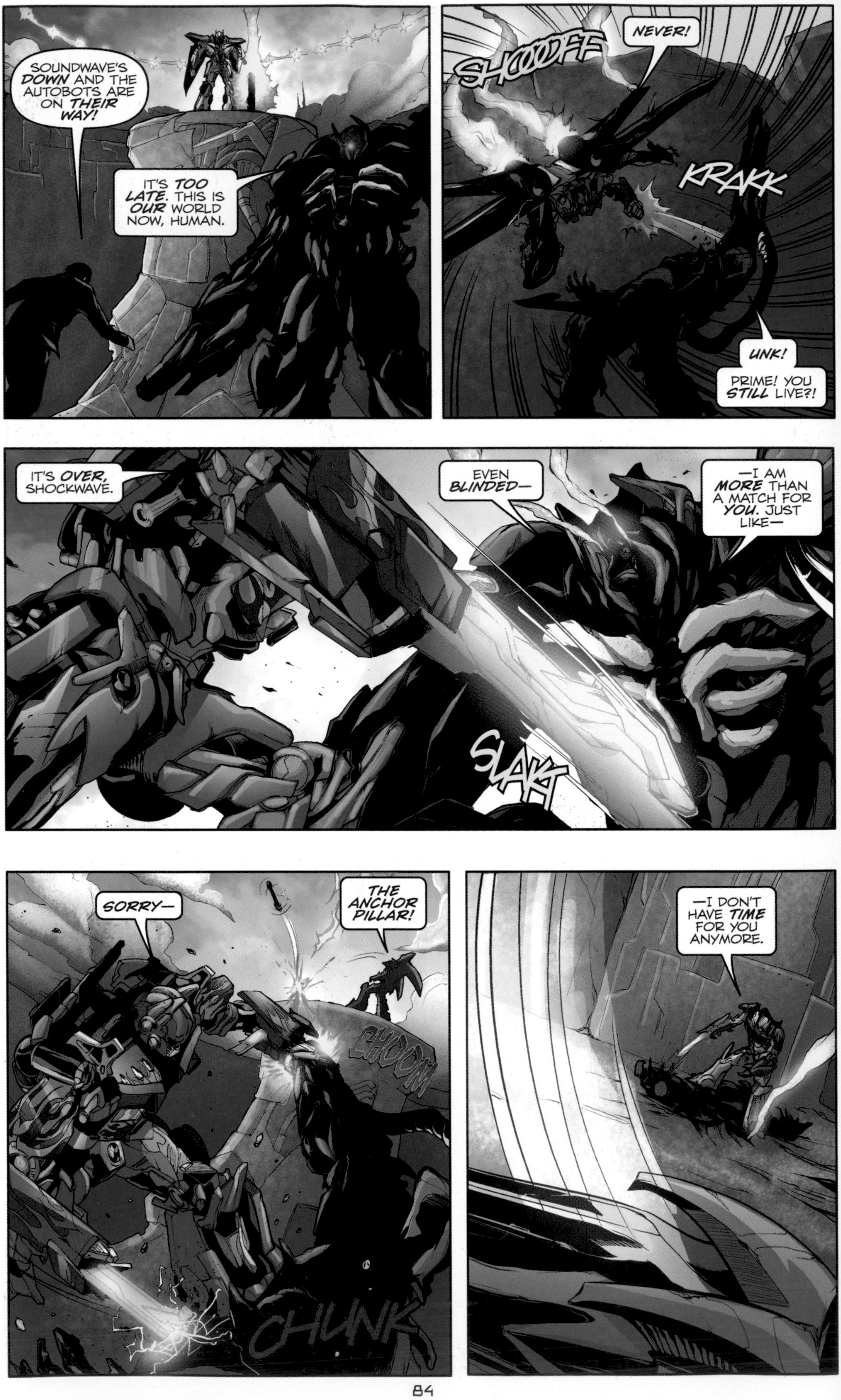
SOUNDWAVE'S DOWN AND THE AUTOBOTS ARE ON THEIR WAY!
IT'S TOO LATE. THIS IS OUR WORLD NOW, HUMAN.
SHOOOFF
NEVER!
KRAKK
UNK!
PRIME! YOU STILL LIVE?!
IT'S OVER, SHOCKWAVE.
EVEN BLINDED—
—I AM MORE THAN A MATCH FOR YOU. JUST LIKE—
SLAKT
SORRY—
THE ANCHOR PILLAR!
CHOOM
CHUNK
—I DON'T HAVE TIME FOR YOU ANYMORE.

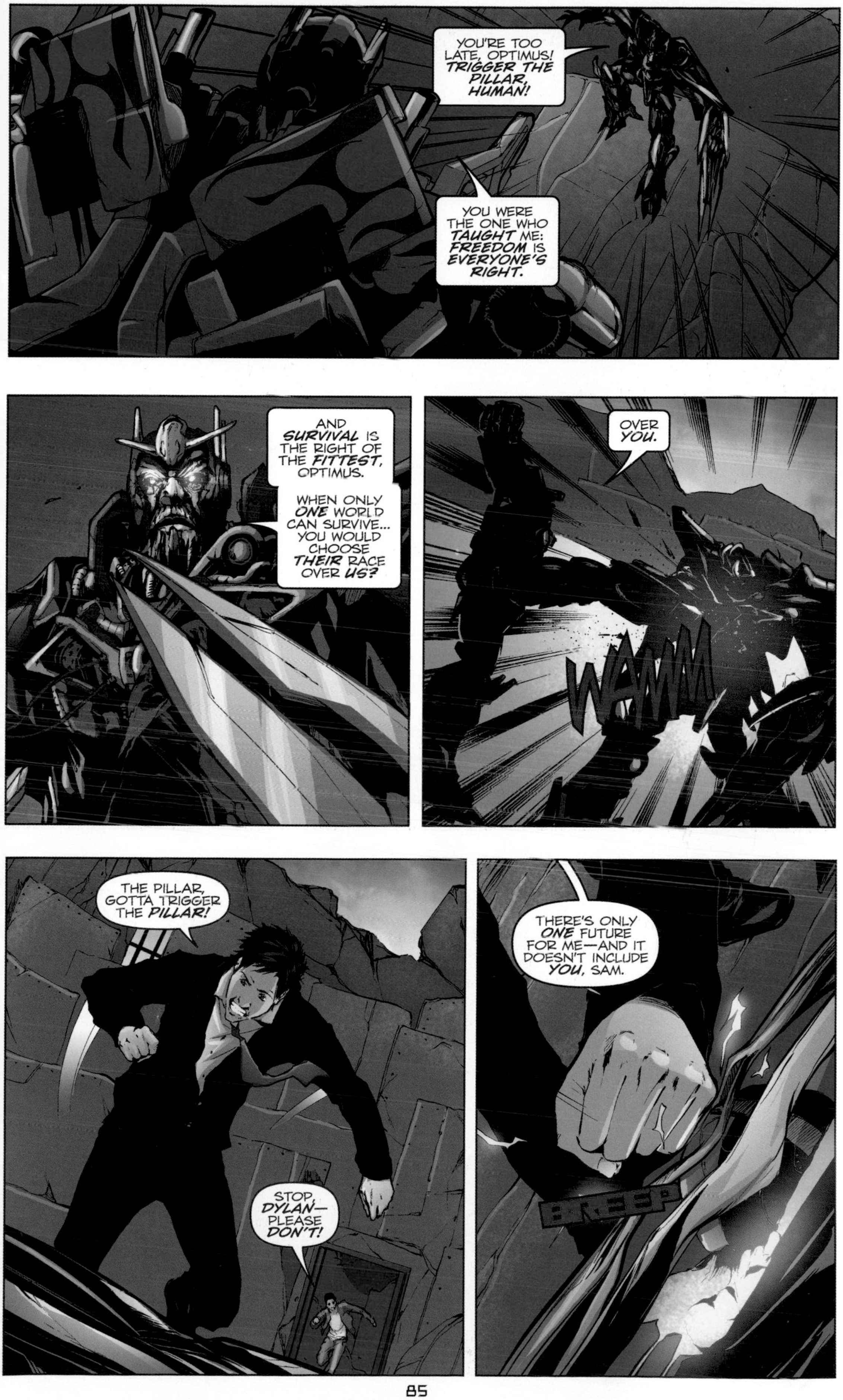
YOU'RE TOO LATE, OPTIMUS! TRIGGER THE PILLAR, HUMAN!
YOU WERE THE ONE WHO TAUGHT ME: FREEDOM IS EVERYONE'S RIGHT.
AND SURVIVAL IS THE RIGHT OF THE FITTEST, OPTIMUS.
WHEN ONLY ONE WORLD CAN SURVIVE... YOU WOULD CHOOSE THEIR RACE OVER US?
OVER YOU.
WAMM
THE PILLAR, GOTTA TRIGGER THE PILLAR!
STOP, DYLAN— PLEASE DON'T!
THERE'S ONLY ONE FUTURE FOR ME—AND IT DOESN'T INCLUDE YOU, SAM.
BREEP

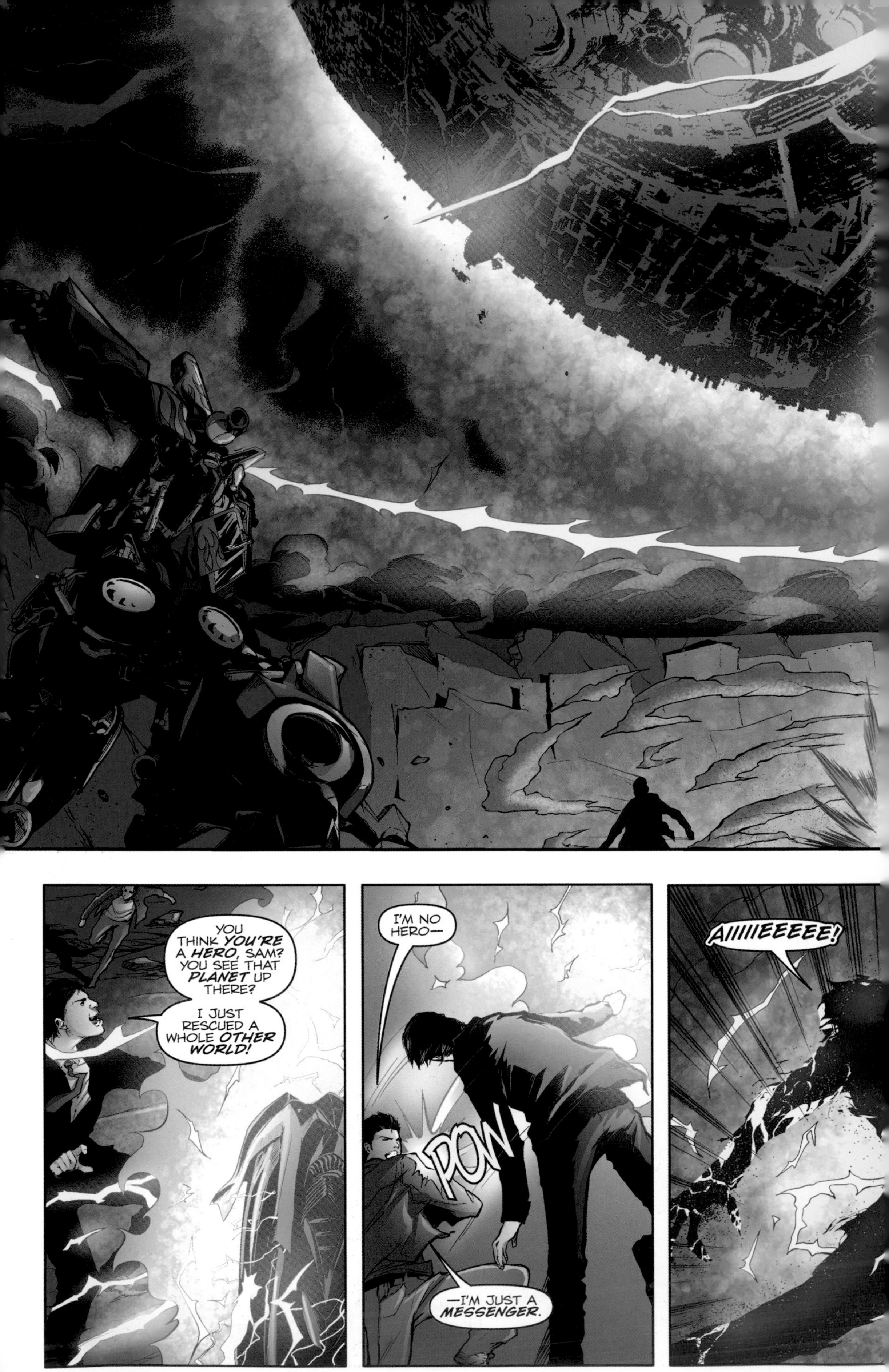
YOU THINK YOU'RE A HERO, SAM? YOU SEE THAT PLANET UP THERE?
I JUST RESCUED A WHOLE OTHER WORLD!
I'M NO HERO—
POW
—I'M JUST A MESSENGER.
AIIIIEEEEE!

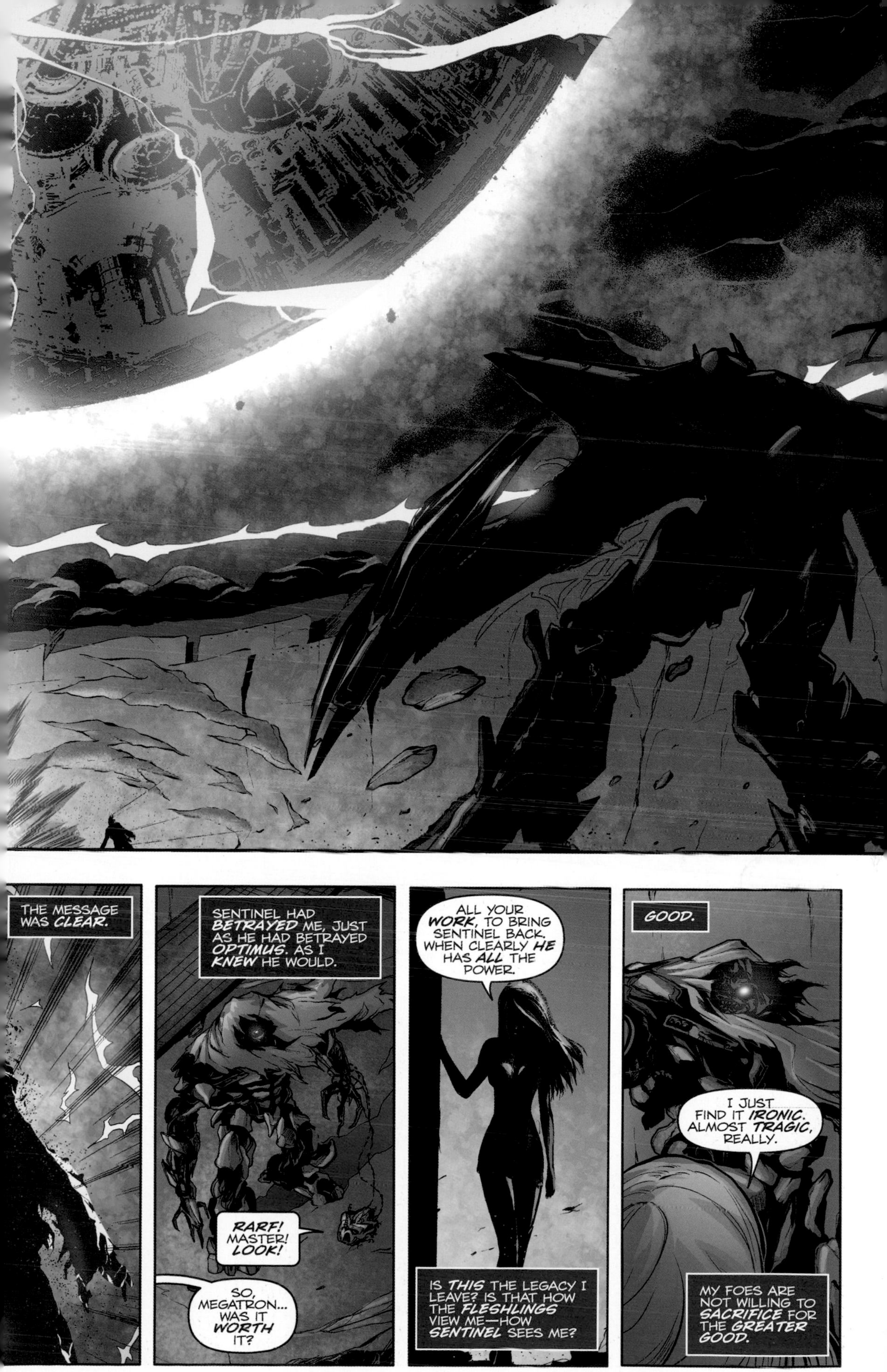
THE MESSAGE WAS CLEAR.
SENTINEL HAD BETRAYED ME, JUST AS HE HAD BETRAYED OPTIMUS. AS I KNEW HE WOULD.
RARF! MASTER! LOOK!
SO, MEGATRON... WAS IT WORTH IT?
ALL YOUR WORK, TO BRING SENTINEL BACK. WHEN CLEARLY HE HAS ALL THE POWER.
IS THIS THE LEGACY I LEAVE? IS THAT HOW THE FLESHLINGS VIEW ME—HOW SENTINEL SEES ME?
GOOD.
I JUST FIND IT IRONIC. ALMOST TRAGIC, REALLY.
MY FOES ARE NOT WILLING TO SACRIFICE FOR THE GREATER GOOD.

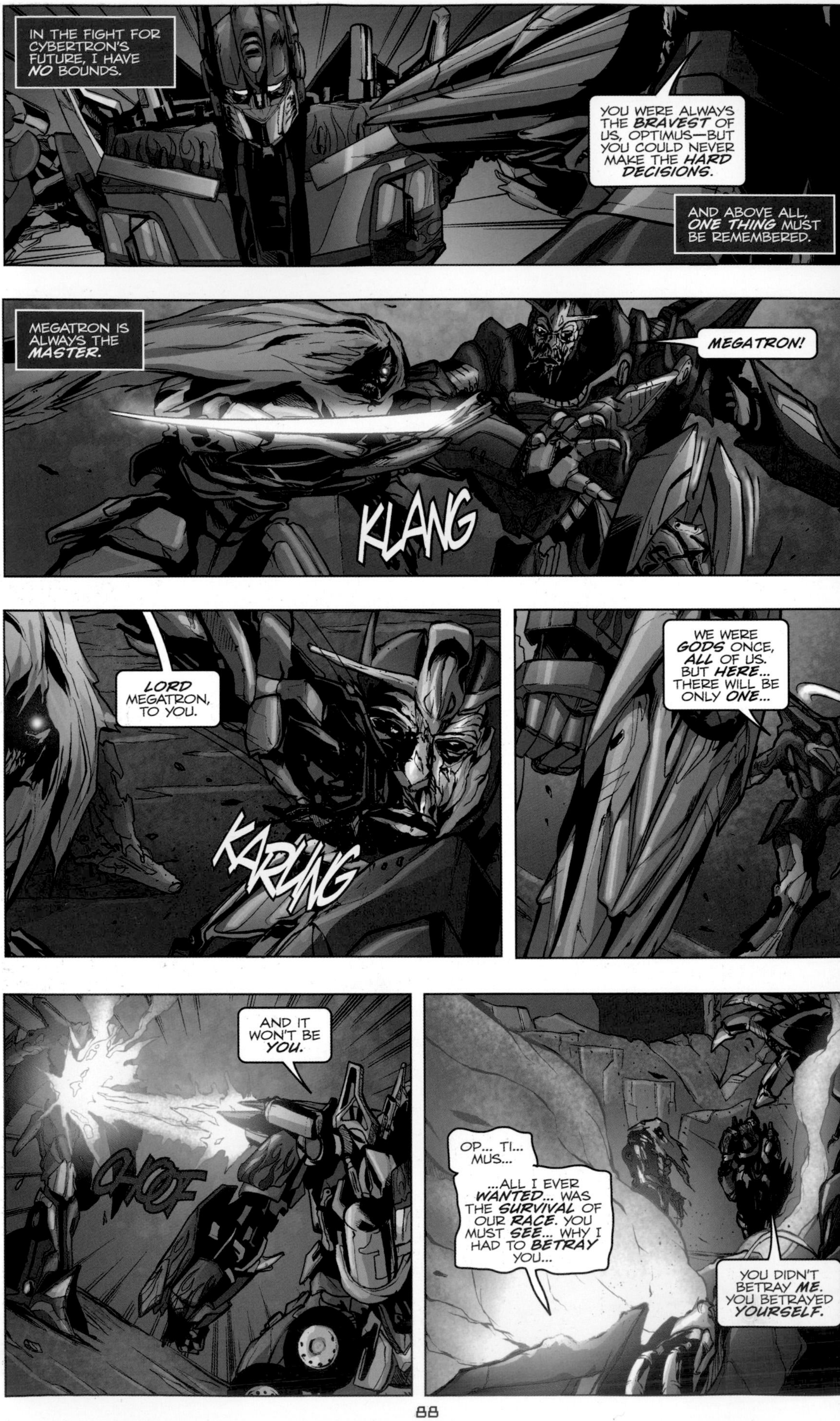
IN THE FIGHT FOR CYBERTRON'S FUTURE, I HAVE NO BOUNDS.
YOU WERE ALWAYS THE BRAVEST OF US, OPTIMUS—BUT YOU COULD NEVER MAKE THE HARD DECISIONS.
AND ABOVE ALL, ONE THING MUST BE REMEMBERED.
MEGATRON IS ALWAYS THE MASTER.
MEGATRON!
KLANG
LORD MEGATRON, TO YOU.
KARUNG
WE WERE GODS ONCE, ALL OF US. BUT HERE... THERE WILL BE ONLY ONE...
AND IT WON'T BE YOU.
CHOOF
OP... TI... MUS...
...ALL I EVER WANTED... WAS THE SURVIVAL OF OUR RACE. YOU MUST SEE... WHY I HAD TO BETRAY YOU...
YOU DIDN'T BETRAY ME. YOU BETRAYED YOURSELF.

SAM— REMEMBER THOSE *CRUISE MISSILES* I MENTIONED?

YOU HEARD HIM—*MOVE* IT, KIDDO!

CRUISE MISSILES, YEAH, SURE...

"...WAIT, *WHAT?*"

KRA-BA-CHOOOM

AND IT'S *OVER.*

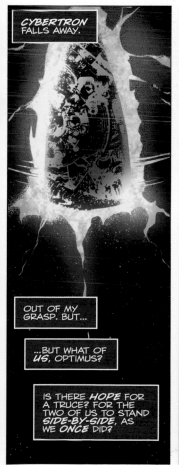

CYBERTRON FALLS AWAY.

OUT OF MY GRASP. BUT...

...BUT WHAT OF *US,* OPTIMUS?

IS THERE *HOPE* FOR A TRUCE? FOR THE TWO OF US TO STAND *SIDE-BY-SIDE,* AS WE *ONCE* DID?

COULD WE REBUILD OUR WORLD, *TOGETHER?*

WOULD YOU *TRUST* ME, MY BROTHER? WOULD I TRUST *YOU?* OR ARE YOU PREPARED TO ANSWER THE *QUESTION...*

...*WHO* WOULD YOU BE WITHOUT ME, PRIME?

CARLY! I *LOVE YOU!* I PROMISE I'LL MAKE ALL THIS *UP* TO YOU.

AND JUST *HOW* ARE YOU GOING TO DO *THAT?*

"SHOW HER HOW MUCH YOU CARE—"

〉*KAUGH*〈

OKAY, *HOLD* ON, *HANG* ON, *BUMBLEBEE...*

"—JUST *SLIP A RING* ON THERE!"

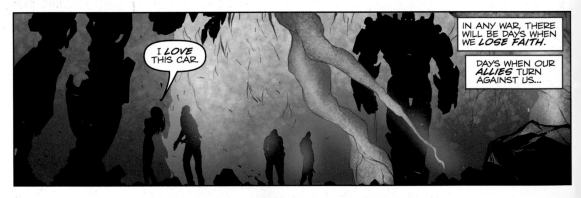

I *LOVE* THIS CAR.

IN ANY WAR, THERE WILL BE DAYS WHEN WE *LOSE FAITH.*

DAYS WHEN OUR *ALLIES* TURN AGAINST US...

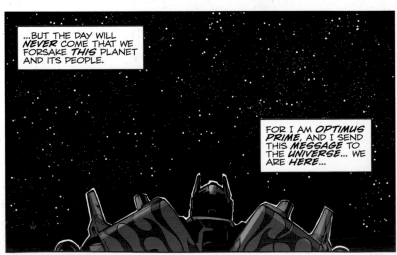

...BUT THE DAY WILL *NEVER* COME THAT WE FORSAKE *THIS* PLANET AND ITS PEOPLE.

FOR I AM *OPTIMUS PRIME,* AND I SEND THIS *MESSAGE* TO THE *UNIVERSE...* WE ARE *HERE...*

...WE ARE *HOME.*

RARF... MASTER?

END...?

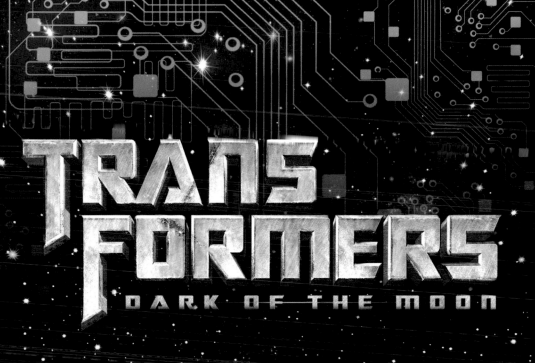

TRANSFORMERS
DARK OF THE MOON

ART GALLERY

ART BY
JORGE JIMENEZ MORENO

COLORS BY
PRISCILLA TRAMONTANO

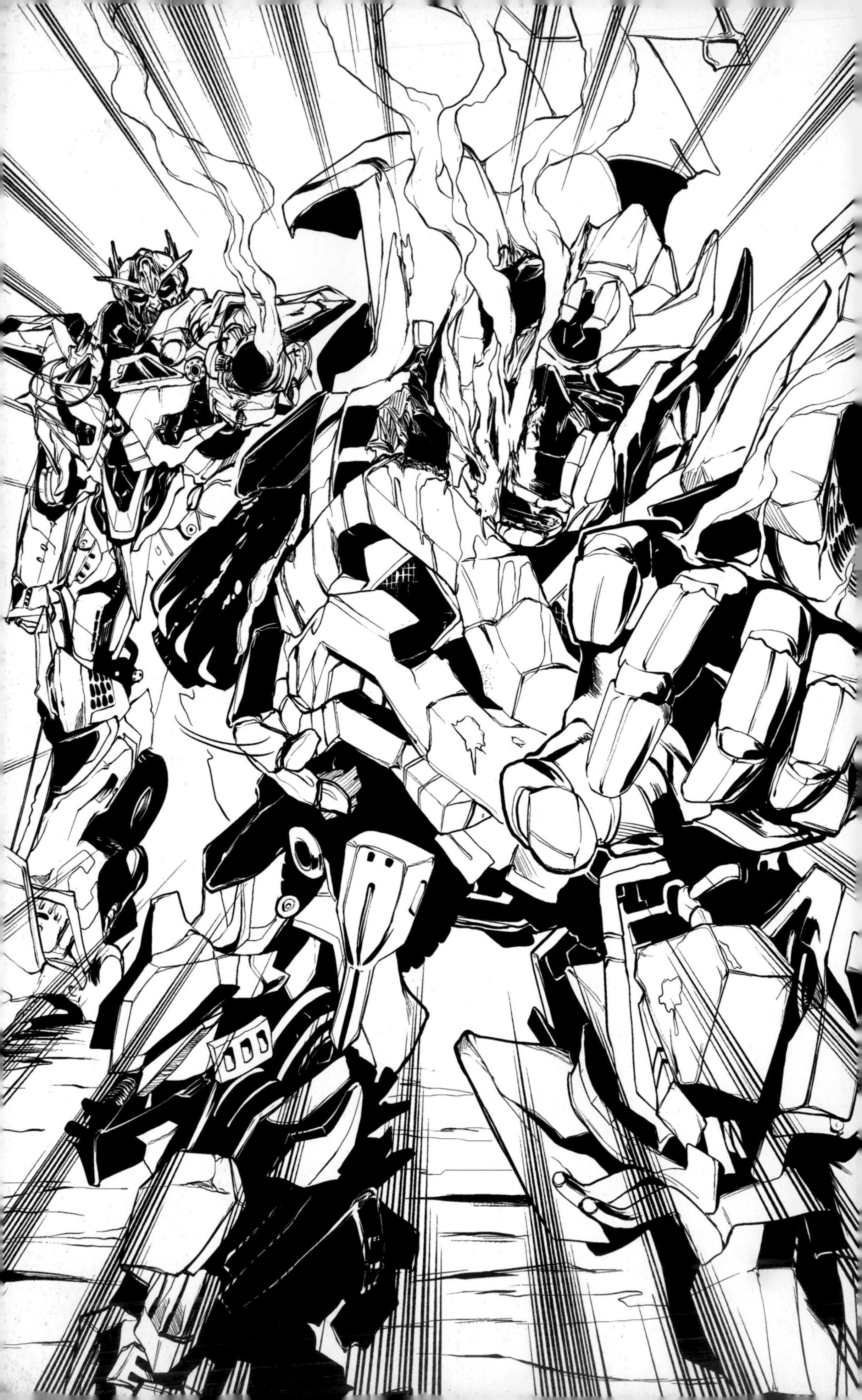

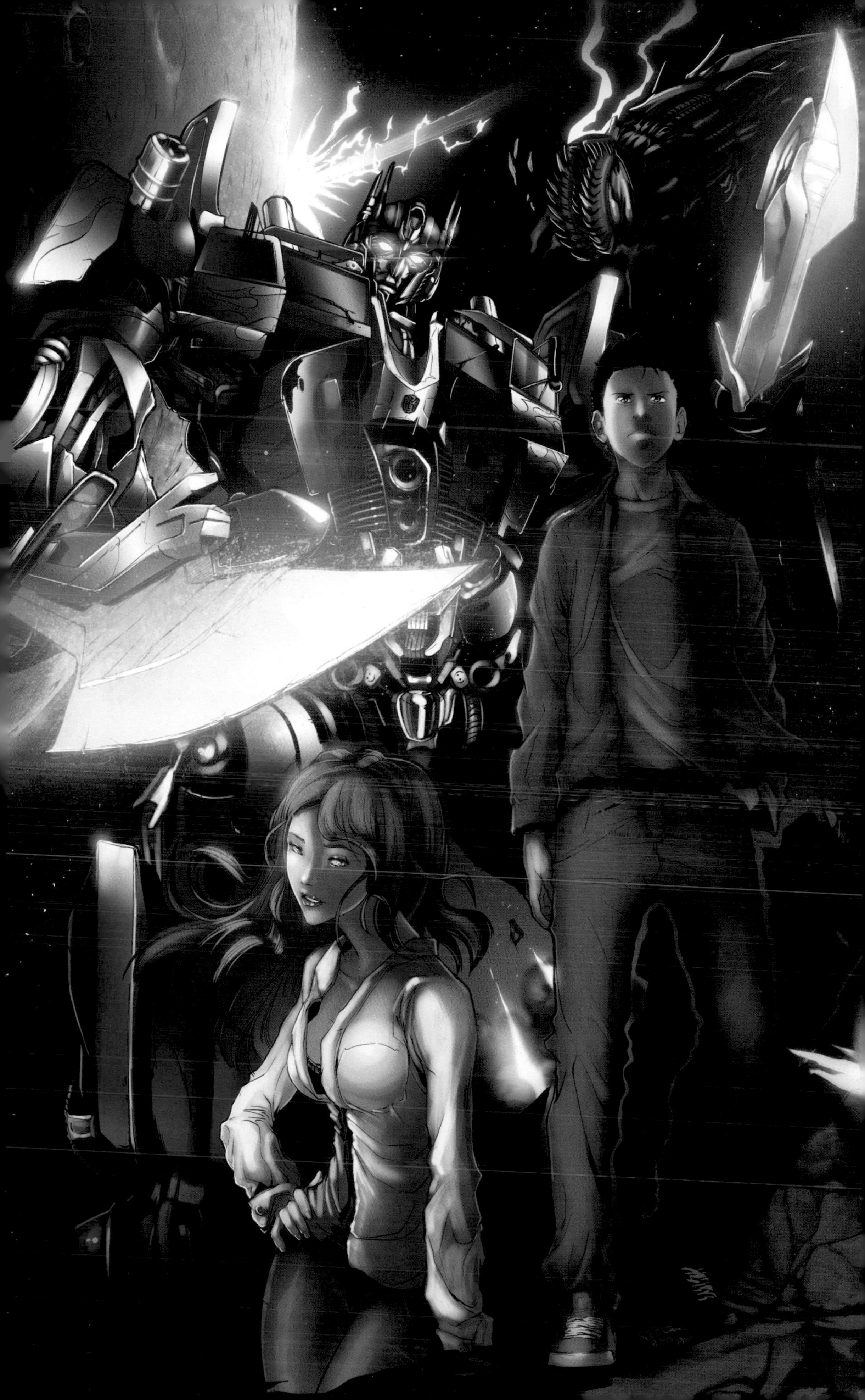

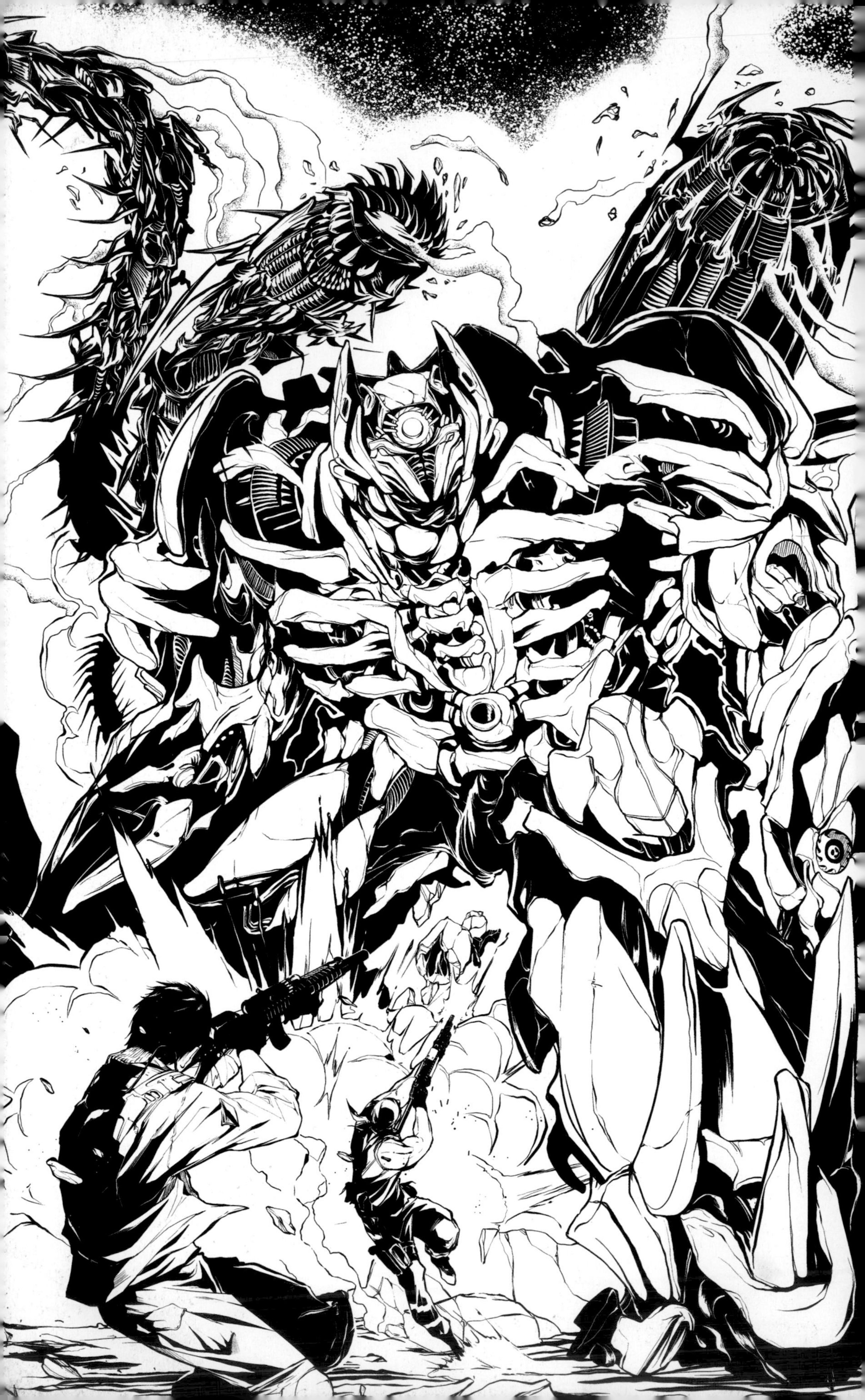

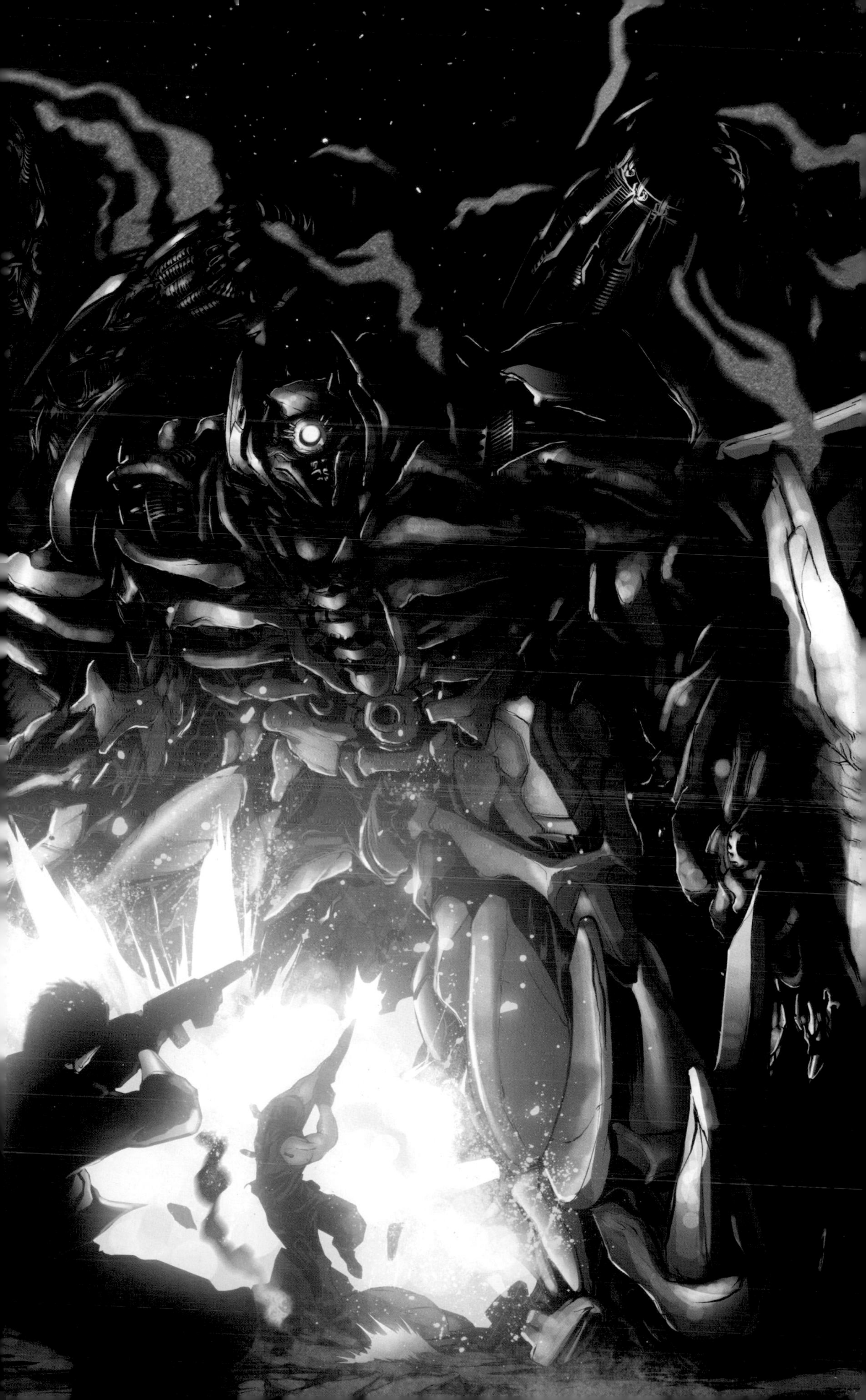

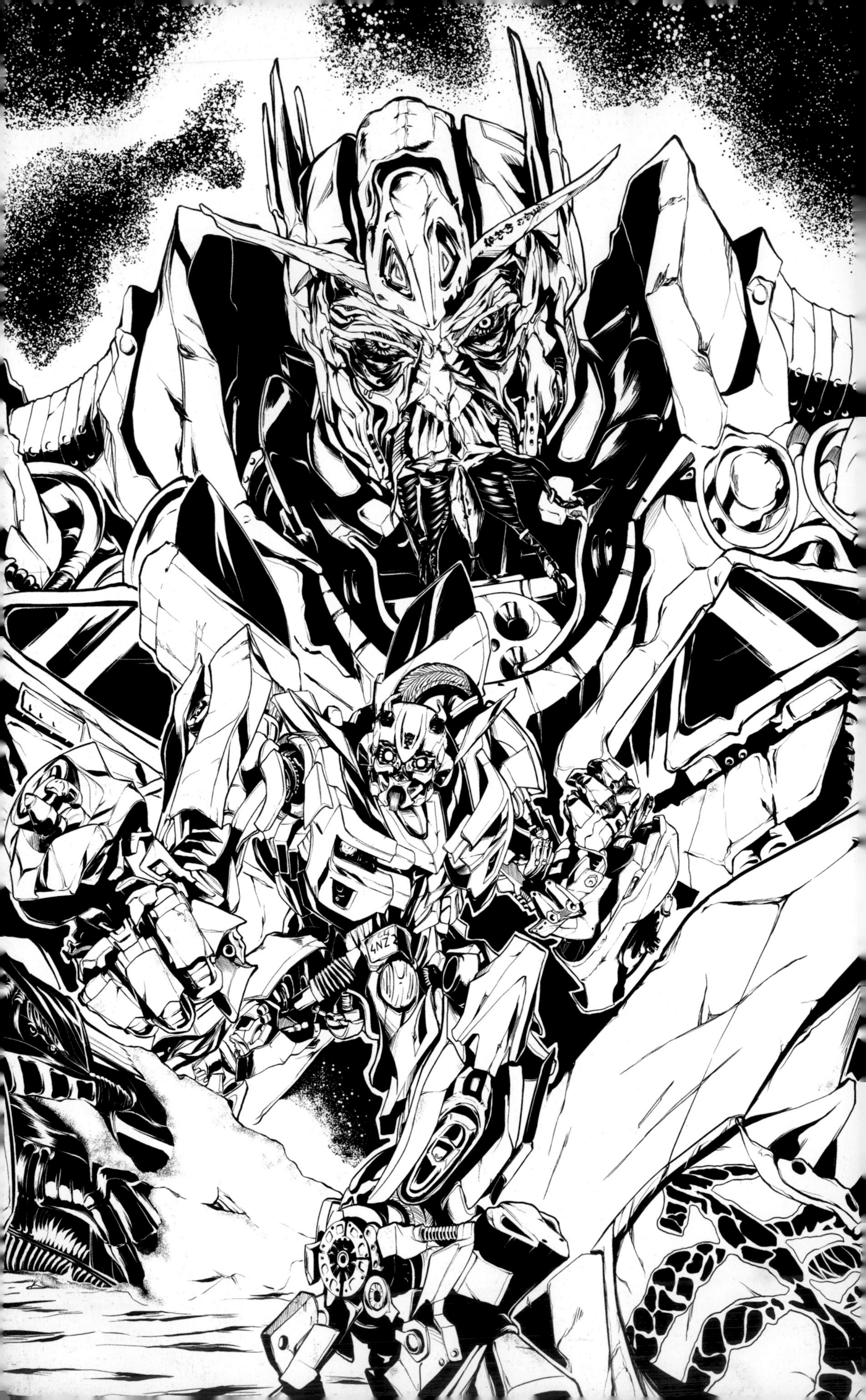

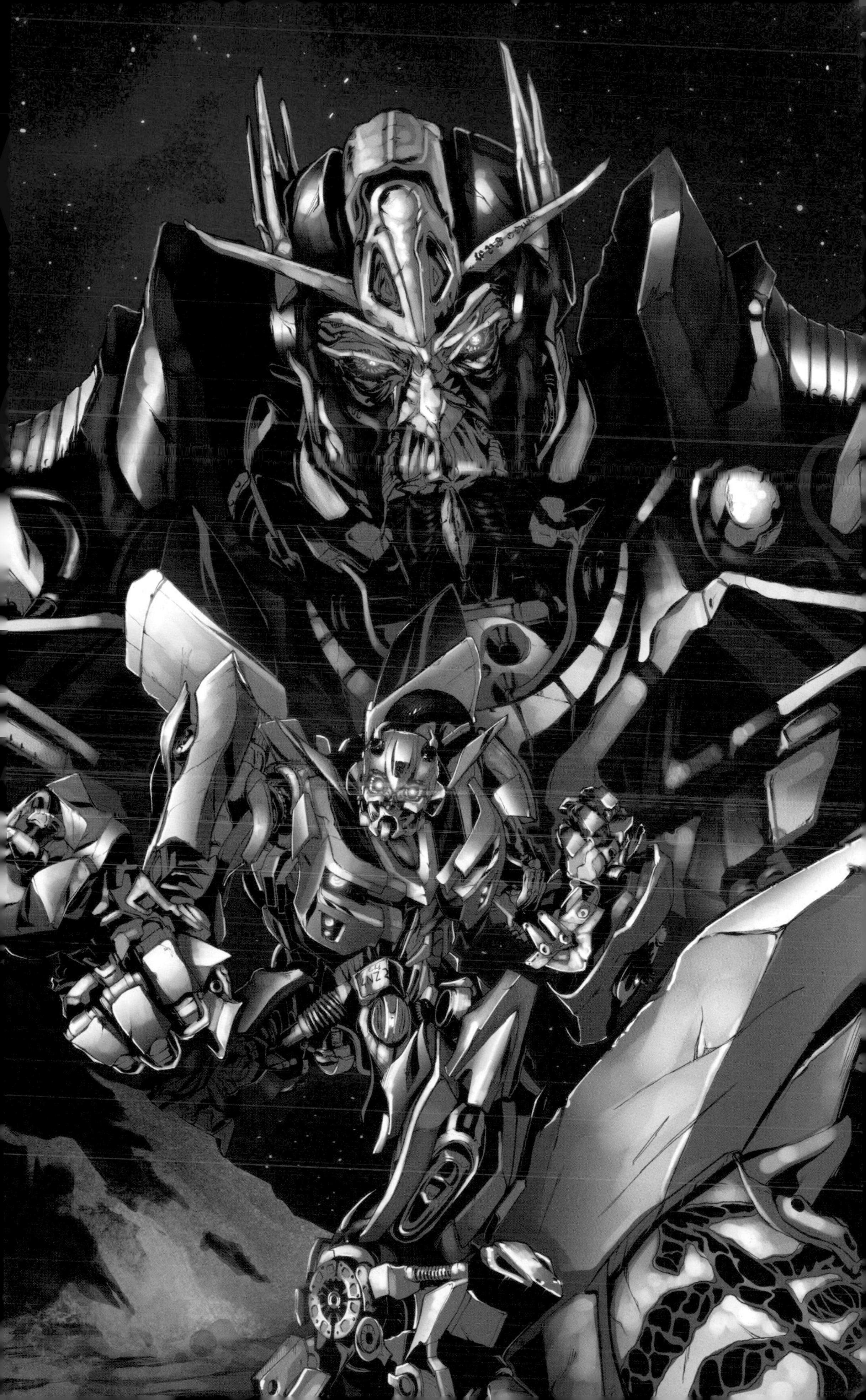

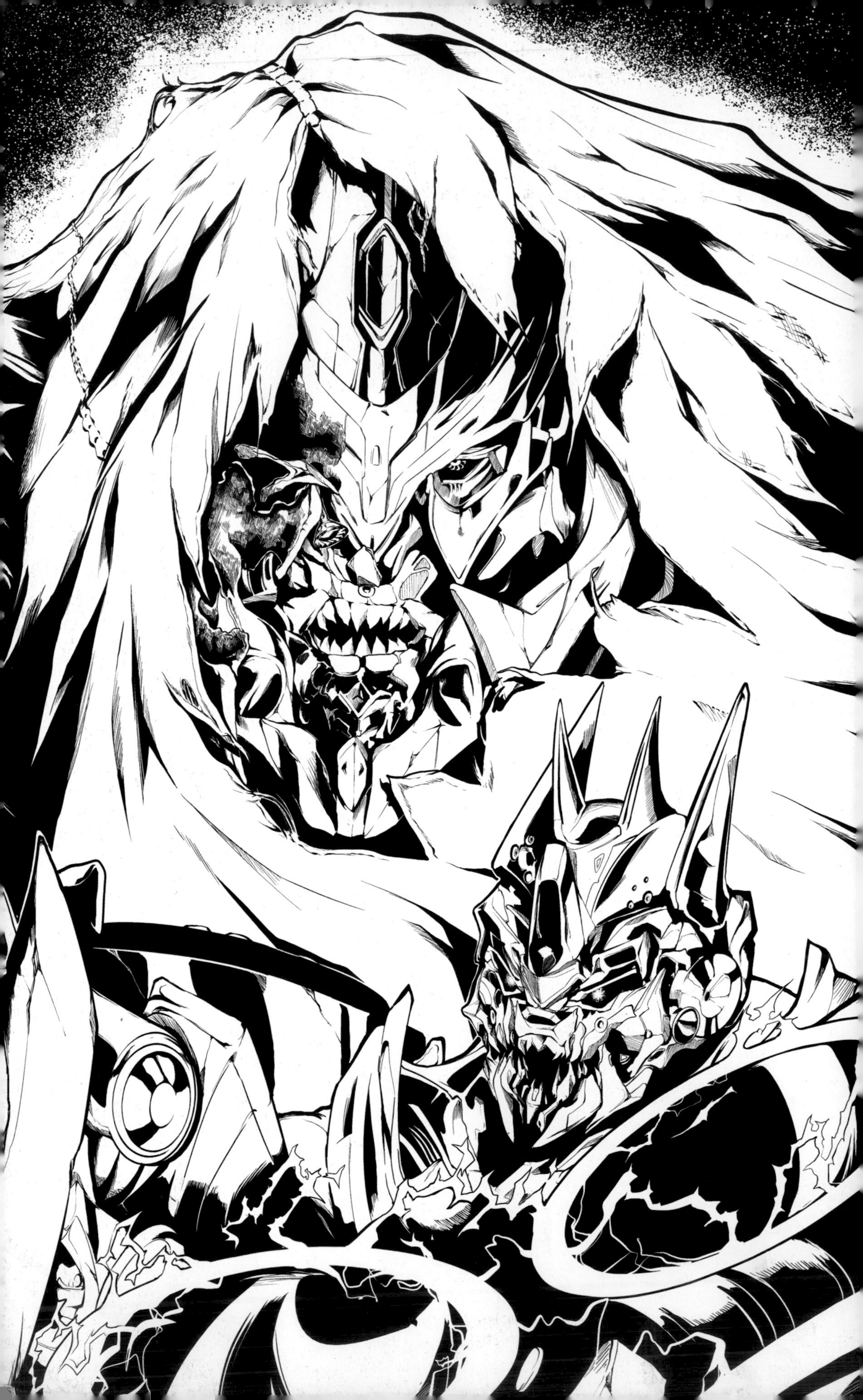

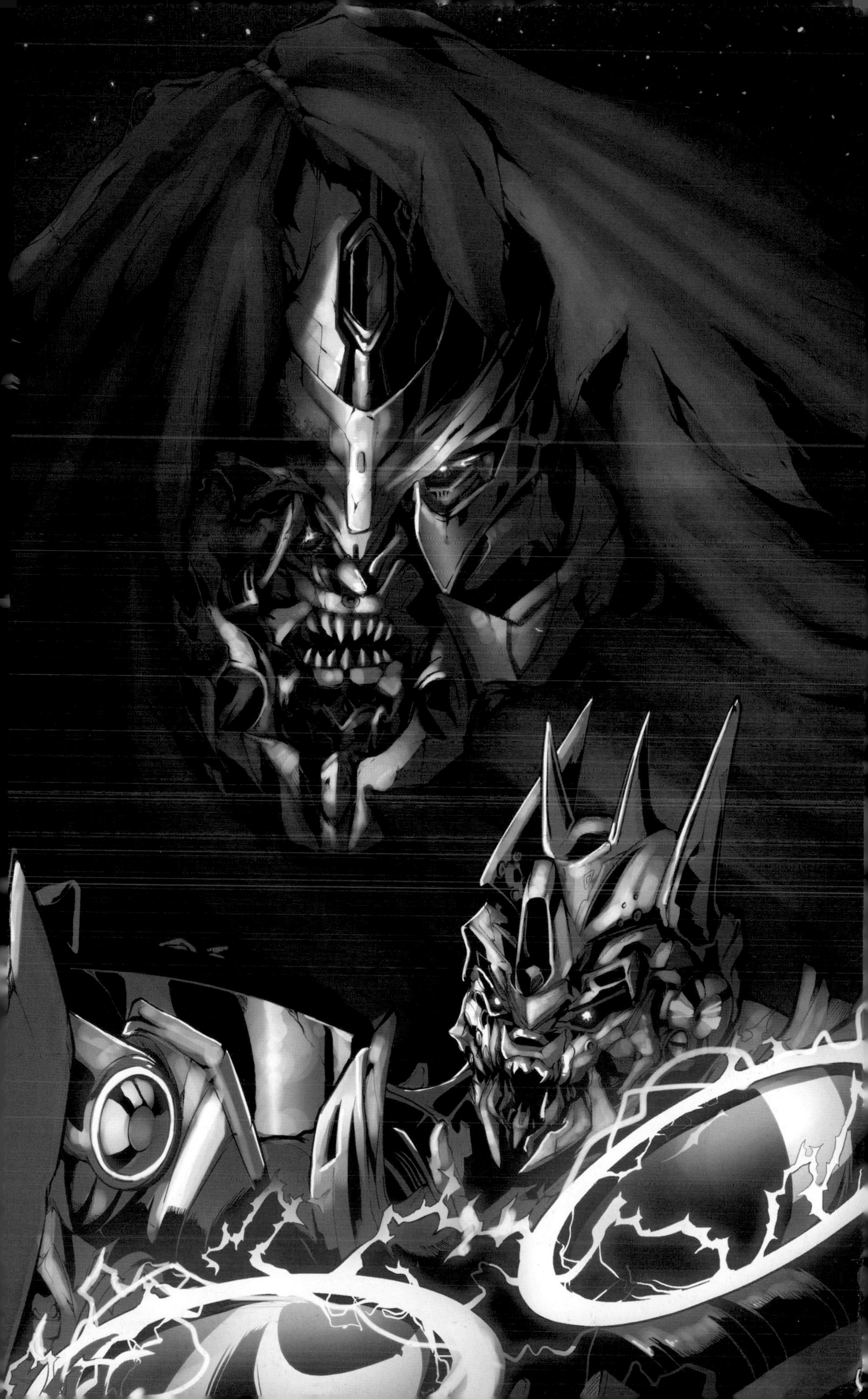

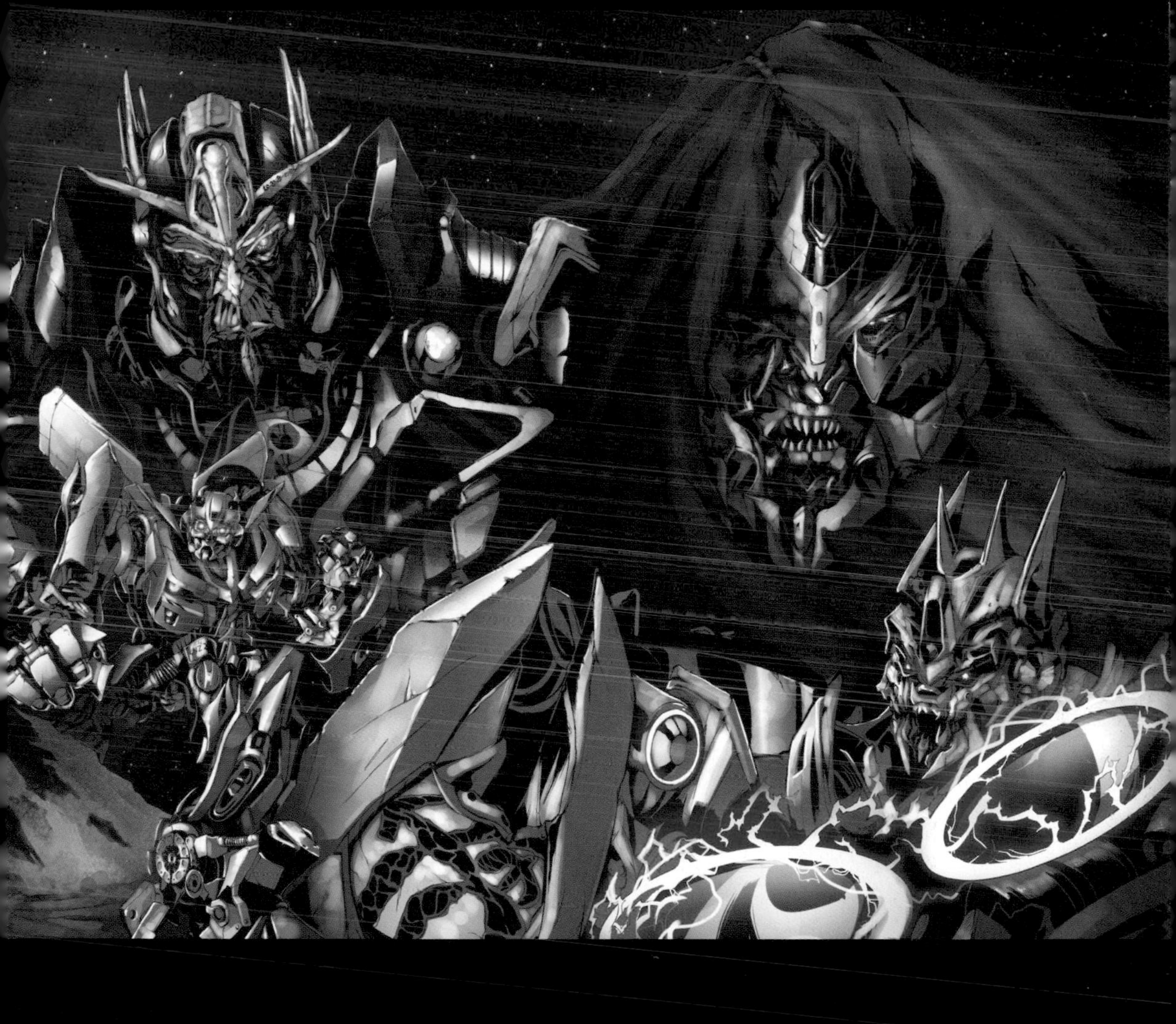

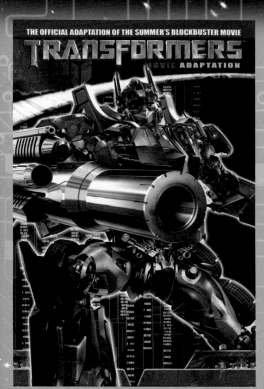

THE OFFICIAL ADAPTATION OF THE SUMMER'S BLOCKBUSTER MOVIE
TRANSFORMERS
MOVIE ADAPTATION

THE TRANSFORMERS: MOVIE ADAPTATION

Kris Oprisko (w) • Alex Milne (a)

Picking up directly where the Movie Prequel left off, in this adaptation of the big-screen TRANSFORMERS blockbuster, the brutal war between AUTOBOTS and DECEPTICONS is rekindled on Earth.

ISBN: 978-1-60010-067-3 • $17.99 • APR073773

THE TRANSFORMERS: MOVIE PREQUEL

Chris Ryall, Simon Furman (w) • Don Figueroa (a)

In this prequel to the TRANSFORMERS live-action movie, discover the secrets of CYBERTRON's past as we see for the first time what momentous events led to the TRANSFORMERS bringing their war to our world.

ISBN: 978-1-60010-066-6 • $19.99
APR073774

THE OFFICIAL PREQUEL TO THE SUMMER'S BLOCKBUSTER MOVIE
TRANSFORMERS
THE MOVIE PREQUEL

TRANSFORMERS
SAGA OF THE ALLSPARK

THE TRANSFORMERS MOVIE PREQUEL: SAGA OF THE ALLSPARK

Simon Furman (w) • Geoff Senior, Nick Roche, Andrew Wildman, Don Figueroa (a)

Originally published monthly in *Transformers Magazine*, as an eight-part movie-based serial.

ISBN: 978-1-60010-358-2 • $17.99
NOV08416

TRANSFORMERS
MOVIE SEQUEL
STARSCREAM

THE TRANSFORMERS MOVIE SEQUEL: THE REIGN OF STARSCREAM

Chris Mowry (w) • Alex Milne (a)

Picking up where the film ended, *The Reign of Starscream* also reveals the fates of other surviving film characters and features both old and all-new TRANSFORMERS characters.

ISBN: 978-1-60010-282-0 • $19.99
SEP084119

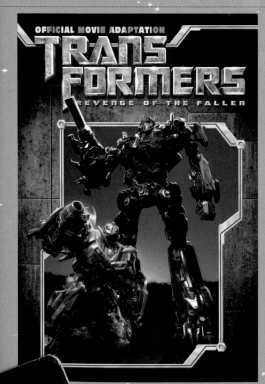

OFFICIAL MOVIE ADAPTATION
TRANSFORMERS
REVENGE OF THE FALLEN

...ORMERS: REVENGE OF THE FALLEN MOVIE ADAPTATION

...Furman (w) • Jon Davis-Hunt, Josh Nizzi (a)

...*sformers: Revenge of the Fallen* picks up directly where the ...ff–THE TRANSFORMERS' brutal war continues, on Earth as the ...n allies to end the DECEPTICONS threat.

...17.99 • APR090859

OFFICIAL MOVIE PREQUEL
TRANSFORMERS
REVENGE OF THE FALLEN
DEFIANCE

TRANSFORMERS: REVENGE OF THE FALLEN MOVIE PREQUEL–DEFIANCE

Chris Mowry (w) • Dan Khanna (a)

This second chapter of the *Destiny* story arc, "Defiance" delves into the very origins of CYBERTRON and the beginnings of the war between the AUTOBOTS and DECEPTICONS.

ISBN: 978-1-60010-457-2 • $17.99
APR090858

OFFICIAL MOVIE PREQUEL
TRANSFORMERS
REVENGE OF THE FALLEN
ALLIANCE

TRANSFORMERS: REVENGE OF THE FALLEN MOVIE PREQUEL–ALLIANCE

Chris Mowry (w) • Alex Milne (a)

In this first chapter of the *Destiny* story arc, "Alliance," readers will learn more about what happened to Sector Seven and the AUTOBOTS, and why their war on our planet is far from over.

ISBN: 978-1-60010-456-5 • $17.99
APR090857

TRANSFORMERS
TALES OF THE FALLEN

TRANSFORMERS: TALES OF THE FALLEN

Simon Furman, Chris Mowry (w) • Carlos Magno, Alex Milne (a)

The characters from TRANSFORMERS: REVENGE OF THE FALLEN reveal events surrounding the film in this collection of the six-issue series.

ISBN: 978-1-60010-628-6 • $19.99
FEB100947

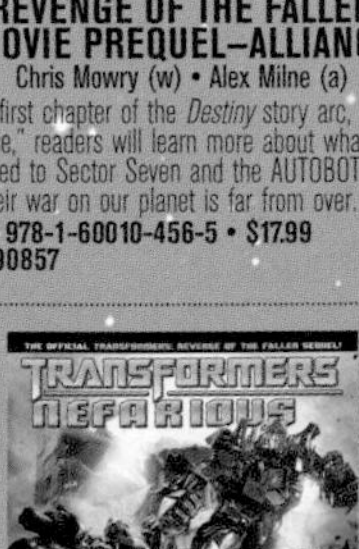

TRANSFORMERS
NEFARIOUS

TRANSFORMERS: NEFARIOUS

Simon Furman (w) • Carlos Magno (a)

The sequel to TRANSFORMERS: REVENGE OF THE FALLEN starts here! The big screen adventures of the TRANSFORMERS continue.

ISBN: 978-1-60010-787-0 • $19.99
SEP100361

MORE TRANSFORMERS GRAPHIC NOVELS FROM IDW PUBLISHING

THE TRANSFORMERS
THE IDW COLLECTION
VOLUME ONE

TRANSFORMERS: THE IDW COLLECTION, VOL. 1 (HC)
Simon Furman, Eric Holmes, Nick Roche, Shane McCarthy (w) • Alex Milne, EJ Su, M.D. Bright, Nick Roche (a)

or the first time ever, the entire IDW TRANSFORMERS UNIVERSE is presented in ardcover, in chronological order!

ISBN: 978-1-60010-667-5 • $49.99 • MAR100992

THE TRANSFORMERS
THE IDW COLLECTION
VOLUME TWO

TRANSFORMERS: THE IDW COLLECTION, VOL. 2 (HC)
Simon Furman, Nick Roche (w) • E.J. Su, Nick Roche, Don Figueroa, Klaus Scherwinski (a)

The re-presentation of IDW's TRANSFORMERS Universe continues in volume 2 of TRANSFORMERS: THE IDW COLLECTION! Includes Stormbringer #1-4, Spotlights: SIXSHOT, ULTRA MAGNUS, KUP, and ESCALATION #1-6.

ISBN: 978-1-60010-751-1 • $49.99 • JUL100297

THE TRANSFORMERS
VOLUME 1
FOR ALL MANKIND
MIKE COSTA
DON FIGUEROA

TRANSFORMERS, VOL. 1: FOR ALL MANKIND
Mike Costa (w) • Don Figueroa (a)

t's been three years since the devastating events of ALL HAIL MEGATRON. The Earth has been rebuilt, the AUTOBOTS are in hiding, and the next great era in the TRANSFORMERS saga is about to begin!

ISBN: 978-1-60010-684-2 • $19.99 • APR100354

THE TRANSFORMERS
MIKE COSTA
DON FIGUEROA
VOLUME 2

TRANSFORMERS, VOL. 2: INTERNATIONAL INCIDENT
Mike Costa (w) • Don Figueroa, Javier Salteres, Guido Guidi (a)

As the AUTOBOTS and SKYWATCH come together against a common enemy, the DECEPTICONS choose to forge their own alliance. However, their involvement with a powerful leader could escalate two countries into war!

ISBN: 978-1-60010-804-4 • $19.99 • OCT100394

idwpub

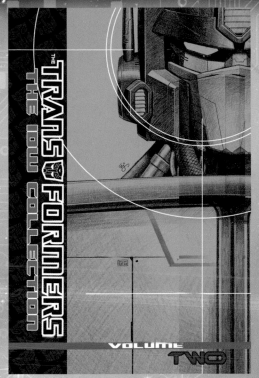

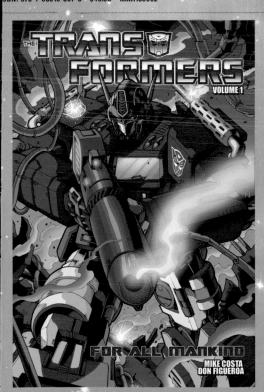

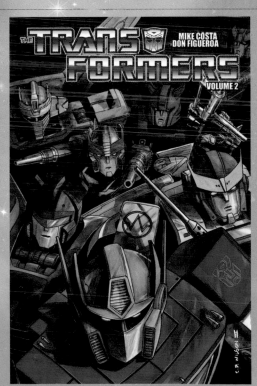

TRANSFORMERS
DARK OF THE MOON

blishing.com